W9-BUL-883

Discovering Jerusalem

by
Nahman Avigad

THOMAS NELSON PUBLISHERS
NASHVILLE · CAMDEN · NEW YORK

Original Hebrew edition published in Israel by Shikmona
Publishing Co., Ltd., Jerusalem.
Copyright © 1980 by Nahman Avigad

Published in the United States in Nashville, Tennessee,
by Thomas Nelson, Inc., Publishers and distributed in
Canada by Lawson Falle, Ltd., Cambridge, Ontario.
First American printing: 1983.

Library of Congress Cataloging in Publication Data

Avigad, Nahman.
  Discovering Jerusalem.

  Translation of: ha- 'Ir ha-'elyonah shel Yerushalyim.
  Bibliography: p.
  Includes index.
  1. Jerusalem—Antiquities.   2. Excavations
(Archaeology)—Jerusalem.   I. Title.
DS109.A74813   1983   933   83-17220
ISBN 0-8407-5299-7

Printed in the United States of America.

OUR FEET HAVE BEEN STANDING
WITHIN YOUR GATES, O JERUSALEM,
JERUSALEM, BUILT AS A CITY
WHICH IS COMPACT TOGETHER

Psalms: 122

7/2/7

CONTENTS

11 PREFACE

13 INTRODUCTION

CHAPTER ONE
THE PERIOD OF THE FIRST TEMPLE
23 1. Jerusalem in the Bible and in Other Ancient Sources
26 2. Where was Early Jerusalem Situated?
31 3. Discovering Israelite Remains on the Western Hill
54 4. The Significance of the Israelite Fortifications on the Western Hill

CHAPTER TWO
AFTER THE DESTRUCTION OF THE FIRST TEMPLE
61 An Interlude on the Western Hill

CHAPTER THREE
THE PERIOD OF THE SECOND TEMPLE
64 1. The Hasmonean Resettlement of the Western Hill
81 2. Intense Development under the Herodians
83 3. A Residence from the Days of Herod
95 4. A Palatial Mansion
120 5. The "Burnt House"
139 6. Jewish Ritual Baths
144 7. Early Mosaic Pavements
147 8. The Menorah Graffito and Fresco Fragments
150 9. Remnants of Monumental Architecture
165 10. The Crafts of Jerusalem—Stone, Pottery, Glass
193 11. Odds and Ends—"Theater Tokens," Coins, Inscriptions

CHAPTER FOUR
AFTER THE DESTRUCTION OF THE SECOND TEMPLE
205 The Roman City—A Second Interlude on the Western Hill

CHAPTER FIVE
BYZANTINE JERUSALEM
208 1. The Flowering of a Byzantine City
213 2. Tracing the Cardo Maximus
229 3. In Quest of the Great Nea Church

CHAPTER SIX
IN THE MIDDLE AGES
247 Muslim and Crusader Remains

259 EPILOGUE

262 CHRONOLOGICAL TABLE

263 SELECTED BIBLIOGRAPHY

The archaeological excavations in the Jewish Quarter of the Old City of Jerusalem have now been in progress for more than ten years running. They have expanded from their modest beginnings in 1969 to embrace a broad scope that encompasses several periods and archaeological strata. The many remains that they have yielded have brought with them a new fund of knowledge on ancient Jerusalem and its history.

The present volume is a general preliminary account of this first decade of our work. Certain matters dealt with in the Hebrew edition of this book (1980) such as the Israelite gate tower, the Cardo, and the Nea church, have been brought up to date, following further discoveries in 1980-1981.

I have sought to tell the story of the excavations in a manner that will allow the general reader to enter into the spirit of our work; at the same time, I have treated the material in such a manner that scholars and students can use the book as a reliable source until the final scientific reports are published. This, I hope, releases me from part of my moral obligation toward all those who cherish Jerusalem and its past, as well as toward the city itself, which has been most generous in yielding up to us its hidden treasures.

Another obligation that it is now my pleasant duty to fulfill is that of expressing my thanks to the many who have lent a hand to our excavations in one way or another. Foremost among those to be mentioned are the institutions upon whose behalf I directed the excavations: the Institute of Archaeology of the Hebrew University, Jerusalem; the Department of Antiquities and Museums of the Israel Ministry of Education and Culture, and the Israel Exploration Society. Joint interests have let the Jewish Quarter Reconstruction and Development Company become a partner in our work, and it has borne most of the financial burden of the excavations. Without the cooperation of the Company and its successive directors and senior staff, our achievements in the field would have been unattainable.

Financial assistance was also forthcoming from the America-Israel Cultural Foundation, the Ambassador International Cultural Foundation (Pasadena, California) and, in the initial years of our work, from Dr. Reuben Hecht of Haifa. Professor Avraham Biran, former Director of the Department of Antiquities and Museums, Abraham Eitan, incumbent Director, and District Archaeologist Amos Kloner all lent their support, especially in overcoming the web of administrative and legal problems that arose during the course of work. Mr. Joseph Aviram, Director of the Institute of Archaeology and Honorary Secretary of the Israel Exploration Society, was of invaluable assistance in many areas of our work, including the furtherance of the English edition of this book.

The success of any archaeological excavation depends largely upon team work, and our expedition was blessed with a loyal and devoted staff whose members, all former students of mine, were fully aware of the significance of the task entrusted to them. The present volume is, to a great extent, the fruit of our joint effort, both in the field and in staff discussions. Dr. Amihai Mazar, the first of the staff to join us, served ably as chief field supervisor for the first two years. He was succeeded by Hillel Geva, the only staff member who has remained with the excavations throughout. Ronny Reich, who was with us for nine years, served as chief surveyor and, on occasion, as an area supervisor as well. The senior staff was rounded out by area supervisors Shlomo Margalit and Zvi Maoz. Over the years others joined the staff for a season or so; they are, in chronological order: Dan Zipper, Yitzhaq Levy, Nahman Gershon, Dan Behar, Benjamin Zass, Nadav Lepinski, Rekhav Rubin (area supervisors); Doron Chen (architect); and Leen Ritmeyer (surveyor and draughtsman). The registration of our finds was undertaken, in succession, by Dina Kastel, Sara Hofri, Atzmona Wachsman-Perl, Hagit Mashat and Martha Goldberg. Dr. Yaakov Meshorer kindly served as numismatic advisor. Avinoam Glick took most of the field photographs. The actual labor in the field was carried out by Arab workmen from Jerusalem and the vicinity. Veteran head foreman Ibrahim Ghassuli, called Abu Ribhi, must be especially commended for his loyal and efficient work; his archaeological career began in 1930 under the late Sir William Flinders Petrie.

An exhibition of archaeological finds from the Jewish Quarter excavations, held at the Israel Museum in Jerusalem in 1976, was organized by Mrs. Yael Israeli, Curator. This most successful exhibition was designed to emphasize the potential of the finds in helping to reconstruct chapters in the daily life of ancient Jerusalem. The exhibition catalogue which I then wrote was the seed from which the present volume grew. The preparation and publication of the present volume has been a team effort. Its rich illustrative material is the work of several photographers (see the Photo Acknowledgements). Hillel Geva, Ronny Reich and Zvi Maoz read various chapters of the Hebrew manuscript and made valuable comments, and Professor Dan Barag kindly read the section on the glass. Mr. R. Grafman has translated the Hebrew text into English, offering many suggestions in the process; the material was hardly new to him, for he also translated the exhibition catalogue for the Israel Museum. Miss Norma Schneider read the English text and gave it a more readable style. The Shikmona Publishing Company has been unstinting in the production of this book, and Judy Silverstein has given it its attractive design.

Finally, I must express my deep appreciation to my wife, Shulamith, who was a never-failing source of encouragement and assistance throughout the many years of excavations. In typing out the manuscript of the Hebrew version of this work, her judgment often led to a better balance between professional jargon and normative language.

I wish to express my deepest gratitude to all the above for their cooperation and assistance. I am sure that, upon opening the present volume, each of them will feel a sense of satisfaction and pride in the part he or she played in shedding new light on the Upper City of Jerusalem through the ages.

Jerusalem   N. Avigad

INTRODUCTION

The reunification of Jerusalem in 1967 was not only a great historical event — well expressed in the Bible by the Psalmist: "Jerusalem, built as a city which is bound firmly together" (122:3) — but was as well an event that will long be remembered as a turning point in the archaeological exploration of the city. The vast increase in archaeological excavations conducted in Jerusalem since the reunification, in locations not even dreamt of previously, has resulted in an unanticipated growth of our knowledge of the city's past.

Jerusalem, shrouded in sanctity and historical glory, was always a symbol of deep emotional significance for the Jewish people and for much of mankind. The desire to depict the abstract image of the Holy City has long found expression in the imaginative and symbolic art illustrating Jerusalem and the Holy Temple, while interest in the earthly Jerusalem has engendered an extensive literature of pilgrims and explorers who have described the city and its monuments, tombs, peoples, and daily life. It is therefore not surprising that Jerusalem — the Holy City — was the foremost target of the excavator's spade when archaeologists began to explore the Holy Land in the mid-nineteenth century. The explorer F. de Saulcy took a first step when he cleared the so-called Tomb of the Kings in 1863; and the first series of systematic excavations were those undertaken by Charles Warren around the Temple Mount, on behalf of the Palestine Exploration Fund in London, in 1867. The expectations of these early explorers, as well as their limited professional qualifications, are underscored by de Saulcy's having identified a tomb built in Hellenistic-Roman style as the tomb of the kings of Judah, missing the mark by at least six centuries, and by Warren's ascription of the Herodian stones of the Temple Mount to Solomon's Temple, which was built nine hundred years earlier.

Since Warren's pioneer excavations, Jerusalem has been the ultimate aim of many excavators. No other city has had so many excavations, nor is any other site so difficult to excavate. And in addition to the political and religious obstacles placed before the early archaeologists, there were the objective deterrents of the site — spreading over hill and dale, having been destroyed and rebuilt innumerable times in the long course of its history, and whose builders were often no less destructive than the warriors who razed it. This cyclic process has left only a few early remains intact, and those still extant are often covered by huge accumulations of debris, which in turn have been sealed off by the densely built residential quarters seen today. Very few open areas have remained for archaeological excavations in the Old City of Jerusalem, within the present city walls.

In the past, Muslim religious authorities, ever suspicious of archaeologists, imposed harsh restrictions which hindered excavators working in the remaining open areas such as the vicinity of the Temple Mount. In fact, Warren and the Bliss-Dickie expedition, during the "heroic" period of the rediscovery of Jerusalem, were forced to burrow like moles beneath the surface in order to avoid the "evil eye." Added to the above, the early excavators of Jerusalem were plagued by a lack of funds which, together with their generally insufficient qualifications, prevented them from coming to proper terms with the enormous task before them.

The obstacles involved precluded most of the sensational discoveries that had been anticipated. And soon, excavating in Jerusalem lost the priority it had had for the various international bodies which had been sponsoring excavations in the Holy Land. The institutions and individual scholars which did continue to meet the challenge of Jerusalem should therefore be commended most heartily, especially the Palestine Exploration Fund in Britain which repeatedly and tenaciously attacked this beckoning target despite the limited means at its disposal. I am in deep sympathy with the pioneer, Charles Warren — a great excavator despite his chronological errors. He carried out his work under the most trying and dangerous conditions. (Once, after his assistant had been buried alive by a cave-in far underground, Warren reported that: "Sergeant Biddles was inconvenienced for three hours!") He even depleted his own pocket in order to complete his first season of excavations. And, when the functionaries of the Palestine Exploration Fund wrote: "Send us results and we shall send you money," Warren replied: "Give me tools, materials, money and food and I will get you results." While we, today, are not so bold in our words, we are still in the position where funds often depend upon "results."

In the best of British tradition, the British Schools of Archaeology in Jerusalem sponsored the last and very successful excavation undertaken by the late Dame Kathleen Kenyon, on the "Ophel" in the city of David, in the 1960s. But the lion's share of ancient Jerusalem — the Old City within the walls — was barely touched and remained a hard nut to crack. It is natural that excavations within the walls were concentrated around the periphery of the city, along the walls and around the Temple Mount. Sites in the residential quarters inside the densely populated areas of the Old City were explored only very sporadically. We therefore had fragmentary and quite faulty knowledge of the city itself, in regard to both its stratigraphic history and its material culture in the various periods. We felt that the soil of the Old City might never yield its secrets, and that it would take an extraordinary occurrence to bring about the circumstances prerequisite to large-scale, systematic excavations in Jerusalem.

Such conditions did indeed evolve in the wake of the 1967 Six-Day War. After Israeli sovereignty over the Old City was established, a broad plan was laid down for the improvement and embellishment of Jerusalem, including a declaration to the effect that the Old City was to be a protected antiquities site. This was done to prevent historical buildings from being damaged and archaeological remains from being destroyed. New construction would be permitted only after archaeological investigation of each proposed building site. The Israel Archaeological Council took up the challenge of the new circumstances with gusto, formulating a plan that

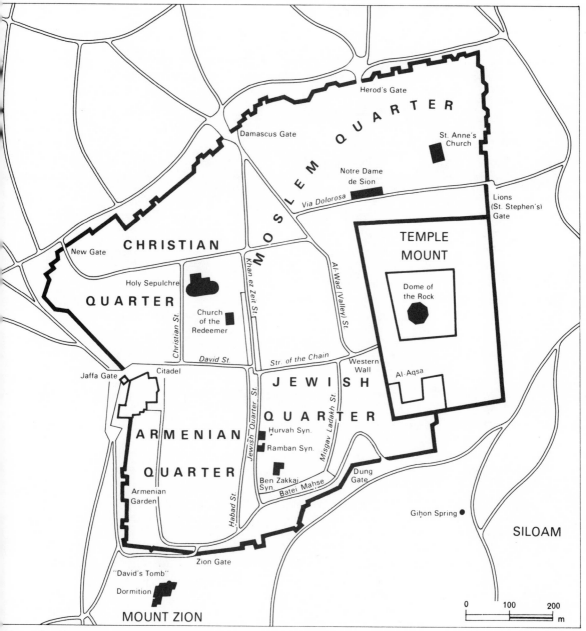

Plan of the Old City

15

3. Bird's-eye view of the Jewish Quarter, looking west; at center, excavation Areas F and P, the construction site of the Yeshivat Hakotel. Photographed in 1974

4. Bird's-eye view of the Jewish Quarter, looking east toward the Temple Mount. Photographed in 1974

called for salvage excavations as well as specific archaeological projects. This created an atmosphere in which widespread archaeological activities were initiated on a scale never before seen in Jerusalem.

The first Israeli expedition in the field was directed by Professor Benjamin Mazar. In 1968 he began excavating south and southwest of the Temple Mount, in areas which had hitherto been "taboo" for archaeologists. Many important remains came to light during the course of these excavations, which continued until 1977, without infringing upon the sanctity of the adjacent holy sites. Mazar was able to do openly what Charles Warren and his colleagues had been forced to do secretly: he exposed large portions of the Western and Southern Walls of the Temple Enclosure, laying bare the area of "Robinson's Arch" and uncovering the paved streets leading to it. He also discovered a monumental staircase leading up to the "Double Gate" in the southern wall, various other structures, and carved stones from Herod's "Royal Portico" in the outermost court of the Temple.

Several more modest excavations were conducted after 1967, including work at the Jerusalem Citadel (under Ruth Amiran and Avraham Eitan), near the southern and western Turkish city walls (under Magen Broshi, Dan Bahat, and Yizhaq Margovsky) and on Mount Zion (under Broshi), and will be referred to later on.

Another major expedition was entrusted with the task of excavating in the Jewish Quarter, alongside the contractors rebuilding the damaged quarter. Since these latter excavations are the subject of this book, and since they were directed by the present writer, I should like to present some of the background for the undertaking at the outset. The Jewish Quarter is one of the four principal residential quarters within the present walls of the Old City (the others are the Muslim, Christian and *2* Armenian Quarters). Located in the southeastern part of the city, the Jewish Quarter sits astride the northeastern knob of the Western Hill of ancient Jerusalem, opposite the Temple Mount. During the period of the Second Temple this was an important residential area of the Upper City, the houses standing atop a lofty cliff overlooking the Temple courts to the east. Never having been excavated by archaeologists, the quarter was a blank page, *terra incognita* about which we knew nothing. Nonetheless, it was generally regarded as one of the main locations for an understanding of the Upper City and the key to a solution of topographical problems which had long confronted scholars investigating Jerusalem. Whoever thought that it would be possible to conduct archaeological excavations there, in the most densely built up of all the city's quarters? But here a popular saying, that archaeology is built on destruction, proved to be true. If the quarter had not been destroyed to such a great extent, it would not have been possible to excavate there.

In the war of 1948, the Arab Legion of Transjordan captured the Jewish Quarter, and its inhabitants were taken prisoner. After the battle for the quarter was decided, all of its many synagogues were systematically destroyed and many of the houses fell into ruin. With the return of the Jews to the Jewish Quarter in 1967, the Government of Israel set up the "Company for the Reconstruction and Development of the Jewish Quarter" to restore the area. During the course of clearing away the ruins and demolishing those buildings on the verge of collapse, many open spaces were created. This provided us with the unexpected and unique opportunity of conducting large-scale systematic excavations before new construction was begun on each individual site. The dream of several generations of archaeologists was about to come true.

Three archaeological institutions underwrote the project—the Institute of Archaeology of the Hebrew University in Jerusalem, the Department of Antiquities and Museums of the Ministry of Education and Culture, and the Israel Exploration Society. An interinstitutional committee, on which I was a representative of the Hebrew University, was formed. When this committee offered me directorship of the excavations, my first reaction was to express my appreciation for the trust placed in me to conduct such a difficult and responsible task. And then, I turned the offer down. After my colleagues on the committee asked me to reconsider, I pleaded for time. I was in an embarrassing position, for I had planned to go abroad on sabbatical leave in order to complete research on a project which had occupied me for years. If the excavations continued for longer than anticipated, what would become of my sabbatical and of my long-standing research project, and what would become of my other commitments? Besides, I was nearing retirement age! And anyone perusing the ruins of the Jewish Quarter at that time would have envisioned lengthy excavations, full of difficulties and ending in inconclusive results. The trial excavations conducted there by the Department of Antiquities were hardly encouraging, to say the least.

On the other hand, as a veteran citizen of Jerusalem, I regarded the very idea of excavating in the Old City as a great privilege and worthy of challenge. Since my earliest days in archaeology this city has occupied an important place in my scientific endeavors. During the many seminars I have conducted with my university students on various facets of the archaeology and topography of Jerusalem, we were constantly faced by a serious lack of basic data and an urgent need for further excavations. And now I was suddenly being presented with the opportunity to excavate on a site which might solve even one of the significant topographical problems of the city. How could I refuse? I decided to postpone my sabbatical leave and my other plans indefinitely, and to take upon myself this fascinating task.

We commenced the first season of excavations in the Jewish Quarter on the first of September 1969; and the 1978 season was our tenth. In retrospect, the decade between seems to have been a single, long season of work. We generally labored in the field for about eight months of the year, utilizing the rainy months to clarify the problems which had arisen during the preceding season, to organize the finds (registration, photographing, and drawing), and to prepare for the coming season. In urgent cases we continued to excavate even in the winter months. A normal season of archaeological excavations on other sites in Israel generally lasts for about two months. On this basis, we chalked up at least forty such "seasons" of work. While our capacity was tremendous, I must admit that such continuous digging is not the ideal way to conduct archaeological work, if for no other reason than the fact that it prevented us from finding the time to study the steadily accumulating material. However, this work schedule was necessitated by the fact that these were salvage operations which could not be suspended without holding up the reconstruction of the quarter.

Frankly, the entire undertaking was difficult and exhausting, and exacerbated by the peculiar circumstances of excavating alongside construction work. The bustle

5. The Jewish Quarter from the east, prior to the destruction of the "Tiferet Israel" (right) and "Porath Yoseph" (left) synagogues. Photographed by Kalter

of building and the noise of the jackhammers, bulldozers, trucks and cement-mixers was our daily lot the year round. We reminisced nostalgically about digging under normal conditions at remote sites. One might swallow some dust there, but it was possible at least to concentrate on the task of revealing the past without such nervewracking intrusions. On such sites there is no danger of houses collapsing into the excavations, of sewage swirling into the trenches, of wet concrete splashing over an ancient wall uncovered the day before, of boards placed to protect such walls suddenly disappearing into the form for a new concrete wall, or of the hundred other little "hitches" which were our daily fare. Here we also had to devote much time to conferences with the Company and its architects and engineers, to coordinate activities and deal with technical problems relating to excavating within a built-up area. For example, our excavations and the subsequent construction work had to be scheduled in advance, and we had to know how near our dig could approach adjacent houses without causing them to collapse, or the location of areas where we could not dig because of sewage or other piping, and so forth. We also conferred on the important subject of preserving the ancient remains which we had uncovered and the modifications in construction which their preservation entailed. We sought to preserve worthy remains within the basements of new structures, or in open spaces, and to allow for their eventual preparation for tourism. While the Company displayed understanding and good will in most instances, in some cases our demands were contested on grounds of planning and budget. But even here we generally found a successful way of compromising, and all such decisions were arrived at in cooperation with the Department of Antiquities, in accord with the guidelines set down by the Archaeological Council of Israel prior to commencement of our work. At present, all the excavated sites that have been scheduled for preservation have been covered over or temporarily enclosed; eventually they will be developed appropriately and opened to the public.

CHAPTER ONE

THE PERIOD OF THE FIRST TEMPLE

1. Jerusalem in the Bible and in Other Ancient Sources

The distant past of Jerusalem is shrouded in mist. We know that the city's history goes back some five thousand years—on the basis of a small group of pottery vessels from the Early Bronze Age I (about 3000 B.C.) found on the slopes of the hill on which earliest Jerusalem rose. However, archaeology has not yet been able to tell us whether these finds point to a proper settlement or merely to a group of squatters settled around the Gihon Spring. And the historical sources of this early period are still silent concerning the city.

The first written mention of Jerusalem may possibly be contained in the documents recently discovered at Tell Mardikh, ancient Ebla, in northern Syria. These clay tablets are written in cuneiform script, in a West Semitic language, and are ascribed to around the middle of the third millennium B.C. According to initial reports, the name Salim (Jerusalem?) is found alongside several other city names, such as Hazor, Megiddo, Lachish, Jaffa, and Ashdod, all famous in the Bible. But no archaeological remains of the Jerusalem of that period have come to light on the site itself.

Jerusalem is mentioned in ancient Egyptian sources of the 19th-18th centuries B.C. The "Execration Texts," written in ink on pottery bowls and figurines, contain incantations against the enemies of Egypt. The "kings" of Jerusalem (*Rushalimum*) appear there among the various city rulers in Canaan and Syria. Tombs and pottery from this same period (the Middle Bronze Age I) have been discovered on the slopes of the Mount of Olives, opposite the Old City.

In the Bible, Jerusalem is first mentioned in the story of Abraham's meeting with "Melchizedek, king of Salem" (that is, Jerusalem)... "priest of God Most High" (Genesis 14: 18-20). According to this tradition, Jerusalem was known in the period of the Patriarchs (around the 18th century B.C.) as a city-state and the site of a cult dedicated to the deity called *El-Elyon*, "God Most High," who bore the epithet "Creator of heaven and earth." Remains of the eastern city wall of this period have been discovered in archaeological excavations.

Evidence of Jerusalem in the days of Egyptian rule over Canaan, in the Late Bronze Age (around the 14th century B.C.), is found in letters from various Canaanite rulers to their Egyptian overlords, whose capital was then at el-Amarna. Among these clay tablets, written in cuneiform Akkadian, are six from Abdi-ḥeba, King of Jerusalem (*Urusalim*). Archaeologists have found tombs and pottery of this period close by the city.

The next chapter in the history of Jerusalem, the Israelite period, is much better documented, both in biblical sources and by archaeological evidence. The following brief review presents a few select highlights on the city in this period. In the days of the Israelite conquest of Canaan (around the 13th century B.C.), Adonizedek, King of Jerusalem, led a league of Amorite kings opposing Joshua. Jerusalem remained a Jebusite city during the subsequent period of Israelite settlement in Canaan, and was conquered only later, by David (around 1000 B.C.). The "City of Jebus," also called the "Stronghold of Zion," was renamed the "City of David" after he captured it. David soon made it the capital of his kingdom, transferring the Holy Ark of the Covenant there from Shiloh. Further, he built an altar dedicated to the God of Israel atop Mount Zion (known as Mount Moriah), at the threshing-floor purchased from Araunah the Jebusite. This act laid the foundations for Jerusalem as the center of worship of the God of Israel. Solomon brought his father's plans to fruition by building the Temple and a palace on the mount, expanding the city northward. Jerusalem thereby became a Holy City, the national and cult center of the Kingdom of Israel.

After the death of Solomon (around 930 B.C.), the United Monarchy split into the northern Kingdom of Israel and the southern Kingdom of Judah, with Jerusalem remaining the capital of Judah alone. This split greatly reduced the political and economic stature of Jerusalem, and smaller cult centers with sanctuaries sprouted up throughout Israel. After the northern Kingdom of Israel was conquered by the Assyrians in 722 B.C., Jerusalem regained its position as the center of religious and national life for all the people of Israel, the focal point of its sanctity and greatness being the Temple.

The ancient sources tell us little of the physical development of Jerusalem in this period. References in the Bible to new residential and commercial quarters — the *Mishneh* and the *Makhtesh* — hint vaguely at the expansion of the city. Among the building projects of the various kings, the Bible notes the *millo*, apparently the built-up terraces on the eastern slope of the Eastern Hill, on which other structures were then built; the *ophel*, an inner citadel built at the northern end of the City of David (thus leading to the use of the name Ophel Hill for the entire spur); and especially the city walls, which were often repaired and expanded. Uzziah, Hezekiah, and Manasseh were among the kings mentioned to have built these fortifications.

Jerusalem gained greatly in stature — political, economic, and spiritual — in the days of Hezekiah. His deeds on the eve of the invasion of Sennacherib, King of Assyria (in 701 B.C.) involved the building of "another wall" and the diversion of the waters of the Gihon Spring into the city through the now famous Siloam Tunnel (also known as Hezekiah's Tunnel). Hezekiah's son, Manasseh, strengthened the Ophel and built a new city wall "west of Gihon." King Josiah instituted a religious reform, smashing unauthorized altars, uprooting pagan cults, and focusing worship of the god of Israel on the Temple at Jerusalem. It was under him that Judah freed itself from the Assyrian yoke, expanded its territory and influence, and enjoyed a period of economic and spiritual prosperity.

Jerusalem was captured for the first time by Nebuchadnezzar, King of Babylon, in 597 B.C., in response to the anti-Babylonian policies of Jehoiakim and Jehoiachin. On this occasion he sent King Jehoiachin and the nobles of Jerusalem into exile in Babylonia. Nebuchadnezzar once again conquered Jerusalem in 586 B.C.,

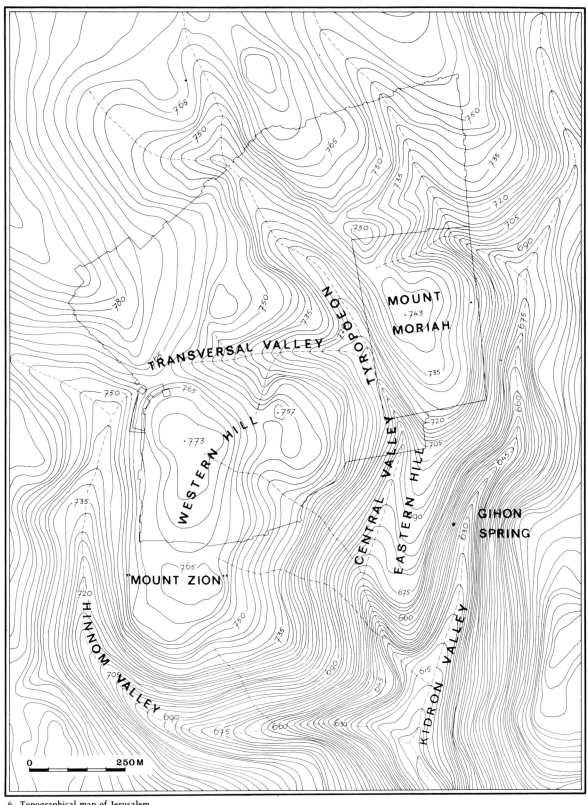

6. Topographical map of Jerusalem

25

and this time the Temple was burnt, the city razed, and the people sent into exile in Babylonia, along with Zedekiah, last of the kings of Judah.

2. Where was Early Jerusalem Situated?

The character of any city, its development and its history, are determined to a great extent by geographical situation and topographical structure. This is especially true of Jerusalem, which not only has "mountains round about it" (Psalms 125: 2), but also spreads over several hills divided by steep valleys. It is therefore important to familiarize ourselves with this aspect of the city and to learn its various features.

Early Jerusalem spread over two (some say three) hills. Our point of departure is *6* the spot known to all as Mount Moriah (743 meters above sea level), the site of the Temple. A long and narrow spur descends to the south. The saddle between the hill and the spur has filled up over the centuries so that today they form a single hill, called the Southeastern or Eastern Hill, and popularly, the Ophel Hill. This spur is flanked on the east by the Kidron Valley and on the west by the Central or Tyropoeon Valley (*ha-gai*); these two valleys meet at the southern end of the spur, where they join the Hinnom Valley coming from the west.

The Southwestern or Western Hill (763 meters above sea level), on the other side of the Central Valley, is much larger and higher than its eastern counterpart. This hill is flanked on the east by the Central Valley and on the south and west by the Hinnom Valley. On the north, it is bordered by a shallow valley which runs perpendicular to it, from the site of the modern Jaffa Gate to the Temple Mount; this is sometimes called the Transversal Valley. The Eastern and Western Hills are thus well protected on three sides by rather steep slopes and valleys, while on the north the natural defences are less effective.

At the foot of the eastern slope of the Eastern Hill there is a gushing fountain—the Gihon Spring—Jerusalem's only supply of fresh water in early antiquity. South of this hill is another minor water source, the Rogel Spring, which is actually only a well.

Any discussion of the Jerusalem of First Temple times is foremost a discussion of its topography. One of the most difficult and significant topographical-historical problems is that of the extent of settlement in that period. This matter has been debated for as long as there have been archaeological investigations in the city. Many scholars have entered into this controversy and a large body of literature, scientific and not so scientific, has grown up around it. A brief look at the basic problem will help us comprehend the contribution of our recent excavations toward a solution.

The first question which arose related to the location of the earliest Jerusalem—the city of the Jebusites, of David and Solomon, and of the later kings of Judah. An early tradition stemming from the ancient Jewish historian Flavius Josephus identified the City of David with modern "Mount Zion," which led to the misnaming of this hill and to the traditional identification of "David's Tomb" there. For Josephus mistakenly identified the biblical "Stronghold of Zion" with the Upper City of his day, which was located on the Western Hill.

This problem was solved long ago by archaeological excavations carried out on the Eastern Hill, which proved that Jerusalem began its long journey through history at this site, near the spring. Any remaining doubts were quelled by the discovery of Hezekiah's Tunnel, leading from the Gihon Spring on one side of the spur to the pool on the other side. The tunnel, and the famous Hebrew inscription describing its hewing, connect the site with King Hezekiah's hewing a water conduit as mentioned in the Bible, to bring the waters of the Gihon within the walled city. This project was carried out somewhat before 700 B.C.

From the Early Bronze Age I pottery found on the eastern slope, it would appear that man had already been settled there by the beginning of the third millennium B.C. On this same slope, Dame Kathleen Kenyon discovered part of a Middle Bronze Age II wall (18th century B.C.), which was apparently reutilized in the Jebusite city wall captured by David. The City of David initially encompassed an area of about 11 acres; after the Temple Mount had been encompassed by Solomon, the city had a total area of about 32 acres. A new city wall was built in the 8th century B.C. along the line of the earlier walls, and thus the area then enclosed did not appreciably grow. Jerusalem now covered about the same area as the average Canaanite and Israelite city in Eretz-Israel, "the land of Israel." The fact that it was confined to a narrow, sloping spur with a maximum width of no more than some 130 meters was decisive in limiting the development and expansion of the city, as well as its supply of vital necessities.

THE PROBLEM OF THE WESTERN HILL How could this city, with all its topographical limitations, have functioned for so long a period as capital of the country and the royal residence, as a national and spiritual center as well as dwelling place for its inhabitants? We must therefore question whether Jerusalem did in fact remain confined to these narrow limits until the very day of its destruction in 586 B.C. Or did it expand under the urban and demographic pressure, and spread beyond the early walls long before that fateful year? This query brings us to the very core of the second topographical problem facing us: was the Jerusalem of the First Temple period built on only one hill, or did it spread to the second hill? Flavius Josephus, the only historian to describe the topography of the city (albeit in the 1st century A.D.), writes: "The city was built upon two hills, which are opposite to one another, and have a valley to divide them asunder... Of these hills, that which contains the upper city is much higher, and in length more direct... The other hill... sustains the lower city, (and) is of the shape of a moon when she is horned..." (*Wars of the Jews* V, 4, 1).

Josephus' description of an upper city and a lower city is of great significance; the center of gravity of the city in his day had shifted to the Upper City on the broad Western Hill, apparently leaving the Lower City on the small Eastern Hill secondary in importance. One must then ask when the City of David (here used in the geographical rather than chronological sense) commenced, and when did Jerusalem expand to the Western Hill? Did this occur in First Temple times, or only in the days of the Second Temple? Scholarly opinion has long been divided over this question, the controversy often becoming rather heated. But a decisive answer was not forthcoming.

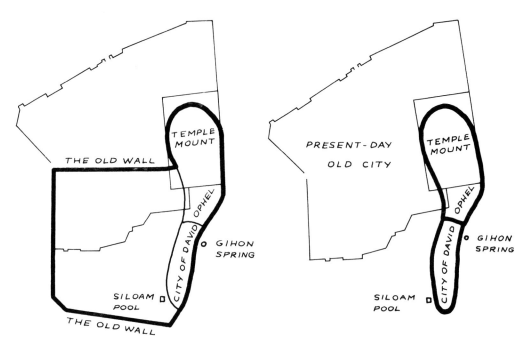

7a. The maximalist view of early Jerusalem   7b. The minimalist view of early Jerusalem

There were only two ways this question could be solved—either through reliable information from historical sources, or through archaeological excavations. Until recently, neither of these provided sufficient information to arrive at an unequivocal answer. Two major schools of thought arose, one historical and the other archaeological, but the paucity of evidence prevented the scales from tipping in either direction, and the controversy raged on. There arose "maximalist" and "minimalist" camps, concerning the size of the city advocated by each: the maximalists included both hills in the city of the First Temple period, while the minimalists excluded the Western Hill. And the variety of opinion which ranged between these two stances was very broad indeed.

The maximalists held that, throughout the period of the First Temple, Jerusalem spread over both the Eastern and the Western Hills. (The Temple Mount has never entered into the controversy, as it is not in dispute.) This view was based primarily on Josephus' description of the course of the first (or early) wall of the city as encompassing the Western Hill on the north, west, and south. Josephus ascribes this wall to David and Solomon and the kings who succeeded them. The maximalists accept Josephus' description at face value, and take the biblical references to the *Mishneh* and the *Makhtesh*—generally considered to have been new quarters somewhere outside the early city confines—to indicate that there had been suburbs outside the City of David. According to this concept, Jerusalem was an extensive city spreading over some 150 acres. In this view only such a large city could have suited the capital of the Kingdom of Israel and Judah. The reliance here was upon the not too lucid historical-literary sources, and a reasoning tainted by emotional factors. Despite the fact that highly respectable scholars held this view, especially in the initial phases of research on Jerusalem, there was no tangible basis or archaeological evidence to support it, and the number of its adherents gradually dwindled.

THE "MAXIMALIST" VIE

The "realistic" minimalists rejected the above map of Jerusalem out of hand. In their opinion such a large area was too much for a city of the Iron Age, and the first

THE "MINIMALIST" VIEW

wall, which Josephus ascribed to the kings of Israel, should properly be attributed to the Hasmoneans. They based their ascription on fragments of walls from the Hellenistic period which were visible within the later city walls encompassing the Western Hill on the west and south. But their contention rested mainly on negative archaeological results, for no decisive remains from the period of the Israelite or Judean Kingdom had ever been found on the Western Hill. Of course, only very limited trial excavations had been conducted there, but this lack of evidence led them to conclude that the Jerusalem of the First Temple period was limited to the Eastern Hill up till the time of its destruction by the Babylonians. Only in Second Temple times, from the Hasmoneans on (2nd century B.C.), did it become a truly large city, spreading to the Western Hill and encompassing also what Josephus calls the Upper City.

There was a third view between these two extremes, according to which the early city expanded only at the end of the Judean monarchy, but only to the northeastern part of the Western Hill adjacent to the Temple Mount. This too was only an unproven conjecture, and the controversy continued, feeding on the lack of evidence. In final analysis, the dispute revolved on the prestige ascribed to Jerusalem as a capital. Could it have been a small, restricted town till its very end? Or did it grow into a large city at least under the late Judean monarchy?

KENYON EXCAVATIONS   The controversy came to the fore once again during the 1960s, with the excavations of the renowned British archaeologist, the late Dame Kathleen Kenyon. Her work, which concentrated mainly on the Eastern Hill, led her to important new conclusions concerning the history of the City of David and its boundaries during the Israelite period. She demonstrated the advantages of modern methods of excavation, correcting many of the serious distortions which had grown out of the mistaken conclusions of her predecessors.

New excavations revealed that the fortifications on the eastern flank of the Eastern Hill, previously ascribed to the Jebusites and to David and Solomon, were built over the ruins of houses from the 7th century B.C. She therefore concluded that these defences must be dated to the Hasmoneans, in Second Temple times. The Israelite city wall was not at the top of the eastern slope, but at its middle. And though the early city did not have as narrow a "waist" as thought earlier, it actually encompassed no more than some 15 acres (excluding the Temple Enclosure).

Dame Kenyon did not rest on these impressive results, which truly revolutionized our knowledge of the City of David. She also sought to solve, once and for all, the problem of the stratigraphy of the Western Hill, seeking a key for determining the extent of Jerusalem in the days of the First Temple. To this end, she conducted several trial excavations on the eastern slope of the Western Hill, within the Central Valley, and (with A.D. Tushingham) in the open area known as the "Armenian Garden," just within the modern city walls on the west. She also dug a deep trial pit in the heart of the Christian Quarter, near the "Muristan." Dame Kenyon claimed to have found no occupation remains outside the walls earlier than the time of Herod Agrippa I (1st century A.D.). Inside the Old City, she did find earth fills containing large quantities of mixed pottery from the Herodian and Israelite periods. Moreover, directly on the bedrock thick layers of earth were found containing potsherds, all from the Iron Age II (8th-7th centuries B.C.). In the Armenian Garden this layer contained a wall (the thickness of which could not be determined) built of large boulders, also ascribed to the Iron Age. Dame Kenyon interpreted these finds as traces of Israelite quarries, which had subsequently been filled in with earth containing Israelite pottery, probably brought from some spot outside the Western Hill. The wall which she found was, in her opinion, no more than a supporting terrace wall built by the quarrymen outside the area settled in the Israelite period.

As a result of her excavations, Dame Kenyon arrived at the far-reaching conclusion that there had been no settlement whatsoever on the Western Hill during the Israelite period, and that the summit of the hill was first settled in the Hellenistic period, more precisely in the period of the Hasmoneans (2nd century B.C.); and that its eastern slope was not occupied prior to the 1st century A.D. It thus seemed that the last nail had been driven into the coffin of the maximalist concept of a greater Jerusalem. Because Dame Kenyon was an authority of the highest order in the realm of stratigraphic excavation, her conclusions were accepted fully, and with a sense of relief, even by those who had previously been in some doubt. It was finally possible to rely upon an authoritative stratigraphic opinion, founded on systematic excavations on the Western Hill. The lengthy controversy concerning the boundaries of Jerusalem in the period of the First Temple had at long last been settled, almost decisively, in favor of the minimalist camp. It seemed as if the royal Jerusalem was fated to remain in our consciousness as a small, narrow town up to its very destruction in 586 B.C.

Much to the good fortune of both Jerusalem and historical truth, the reunification of the city in 1967 enabled widescale excavations in the Upper City. They have since shown that Dame Kenyon made a basic error — not concerning stratigraphy but one of interpretation — and this led her to mistaken historical conclusions. She had relied mainly upon the results of trial excavations in sporadic, minor trenches, results which she regarded as negative. In interpreting the finds on the summit of the Western Hill, she failed to consider the likelihood that such large quantities of earth containing Israelite pottery could not have been brought from the far-off, small Eastern Hill. In fact, this pottery must have come from the Western Hill itself, and therefore there must have been an Israelite settlement there.

In our experience, decisive and far-reaching conclusions should not be arrived at solely on the basis of trial pits and trenches. There were spots in our excavations where the earliest remains, found directly on the bedrock, dated from as late as the Byzantine period. What false and misleading conclusions would have resulted if we had been so unlucky as to dig only at such spots! At other places on the rock we uncovered remains from the Herodian or Hasmonean period — and at many others, we found Israelite remains, in the lowermost stratum, albeit often only in small, sporadic patches. The absence of an Israelite stratum in other areas can be explained by the fact that building activities in later periods often led to the surface being scraped down to bedrock. Much of the Israelite remains were cleared away during the extensive building projects in the period of the Second Temple, when huge quantities of earth were transferred from one spot to another in order to level the ground or to obtain large structural fills. This shows the true origin of the many Israelite sherds in the earth fills found in the excavations carried out on the Western Hill by Dame Kenyon and others.

RECENT EXCAVATIONS Our excavations, conducted at many different spots and in wide areas scattered over the entire Jewish Quarter, have swung back the pendulum of the controversy over the first settlement on the Western Hill. We have now proved that this hill was indeed populated and encompassed by a city wall in the period of the First Temple, at least from the 8th century B.C. on. We are still far from a clear and final picture, and the field data are as yet fragmentary; but for the first time in modern research on Jerusalem we have arrived at a solid point of reference for the serious discussion of this topic of major importance. In the following pages we shall review the results of our explorations into the Israelite period and examine their historical significance. But it should be emphasized that the scientific evaluation of our findings has not yet been completed: the chronology referred to here is still approximate, and several of our dates may have to be revised in the future, in the interest of a greater degree of accuracy. What is important at this stage is the very fact that we have been able to determine that Israelite occupational strata do exist on the Western Hill.

3. Discovering Israelite Remains on the Western Hill

Over our years of work in the Jewish Quarter, we have managed to excavate many extensive areas—as the plan of our excavation areas shows. The fact that these sites are scattered over the entire quarter makes it clear that our stratigraphical conclusions can hardly be considered haphazard, but reflect an accurate and typical cross-section of the history of this locale.

In most of the sites where we excavated down to bedrock or virgin soil (and we generally did reach bedrock where possible), we found the earliest occupational level to be from the Late Israelite period (Iron Age II; 8th-7th centuries B.C.). The Western Hill had not been settled prior to this. The most apparent outward feature of the Israelite stratum was the fresh red color of the earth, this *terra rossa* typifying the virgin soil of the Jerusalem region. This earth—either immediately overlying the bedrock, or used as fill and generally containing Israelite pottery—served as a guide and signpost to the Israelite level.

STRUCTURES The Israelite stratum was generally poor in building remains and smaller objects, for it had often been nibbled away in later periods. This layer had sometimes been disturbed by later building foundations; at other times, especially in the period of the Second Temple, it was removed entirely, exposing the bedrock for the hewing of cellars, cisterns, and baths. Although this left insufficient remains of walls to enable us to reconstruct the plans of individual Israelite buildings, or even of single rooms, the remains were indeed sufficiently extensive to indicate that a permanent settlement had indeed existed here. It makes little difference to the stratigrapher-archaeologist whether only fragments of walls and associated floors are found, or

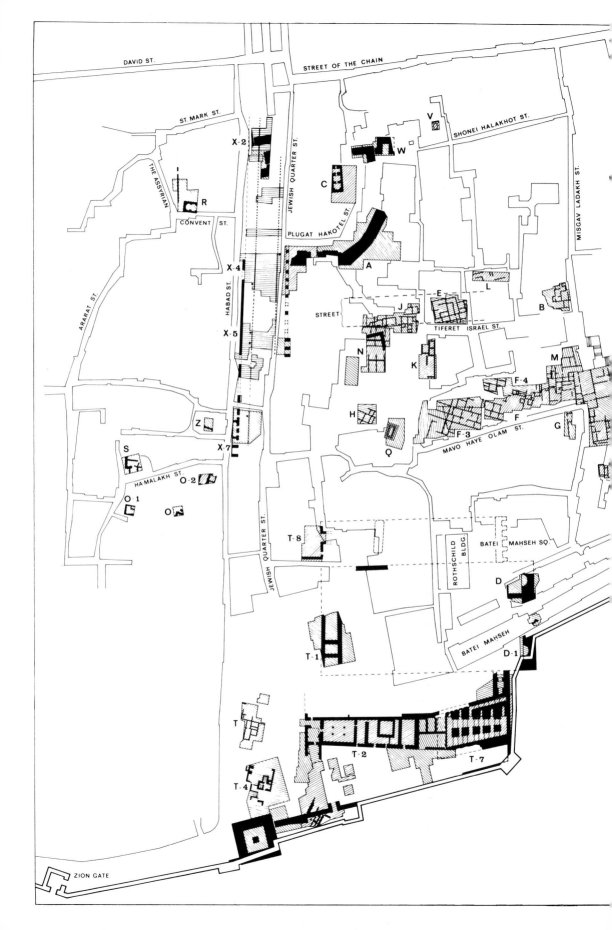

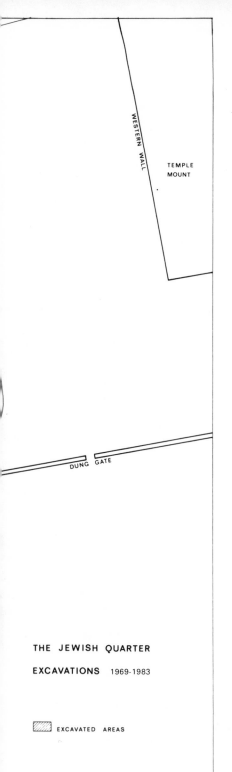

THE JEWISH QUARTER

EXCAVATIONS 1969-1983

EXCAVATED AREAS

0   50 M

whether entire buildings are brought to light intact. The sherds found above and beneath the floors provide ready evidence for the period of construction and for the most recent occupation.

Our strong desire to find a solution to the problem of settlement on the Western Hill led us, from the very beginning of our work, to search for such remains from the period of the First Temple. Green lights began flashing shortly after we began our first year in Area A, when we discovered the first meager remains of a wall with an attached floor, alongside Iron Age sherds. At first we thought that this wall was nothing more than a bit of some farmer's hut, hardly indicative of a true settlement on the spot. But the more we were able to trace such remains, together with complete pottery vessels and other objects, the clearer it became that we had come across evidence of a true Israelite settlement. The buildings here were built of undressed stones and had plastered walls. The finer floors were of a thick layer of crushed and tamped chalk (ḥawār), while the poorer ones were of beaten clay with a coating of lime. The fill beneath the floors was generally of the common red earth.

9. The beginning of our excavations: Area A (1969), where the Israelite city wall was discovered (see p. 32)

MISCELLANEOUS FINDS

In the light of the destruction and scraping which eradicated much of the Israelite stratum, it is not surprising that the smaller finds reflecting daily life were also few and far between. What is surprising is that, despite all, we uncovered a considerable number and variety of finds in the fragmentary Israelite occupation layer. These enabled us to determine the nature of the stratum and of various aspects of the material culture of Jerusalem at that time. In general these finds conform with those from other contemporaneous sites in Judah.

Building remains from the Israelite period (Area F, p. 32)

POTTERY   Potsherds were found in greatest quantity, for pottery vessels were the most common commodity, continuously broken and replaced. The number of complete vessels found is not large, though the abundance of sherds and fragments encompasses the entire range of pottery ware and forms in use at that time. These were ordinary household vessels, especially kitchen utensils of the sort usually found on any Judean site of the 8th-7th centuries B.C.: bowls, kraters, jugs and juglets, cooking pots and storage jars. Many of them had an outer red coating, what potters
16 call a slip, and were burnished over their entire surface or in bands, as is so typical of Iron Age II pottery from Judah. Pottery oil lamps are represented by bowl-like vessels — with rounded bases typical in the 8th century B.C., flat bases in the 7th century B.C. and high bases in the late 7th and early 6th centuries B.C. We should note here that our knowledge of the pottery vessels of this period in Jerusalem has been enriched greatly in recent years as a result of the discovery of contemporaneous tombs close by the city.

FIGURINES   Another category of pottery object quite common in that period includes various figurines and statuettes. Outwardly it seems strange that the Israelites would have used such objects, for there were strong religious injunctions against the making of graven images (though the use of "teraphims" is certainly noted in the Bible, even if in a derogatory manner). However, very few archaeological sites in Judah have
11 failed to yield such figurines, which are either zoomorphic or anthropomorphic, that is in the form of an animal or in that of a human. The animal figurines are rather schematic, depicting horses (sometimes with riders) and other indefinite quadrupeds. Their use is not clear, and they have often been interpreted in this context as toys.

12. The Israelite city wall discov
in Area A (p. 32). Looking north
13. Area W (p. 32) during excav
14. Area W (p. 32) after clearan
of the Israelite tower and the
Hasmonean tower (in foreground

11. Animal figurines

The statuettes are more interesting, depicting women supporting their exposed breasts with their two hands; the head is generally molded separately and then attached onto the cylindrical body. These pillar-shaped statuettes are very common in Judah and are often found within the remains of private houses. It is doubtful that they served for worship, and it is assumed that they were a hand-down from Canaanite times, used in folk magic and as talismans for fertility, in pregnancy, and during birth. They thus symbolized the goddess of fertility, who was held in esteem by all the peoples of antiquity—not least by Israelite women who were hardly exceptional in holding such superstitious beliefs.

We have been able to restore one broken figurine, the nicest one we found. Its arms were missing, which led us to dub it "The Venus of Jerusalem." After the arms *15* supporting the bosom had been restored, we were well able to understand the delicate smile on the figure's face: she was simply pleased with the abundance she held in her hands, far more than usually possessed by most of these figurines.

15. Israelite fertility figurine

15a. A unique figurine with pinched, bird-like face
and arms stretched forward in blessing (?),
or possibly exaggerated breasts symbolizing fertility (7th century B

16. Israelite pottery (Iron Age II)

17. Jar fragment bearing ancient Hebrew inscription: [*El*] *qoneh aretz*

INSCRIPTIONS Every archaeologist is especially delighted by one particular type of find — inscriptions. The written word does so much to enliven the other "silent" finds, creating a "personal" contact with ancient man and his deeds. Nothing else expresses so very closely the Israelite character of a stratum as an inscription in ancient Hebrew. And, of course, every additional Hebrew inscription found in Jerusalem is of even greater importance, for very few Hebrew inscriptions from the days of the First Temple have come to light here. The Hebrew epigraphic material found in our excavations was indeed a significant supplement to the archaeological evidence, confirming the existence of a settlement on the Western Hill in Israelite times.

Our most interesting epigraphic find is a fragment of a storage jar bearing three lines of script in black ink. The ancient Hebrew script is in the fine hand of a skilled scribe, and its form indicates that it was written in the late 8th or early 7th century B.C. The script is partly effaced, and the only thing legible in the first line is the end of a name: ...*iahu*. In the second line we can clearly read the name *Michaiahu*, and in the third line the surviving letters *qn'rṣ* can be restored to read *(El) qoneh aretz*, which translates as "(God,) Creator of Earth." An identical phrase is found in a Phoenician inscription of the 8th century B.C. from Karatepe in Turkey: "Baal shamem and El qoneh aretz." In the Bible the phrase appears as an epithet of God in the words of Melchizedek, King of Salem (Jerusalem) and priest of *El Elyon* ("God Most High"): "Blessed be Abram by God Most High, Creator of Heaven and Earth" (Genesis 14:19). In an oath, Abraham himself identified *El Elyon* and his epithet with "the Lord" (that is, Yahweh; Genesis 14:22). In our inscription, the expression "Creator of Earth" appears for the first time in a later Hebrew context, indicating that this was indeed also the epithet of the God of Israel. Just what the significance was of such an epithet on a pottery storage jar is unclear; the jar may have contained an offering intended for the Temple.

41

18. Hebrew ostracon

Another inscription found written on a potsherd was a letter apparently concerning inspection or control. This ostracon is written on both sides, five lines of ink script on the face and two on the back (though it is incomplete). The script is partly blurred, but on the front it is possible to read (tentatively) the following words:

]ṙḥ . šl ......
]n . wlbqr ....
]'l . bqy . byt
].............l'
]ḃms . lbq̇ṙ

The word *lbqr* (in lines 2 and 5) in biblical Hebrew is generally interpreted as meaning "to investigate," "to examine," or "to control." The word *bqy* (line 3) appears in the Bible as the name of a prince of the tribe of Dan: "Bukki the son of Jogli" (Numbers 34:22). The word *byt*, "house," after his name might be the beginning of the name of his place of origin, as we read of other persons in the Bible (for instance, "Jesse the *Beth*-lehemite"). Whether the bottom line referred to taxes (Hebrew *mas*) cannot be determined. The words of the inscription are separated by dots, and the cursive script is obviously the product of a professional scribe. Certain characteristics of the letters point to the end of the 7th and the beginning of the 6th centuries B.C.

Seal impression: *lamelekh mmšt*, and two-winged sun-disk

20. Seal impression: *lamelekh Hebron*, and two-winged sun-disk, together with incised concentric circles

21. Seal impression: *lamelekh...*, and four-winged scarab

22. Seal impression: *lamelekh Ziph* and four-winged scarab

SEAL IMPRESSIONS Impressions of inscribed seals on the handles of storage jars provide an important source for epigraphic material, especially those bearing the type of seal known as *lamelekh* stamps. The word *lamelekh* is generally interpreted as meaning "of the king" or "royal," that is, the jar and its contents had royal sanction. These seals also bear the name of one of four cities: Hebron, Ziph, Socoh or *mmšt* (the latter an unknown name), as well as the symbol of a four-winged scarab or a stylized two-winged solar disc. Such impressions have been found on almost all the Israelite sites in Judah, and 44 examples came to light in the Jewish Quarter excavations. The significance of the city names and the exact purpose of the jars so stamped is still a matter of controversy. We do not know whether they were intended for taxation, for emergency food provisions for the respective cities or for royal estates producing wine, oil, or other products. Both the two-winged sun and the four-winged scarab are obviously royal emblems. The stamped jars first appear around the end of the 8th century B.C. (the days of Hezekiah, King of Judah), and continue for a time into the 7th century B.C. It is generally assumed that they were superseded by impressions bearing the form of a stylized rosette.

27

43

Occasionally, *lamelekh* handles bear concentric circles incised into the pottery after firing. This mark is usually interpreted as a sign canceling the validity of the royal stamp and thereby indicating that the vessel could be used for private purposes. One of our handles, undoubtedly from a jar of the *lamelekh* type, has the stamp of a private person next to the incised circles. The private seal reads *23* "Belonging to Nera (son of) Shebna," the two names representing shortened forms of the biblical names Neriah and Shebaniah. An identical impression was found at Ramat Raḥel south of Jerusalem, on a handle bearing a two-winged *lamelekh* impression, indicating that this was most likely the stamp of an official responsible for the manufacture of the royal storage jars.

The handle of another storage jar bears a Hebrew seal impression reading *24* "Belonging to Neri son of Shebanio," names identical to those found on the private seal impression just mentioned, but with variant forms given to the endings of the names. Despite the differences in spelling and script, both impressions were apparently made by the same official. The name Shebanio here is of particular interest, for this is the first time that a name terminating in the shortened theophoric element *-io* has been found in Judah in a clear archaeological context. Till now only two seals from Judah are known with this element, both of them of unknown provenance; and both belonged to officials of King Uzziah: "Belonging to Shebanio, Servant of Uzzio" and "Belonging to Abio, Servant of Uzzio." While names ending in the *-io* form were common in the northern Kingdom of Israel—as evidenced by the Samaria Ostraca of the 8th century B.C., in names such as Abio, Gadio, Obadio, Shemario—in the Kingdom of Judah the theophoric element was given a fuller form, *-iahu*—as seen in the Arad Letters of the 8th-7th centuries B.C., and the Lachish Letters of the early 6th century B.C., in names such as Abiahu, Berechiahu, Gemariahu, Obadiahu, and Shemariahu. It has been suggested—and quite properly—that the names Amario, Obadio, and Shemaio occurring in the Hebrew inscriptions of the 9th and early 8th centuries B.C. recently discovered at Kuntilet Ajrud, in northern Sinai, represent persons who may well have been from the northern kingdom. But our new discovery in Jerusalem supports the view that names ending in *-io* occurred in Judah as well as in Israel in the 9th and 8th centuries B.C., under northern influence. After the fall of Samaria in 722 B.C., the *-io* form ceased to be used in Judah, as in the north. It is of note that names such as Urio and Aḥio reappear again in Judah in the post-exilic period.

Two other seal impressions are noteworthy. One of them reads "Belonging to *25* Zaphan (son of) Abimaaz"; Zaphan is a contraction of the name Zephaniah, and Abimaaz is quite similar to the biblical name Ahimaaz (see 1 Samuel 14:50). The second impression reads "Belonging to Menahem (son of) Yobanah"; Yobanah, meaning "God has built," is a variant form of the biblical name Benaiah. Impressions identical to these two, found on storage jars at other sites in Judah, lead us to assume that they, too, are the seals of administrators who had stamped the jars in their official capacity.

We also found one jar handle with a seal impression bearing a work of art. It *26* depicts a very realistically rendered prancing horse, and is of an artistic standard seldom seen in Israel. This motif is a rare one in the glyptic art of the Israelite period.

...ression: "Belonging to Nera/Shebna" and incised concentric circles

24. Seal impression on jar handle: "Belonging to Neri son of Shebanio"

25. Seal impression on jar handle: "Belonging to Zaphan/Abimaaz"

...ression on jar handle depicting a horse

27. Seal impression on jar handle depicting a rosette

SETTLEMENT ON
THE WESTERN HILL

There is no doubt whatsoever that all these finds point to a permanent settlement on the Western Hill. And even though their distribution is rather sparse, the fact that such remains have been found scattered throughout the Jewish Quarter indicates that we are not dealing with mere isolated houses, but rather an extensive settlement. Moreover, remains from the Israelite period have also been found in the limited excavations on the Western Hill outside the Jewish Quarter — in the court-yard of the Jerusalem Citadel (conducted by S.N. Johns, and later by Ruth Amiran and A. Eitan), in the Armenian Garden (by Kathleen Kenyon and A.D. Tush-ingham), and on Mount Zion (by M. Broshi). The discoveries made there serve to complement our picture, extending the limits of the Israelite settlement to the entire Western Hill.

45

But what sort of settlement was this? Was it a rural village or a town, a minor suburb or an extensive residential quarter, an open settlement or a walled city? Before we had a chance to consider this problem, we discovered an Israelite city wall which served to answer all these questions at one fell stroke. We never expected to find anything like it at that particular spot and, although the unforeseen location of the wall caused us quite a few headaches in trying to determine the continuation of its course, it is one of the most important archaeological discoveries made in Jerusalem in recent times. For only now can we definitively state that Jerusalem did encompass the Western Hill in the period of the First Temple.

This discovery has stirred considerable public interest. In Jerusalem itself, a public row developed over how the wall should be preserved. The planners were forced to change the location of projected buildings to take its preservation into account within a basement, as had been done for other important remains in the Jewish Quarter. When public opinion demanded that more should be done, and that the wall should remain exposed to view, the overall plan for this part of the Jewish Quarter was reconsidered. Finally, the then Minister of Housing, Mr. Zeev Scharef, ruled that all previous plans were to be canceled and that a plaza would be built around the wall, leaving it open to view. This plaza has since been built, but the wall itself has remained covered up, pending completion of construction work around it.

The uncovering of this wall was a slow process which continued with intervals over most of the period of our work in the Jewish Quarter. The main point of interest, the uncovering of the first segment some 40 meters long, running from north to south in Area A, occurred during 1969-1970, under the supervision of Ami Mazar, Hillel Geva, and Ronny Reich. At first we noticed a "paved" area of large stones in several "squares" of excavation, beneath the remains from the period of the Second Temple. We thought that it was a sort of broad platform, built for some unknown purpose. But the further we excavated in other squares, the further this "platform" extended. When we discovered its edge on the west, in one of the new "squares," we were able to dig down along its outer face. From the pottery from this trial pit, we found that the construction was from the Israelite period. At this point we began asking ourselves whether it might be a massive supporting wall, and then our work was halted for a time by the conclusion of our first season of excavations.

During the next season, we found the eastern edge of the "platform" in another new square. The fact that it was rather far from the western edge, some seven meters, now suggested—for the first time—that we might actually have come across a very thick wall. Only after we had uncovered two offsets, one opposite the other, on either side of the "platform," were we sure that this was indeed a fortification wall. Then we were faced with the question whether it truly dated from the Israelite period. The mere possibility was so startling as to be farfetched, even in conception!

With the dismantling and removal of walls built over the "platform," the full *12, 28* view of this impressive mass of city wall was exposed. Now that the huge wall was a reality, we still had to ascertain whether the evidence concerning its date would be

28. The Israelite city wall, looking south

clearcut or ambiguous and conflicting. Obviously, we would have to proceed with the utmost caution. In square after square, we traced the course of the wall as far northward as we could dig, eventually exposing a continuous stretch 40 meters long. The wall was uniform in construction, as was the stratigraphic picture which came to light; the same Iron Age II pottery and the same red earth were found all along the wall's base. Nowhere did we encounter any evidence which might have caused doubt of its Israelite origin. Indeed, every new meter uncovered strengthened our faith in this conclusion. Our excavations here continued for many months, with numerous trials, hesitations, and careful considerations, till finally we were convinced that no doubt was left. After such difficult birthpangs (and no won-

29. The foundation of the Israelite city wall, from the side near the western offset

der—the "baby" was 7 meters wide!), we were able to call the wall by its proper name: the Israelite city wall.

I well remember our hesitations—mine and those of my supporting team—when we were faced by the great responsibility of making our conclusions concerning the identity of the wall public. We were only too well aware of the far-reaching consequences this would have in the historical and topographical realms, and that the eyes of many scholars would be focused upon us. Our conclusions would be placed under minute scrutiny by all concerned, and we could not afford to be wrong in so significant a matter.

Now, several year later, I can note with satisfaction that our results have found general acceptance among my colleagues who have visited the site. Even the late Dame Kenyon, who toured our excavations, was convinced by the now obvious facts. Since seeing is believing, Dame Kenyon did include the Israelite wall in her last book on Jerusalem, although in her revised plan published there the city's boundaries are kept to a minimum.

I must admit unblushingly that I had the feeling that we had indeed "made history." Claims by some of my colleagues that the wall was the most important archaeological discovery of the century in Jerusalem have added to this feeling, immodest as it may seem.

SCRIPTION OF THE WALL

The Israelite wall is situated on the northern edge of the Jewish Quarter, about 275 meters west of the Western Wall of the Temple Enclosure. All in all, we have uncovered a continuous stretch of some 65 meters, 45 meters of which run on a north-south line, with a slight tendency to the southwest along today's Pelugat Hakotel Street. There, the wall turns westward and continues up to Jewish Quarter Street. Its continuation farther west is unknown, for it was destroyed at that point during the construction of the Byzantine *cardo maximus* (see below, p. 213).

8, 12, 28

The wall, which averages seven meters in thickness, is not uniformly preserved. While seven courses of stones have survived in some places, to a maximum height of 3.30 meters, at many spots only one or two courses have remained intact. The two faces of the wall are built entirely of large boulders of hard *mizzi* stone, without mortar, though small stones were used to chink the joints. The core of the wall has mixed stones, also large. Actually, most of the remains found represent only the foundation of the wall—that part which was not originally exposed to view. The upper wall itself is missing, except for a few dressed stones in the northern part.

29

THE DATE OF THE WALL

The ascription of the wall to the Late Israelite period is based on the stratigraphy and the pottery. The wall is founded upon bedrock, *terra rossa* filling the lowermost joints. The deposits of earth found on either face of the wall contained sherds of the 8th-7th B.C. centuries only. Israelite sherds were also found above and below the fragments of two floors built adjacent to the wall. The fact that structures of the Hasmonean period were built immediately over the wall is also of chronological significance, for we have found it to be a rule in the Jewish Quarter that the Hasmonean or late Hellenistic stratum immediately overlays the Israelite stratum, with no other layers intervening.

An especially significant stratigraphic situation was revealed in the southern part of the wall, where it turns to the west. There, the Israelite city wall had cut through and destroyed earlier structures, whose remains could be seen clearly north of the wall. These buildings, too, were definitely of the Israelite period and, according to the pottery evidence, were built no earlier than the 8th century B.C. It thus appears that there had already been a settlement on the Western Hill when the city wall was built, and that the earlier houses were partly demolished in order to make way for the new fortifications. We shall return to the historical implications of this point later on.

35

DISCOVERING
THE ISRAELITE TOWER

Our search for the northward continuation of the Israelite city wall, although at first frustrating, eventually led us to a most dramatic discovery. In fact, our quest for this wall brings to mind the biblical story about Saul, who set out to find his father's donkeys and found a kingship.

We had assumed that the broad wall (1, on the plan, p. 50) extended northward, close to the Street of the Chain, turning east along the Transversal Valley, a natural topographical line quite suitable for a defensive wall. However, we were thwarted in our plan to make a trial probe at what we conjectured was the eastward turn by a

30

36

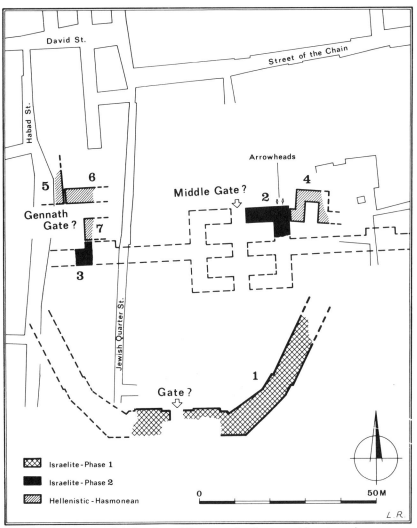

30. Plan of the remains of the Israelite and Hasmonean fortifications, with conjectural reconstruction of the "Middle Gate"

Muslim tomb which had been erected there in Turkish times. When we could find no other spot available farther east, we were forced to abandon our search there for the continuation of the Israelite wall, and we turned to a spot somewhat to the west, where a dilapidated house had just been torn down.

What we expected to find at this spot was the northern line of the defences which encircled Jerusalem in Hasmonean times (2nd-1st centuries B.C.), the line which Josephus called the Early Wall, and has since become known as the First Wall. Although frequently discussed in archaeological literature, no authenticated remains of its northern course had ever been found. However, not only did we uncover the Hasmonean wall, but we also found a completely unexpected fortification from the Israelite period several hundred years earlier. The circumstances surrounding our discovery were so replete with problems and surprises that we feel they are worthy of sharing.

We excavated an area of about 10 by 12 meters on the site marked "W" on the general plan (p. 32), at the corner of Shonei Halakhah and Pelugat Hakotel Streets, reaching a depth of some 15 meters below the modern street level. The great depth involved and the limited area available to us made our seven months of work there a

31. Corner of the Israelite tower. At left, the abutting Hasmonean tower. Hillel Geva and the author are seen standing on the burnt Israelite surface

technical nightmare. The fact that the site was inaccessible to motor vehicles caused us the additional problem of finding a way to dispose of the earth being removed from our constantly growing pit. Here some of "Saul's donkeys" proved an efficient though slow means of hauling it to a dump some distance away. Also facing us, like the sword of Damocles, was the constant danger that the loose earth from the sides of the pit would cave in. The very narrow space, especially at the bottom of the pit, meant that shoring of any sort would leave us no room for digging.

Fortunately, there was only one serious earth-fall, and that occurred after we had completed our work, following a torrential rain. The collapse of a new house on the brink of our pit was, however, diverted only by a skillful feat of emergency engineering. A further aggravation in the face of all these difficulties was the sad fact that the first few months of our work in this probe bore almost no fruit: we dug down for ten meters in the eastern part without striking anything ancient and almost decided to abandon the site in despair. However, our commitment to the principle of reaching bedrock wherever possible proved its worth when the first stones of the very wall we were seeking began to emerge, at a depth of about 12

51

32. Arrowheads scattered among the burnt remains at the base of the tower

meters. Our tenacity had prevailed. We shall return to this wall later on, but let us now continue with the story of the Israelite tower.

AN ISRAELITE TOWER

An entirely different scenario was developing in the western part of the pit, where two massive structures came to light — one Israelite and the other Hasmonean — both of them as fascinating as they are significant. When we removed the uppermost layers, which contained sparse remains from Late Arab times and some *14* walls of the Byzantine period, we revealed the outer corner of a massive structure which continued below the present street level; beneath that it could not be traced. Only in 1980 were we able to follow this wall along 12 meters to the west, where it ends. This structure appeared to be a fortification, probably part of a tower which jutted out from the city wall. Its walls, some four meters thick, were built of large, unhewn stones of the hard *mizzi* type similar to those of the broad Israelite wall. The spaces between the stones were chinked with smaller stones, and no mortar *31* whatsoever was used. The quoins (the stones forming the actual corners) were built of even larger but carefully dressed stones with a slightly convex profile, laid as "headers and stretchers." In front of the northern face of the tower was a floor of beaten earth. The potsherds found both above and below this surface date it to the end of the Iron Age II. This, in turn, provided a sound basis for dating the fortification itself to the Late Israelite period.

After we removed part of the beaten earth surface and dug down to bedrock, we found that the foundations of the tower cut through even earlier buildings and floors. The pottery found here showed that none of the remains were older than the 8th century B.C., the same situation which prevailed at the base of the broad Israelite wall farther south, where the foundations also cut through and destroyed earlier Israelite buildings. The Israelite tower still stands to a height of about eight meters. The quality of its construction and its magnificent state of preservation

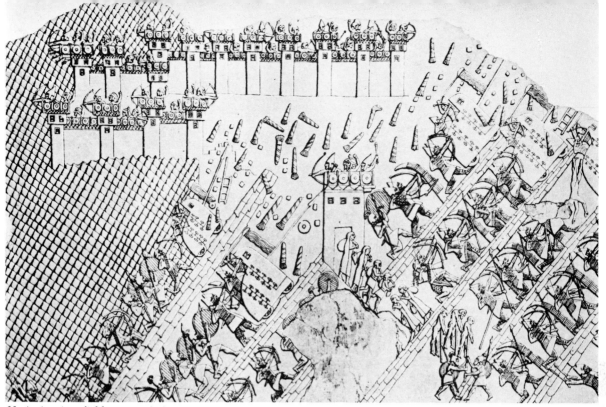

33. An Assyrian relief from Nineveh, depicting the siege of Lachish (after Layard)

render this tower a most impressive example of the monumental architecture of the First Temple period—and it is the only known example of its kind in Jerusalem.

In 1978 another part of a fortification wall came to light some 50 meters west of the Israelite tower, at the northern end of Jewish Quarter Street and just south of David Street. This was apparently part of a city wall and a watchtower or an offset *30* of the wall (3, p. 50). Based on the pottery found there and the similarity of its cornerstones to those of the Israelite tower to the east, it too can be ascribed to the Israelite period. While elements (2) and (3) both form parts of one and the same wall, they have no direct structural connection with the broad Israelite wall to the south (1), and they most probably represent a separate fortification system.

During our clearing of the beaten earth surface in front of the Israelite tower (2)—which was located outside the walled city at the time these fortifications were in use—one particular discovery generated a great deal of excitement: the surface *32* at the foot of the tower was covered with charred wood, ashes, and soot, among which were found a group of arrowheads, four of iron and one of bronze.

The flat, leaf-shaped iron arrowheads are of a type common in this country in Israelite times, while the triple-bladed, socketed bronze arrowhead is of the "Scythian" type and of northern origin. "Scythian" arrowheads, in use from the late 7th century B.C. till sometime in the Persian period, were generally employed by foreign mercenaries. Three factors here—the fortifications, the traces of a conflagration, and the arrowheads—point to a fierce battle for the city walls, in which the foreign attackers used bronze-tipped arrows and the Israelite defenders struck back with iron-tipped arrows, showering the invaders with burning torches as well, in the hope of setting fire to their battering rams, ladders, and shields. Judging by the sheer quantity of charred remains within the small area uncovered, the defenders

34. Two arrowheads: on the right, a bronze arrowhead of "Scythian" type; on the left, an Israelite arrow of iron

53

did manage to burn their attackers' equipment — however, the enemy did eventually succeed in storming the wall. Just such a battle is depicted in the reliefs found in the Assyrian royal palace at Nineveh, which show the siege and capture of the Judean city of Lachish by Sennacherib in 701 B.C.

If we fit these discoveries in with known historical data, it seems likely that they are direct evidence of the siege and final conquest of Jerusalem in 586 B.C., by Nebuchadnezzar, King of Babylon, who:

> burned the house of the Lord, and the king's house and all the houses of Jerusalem; every great house he burned down. And all the army of the Chaldeans, who were with the captain of the guard, broke down the walls around Jerusalem (2 Kings 25:9-10).

It seems that what we found is the first tangible evidence of the fateful battle for the walls of Jerusalem, which terminated in the destruction of the entire city and the burning of Solomon's Temple.

4. The Significance of the Israelite Fortifications on the Western Hill

Our archaeological finds in the Jewish Quarter clearly show that this area was settled in the period of the First Temple, from the 8th century B.C. on. Together with the finds from other minor excavations, in the Citadel, in the Armenian Garden, and on Mount Zion, our evidence indicates that Israelite houses were spread over the entire plateau of the Western Hill. To date, with the exception of a few isolated sherds, no pottery from before the 8th century B.C. has been found here.

As already noted, the Bible hints at the existence of two suburbs outside the City of David — the *Mishneh* ("Second") and the *Makhtesh* ("Mortar"). Huldah the Prophetess, wife of Shallum the keeper of the wardrobe (of the king), is described as dwelling "in Jerusalem in the *Mishneh* (Second Quarter)" (2 Kings 22:14). In the Book of Nehemiah (11:9), an official named Judah, the son of Hassenuah, is denoted *'al ha'ir mishneh*. The interpretation of this Hebrew phrase is open to controversy; it has been regarded as referring either to a secondary city, the *Mishneh*, or to the official position of vice-mayor. Our excavations now point to the *Mishneh* as having been situated on the Western Hill; this hill, set off from the City of David by a deep valley naturally developed into the second quarter of the city, alongside the parent "downtown."

THE MISHNEH

The prophet Zephaniah notes: "'On that day,' says the Lord, 'a cry will be heard from the Fish Gate, a wail from the Second Quarter (*Mishneh*), a loud crash from the hills. Wail, O inhabitants of the Mortar (*Makhtesh*)!'" (Zephaniah 1:10-11). Note the continuity: the Fish Gate — the *Mishneh* — the hills. It truly evokes a vivid picture of ever-increasing distance. To the prophet dwelling in the City of David, the Fish Gate symbolized the old city wall, with the *Mishneh* beyond, and the distant hills still further away. That the *Mishneh* was probably a well-to-do residential quarter is evidenced by the fact that Huldah the Prophetess and her husband, a high court official, lived there. In contrast, the *Makhtesh* was probably a commercial and industrial section located apparently in the lower Central Valley.

The spread of early Jerusalem can be compared to similar developments in modern times, when the population density in the Old City rendered it incapable of absorbing new inhabitants and new quarters were established in more convenient conditions outside the city walls. The first of the modern Jewish quarters, built late in the 19th century, was also located to the west. It can be assumed that the expansion of Jerusalem in biblical times, to an area several times that of the original city, was brought about largely by the influx of refugees from the northern Kingdom of Israel, after the Assyrian conquest of Samaria in 722 B.C., and after Sennacherib's campaign to Judah, in 701 B.C.

NIFICATION OF THE CITY   At first, the new settlement which spread over the entire Western Hill was outside the city wall, isolated from its mother-town, the City of David. Later, the *Mishneh* was enclosed by a wall which joined up with that of the City of David, forming one large, fortified city. It is paradoxical that an event of such significance has not been accorded specific mention in the historical books of the Bible; it is perhaps concealed behind one of the recurring instances of the phrase: "And he (the king) built the walls..." However an echo of this important development does seem to be heard in the psalm: "Our feet have been standing within your gates, O Jerusalem! *Jerusalem, built as a city which is bound firmly together*..." (Psalms 122:2-3). This pilgrim's praise has generally been misinterpreted as allegorical, or as referring to the rebuilding of the city and its walls in the days of Nehemiah. But today, with the two separated parts of the modern city, Jewish and Arab again joined together, following the Six-Day War, we must take the text at face value. Only a city which had been divided could be "bound firmly together" again. Prior to our excavations we knew little of these two separate parts of the ancient city. Now we can understand the awe of the Psalmist at the sight of the city spreading over two hills and encompassed by a single mighty wall — a sight which must have left an overwhelming impression on those approaching its gates for the first time.

N WAS THE WALL BUILT?   Although the pottery found in this area of the city indicates that the city wall must have been built in the late 8th century B.C., there is another chronological indication which should be taken into consideration. A series of tomb-caves hewn into the bedrock was discovered by Mazar on the slopes of the Central Valley west of the southwestern corner of the Temple Mount and ascribed by him to the 8th century B.C.

That spot could not have been a part of the walled city as long as the tombs continued to contain actual burials (unlike the royal tombs), for they would have been thought to pollute the city. Therefore, the expansion of the city may well have begun early in the 8th century B.C., with the new quarter being enclosed within the wall only toward the end of the century. That the quarter on the Western Hill was undefended in its earliest stage is clearly shown by the fact that our wall was built partly over the ruins of earlier Israelite houses. Those houses were disregarded in selecting the line of defence, and were demolished where necessary to make way for
35   the wall. Indeed, Isaiah actually describes the emergency measures adopted in the face of approaching danger, in preparation for war: "...and you saw that the breaches of the city of David were many, and you collected the waters of the lower

35. The Israelite city wall cutting through earlier Israelite house

pool, and you counted the houses of Jerusalem, and *you broke down the houses to fortify the wall*. You made a reservoir between the two walls for the water of the old pool" (Isaiah 22:9-11). Many kings fortified Jerusalem, but Isaiah's words probably refer to Hezekiah, the only ruler to have undertaken such defensive measures including the building of walls and the protecting of the major source of water, in preparation for a siege.

The Bible further relates: "...the deeds of Hezekiah, and all his might, and how he made the pool and the conduit and brought water into the city..." (2 Kings 20:20); "And when Hezekiah saw that Sennacherib had come and intended to fight against Jerusalem, he planned with his officers and his mighty men to stop the water of the springs that were outside the city; and they helped him. A great many people were gathered, and they stopped all the springs and the brook that flowed through the land, saying, 'Why should the kings of Assyria come and find much water?' He set to work resolutely and built up all the wall that was broken down, and raised towers upon it, and outside it he built *another wall*; and he strengthened the Millo in the city of David. He also made weapons and shields in abundance" (2 Chronicles 32:2-5); and he "...closed the upper outlet of the waters of Gihon and directed them down to the west side of the city of David" (2 Chronicles 32:30).

From the above, one would expect that the pool which gathered the waters of the Gihon spring was located within the walled city, but it was actually outside the City

56

of David, west of its southern tip, at the opening out of the Central Valley. Here, the pool would have been exposed to the enemy, in negation of Hezekiah's very intention of denying the enemy access to the water and assuring his own supply. The discovery of our wall now provides a solution to this problem.

In seeking to reconstruct the course and extent of the Israelite city wall, we have two points of reference: the remains themselves and Josephus' description of them in his *War of the Jews*. Josephus describes the three walls of Jerusalem in their chronological order; concerning the earliest of them, he writes:

> Of the three walls, the earliest (elsewhere called the "First wall") was nearly impregnable, owing to the (surrounding) ravines and the hill above them on which it stood. But besides possessing an advantageous position it was also strongly built, as David and Solomon and also the kings after them had taken pride in the work. It began, in the north, at the tower called Hippicus, and ran towards the Xystus. Then joining the Council-house it terminated at the western portico of the temple. On the other side, on the west, it began at the same point and descended through the place called Bethso to the Gate of the Essenes. Then, on the south side, it turned above the spring of Siloam and thence inclined again, on the east side, towards the pool of Solomon, continued to a place called Ophlas and joined the eastern portico of the temple (*War*, V, 4, 2).

According to this description, it appears that the course of the first or early wall was dictated by topographical considerations. It continued along the slopes of the valleys, which supplemented its defensive capacity. On the north it passed along the Transversal Valley from the Hippicus Tower near the present-day Citadel and continued eastward to the Temple Mount; in other words, parallel to and south of the modern David Street and Street of the Chain. On the west, it continued from Hippicus Tower southward along the Valley of Hinnom, on the line of the present city wall. It then turned eastward above the Hinnom Valley, encircling the summit of modern "Mount Zion," and continued till the southern tip of the City.

As we have seen, the remains of the fortifications which we uncovered are located on the northern border of the Upper City, along the Transversal Valley, the weakest flank in its natural defences. They represent two fortification systems, one adjacent to the other: (a) the broad wall to the south (1 on plan 30, p. 50); and (b) the tower 2 and wall fragment 3 to the north. There seems to be no organic connection between them and they were probably used in different periods.

The broad wall was apparently the earlier of the two systems and its peculiar north-south course with a turn to the west can be explained on topographical grounds. It appears to have skirted a minor ravine branching off here from the Transversal Valley, and crossed westward on the saddle between the two "peaks" of the Western Hill, then continuing back northward, curving along a topographically convenient course to a point again above the Transversal Valley.

In contrast, the wall to which the tower (2) and the western fragment (3) belonged did what the broad wall specifically sought to avoid, i.e. it cuts right across the ravine straightening out the northern line of the earlier wall here, thereby canceling the function of the bay-like broad wall to the south. The cause of this major change is difficult to explain.

38

36

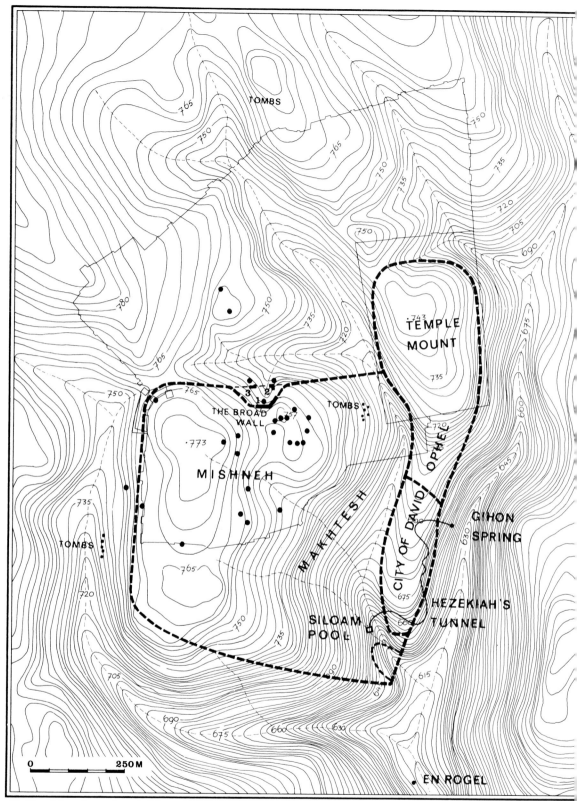

36. Map of Jerusalem at the end of the monarchic period. The dots represent excavated Israelite sites

In the Hebrew edition of this book the opinion was expressed that the topographical formation at this spot is most suitable for a city gate and that there might have been a gate here in the period of the monarchy of Judah. It is to be remembered that the Damascus Gate further to the north is depicted on the Byzantine Madaba map of Jerusalem as the main entrance to the city (see below), and as such it serves even today; all major attacks on besieged Jerusalem in the past came from the north. However, we had no archaeological evidence to support our proposition regarding and Israelite gateway.

Meanwhile additional soundings and investigations were made on the spot and new data were revealed which enabled us to offer tentatively the reconstructed plan as shown in figure 30. The broad wall (1) seems to have had in the center of its southern section an opening. The form of this gate (?) could not be established owing to the poor condition of the remains, which are partly covered by a modern building making further excavations to the south impossible.

30   The reconstruction of the gate of the second phase of fortification which crosses the ravine is based on elements 2 and 3. Structure 2 with its massive corner and the entrance jamb is most probably part of a gate's tower, whereas wall fragment 3 with its projecting pilaster is a section of the associated defence wall. These remains, scanty as they are, are of great significance in their position and shape. Although tentative, this reconstructed four-chambered gateway, proposed by Leen Ritmeyer, looks quite convincing in its setting and fits very well within the framework of typical gates in the late Israelite period. Only the position of the tower outside the line of the city wall is not according to the common practice. Generally gate-towers protrude inside the wall; the gate of wall 1 may have belonged to the latter type.

In trying to identify our reconstructed gate 2 with one of the gates known from the Scriptures, we seem to have no better candidate then the "Middle Gate" (*sha'ar ha-tawekh*) mentioned only in Jer. 39:3. As can be observed on the plan 36 (p. 58), our gate is situated right in the middle of the northern defence wall of the city. The biblical narrator mentions the Middle Gate as the meeting place of the Babylonian generals after the forcing of the north wall of Jerusalem during the siege in 586 B.C. Above we claimed to have found evidence of a battle raging in front of this gate.

Our remains of fortifications are situated exactly along the northern course of the early wall described by Josephus. In the next chapter we shall see that in the same line remains of the Hasmonean defence wall and its gate were discovered. We may therefore assume that the same correlation holds good for other parts of the first wall on the west and on the south. After all, a city's line of defence is generally determined by topographical considerations which do not change with time, except for major developments brought about by extreme changes in the populated area. In Jerusalem, these factors have not changed over the centuries. Following this principle, we now conclude (in slight contrast to my suggestion published soon after the wall was discovered) that the course of the Israelite wall corresponds in general with that of the Hasmonean wall, and that both of these coincide with Josephus' early wall as described above.

No clear remains of the Israelite city wall have yet been revealed in the excavations conducted along the line of the Turkish city wall on the west; but work there has hardly exhausted all possibilities. This subject has recently been treated by

Hillel Geva of our staff, who maintains that underneath the Hasmonean city wall and other building remains excavated there are concealed remains of the Israelite city wall. Future excavations on the spot would undoubtedly clarify the matter. Similarly, no Israelite remains have been found on the south, where Bliss and Dickie excavated by tunneling along the later wall. They uncovered a number of Hasmonean wall fragments there, but made no soundings on either side of this line.

We may therefore assume that in the period of the First Temple our city wall encompassed the entire plateau of the Western Hill, including the Citadel, the Armenian Garden, and the summit of Mount Zion. This actually leads us back to the "irrational" maximalist view in the controversy over the extent of Jerusalem in the period of the First Temple, but now this view is based on new facts and possesses a much higher degree of probability.

Our projected course of the city wall would have the southern line of the wall crossing the Central Valley from the west and joining up with the southern tip of the City of David, thereby placing the Siloam Pool within the protection of the walled city — as it must have been according to the Bible, as well as according to logic. The pool was situated between the old wall of the City of David and the new wall coming from the west, and it was undoubtedly to this wall that the quotation cited above was referring: "You made a reservoir between the two walls...," that is, between the old wall and the new one. Apparently, the new wall was the "another wall" built by Hezekiah, as noted in 2 Chronicles 32:5.

THE SILOAM POOL

36

Dame Kathleen Kenyon was adamantly opposed to this solution, holding that this spot was not settled in the Israelite period, for her trial excavations on the eastern slope of the Western Hill had yielded no remains earlier than the days of Agrippa I, in the 1st century A.D. Therefore, it could not have been included within the walled city of the First Temple. But we have already seen that conclusions of this sort do not always stand the test of scrutiny. In our opinion, even if the eastern slope was not actually settled then, it must have been within the walls, for otherwise the Siloam Pool below it would have been exposed to the enemy. To counter this, Dame Kenyon made the ingenious suggestion that the Siloam Pool was not an open reservoir at all, but rather a subterranean cistern hidden from the eyes of the enemy. There is, however, no evidence whatsoever to support this assumption.

In this connection, it should be noted that a massive wall eight meters thick and built of crude boulders came to light in this area of Dame Kenyon's excavations (her F), near Birket el-Hamra — which is most probably the biblical "Lower Pool" (or the "pool of Shiloah" of Nehemiah 3:15). At first she thought that it was the Israelite wall, which logically should be there even in her view. However, when she subsequently found that the massive wall cuts through a thick accumulation of earth containing Iron Age pottery, she concluded that the wall was a dam of the pool, built in the 1st century A.D. Considering the fact that our Israelite city wall to the north is of similar thickness, and also cuts through an earlier Israelite layer, could not her initial impression have been the more correct? Another question which presents itself here is how a thick Iron Age deposit could possibly have accumulated on a spot which, according to Dame Kenyon, was outside the city in the period of the First Temple. We can only hope that further excavations on the site will provide definitive answers to this most provocative question.

CHAPTER TWO

AFTER THE DESTRUCTION OF THE FIRST TEMPLE

An Interlude on the Western Hill

Less than fifty years after Jerusalem had been destroyed and most of its population exiled to Babylonia, Judea became a province or satrapy of the Persian empire, under the name *Yehud*. In 538 B.C., King Cyrus of Persia issued a proclamation, cited in the first chapter of the Book of Ezra, enabling the exiled Jews to return to Jerusalem and rebuild their Temple there. This ushered in a new epoch in the history of Jerusalem and of the Jewish people.

HE RETURN FROM EXILE The first exiles to return to Jerusalem came under the leadership of Sheshbazzar, who was apparently the son of Jehoiachin, the penultimate king of Judah. Under Zerubabel, grandson of Jehoiachin and Governor of Judea around 521 B.C., and later under Ezra the Scribe (around 458 B.C.) and Nehemiah, Governor of Judea around 445 B.C., the renewed settlement in Jerusalem grew. Zerubabel rebuilt the Temple; Ezra restored the spiritual life of the people; and Nehemiah rebuilt the walls of Jerusalem and reorganized the religious, social, and economic life of the people. One indication of the internal independence of the province in Judea was the privilege granted to it by the Persian authorities to mint its own coinage. These coins bear the name of the province, *Yehud*, and sometimes that of the current Governor, written in archaic Aramaic or Hebrew script. Similar inscriptions in the early Aramaic script have been found stamped on storage jar handles and on blobs of clay which had originally sealed written documents.

NEHEMIAH'S WALL In Jerusalem the most significant development after the rebuilding of the Temple was the reconstruction of the city's fortifications, as related in the Book of Nehemiah. In preparation for this project, Nehemiah conducted a survey of the ruined city walls in order to ascertain their condition. He then organized groups of volunteers from every walk of life to carry out the work, each team being responsible for the rebuilding of a particular segment. Nehemiah lists the various gates and towers by name and in a given order, and relates that the task was completed in 52 days. This detailed description of the wall, which appears in no other source, serves as a basic guide for topographical research into Jerusalem in the period of the Judean Monarchy, for Nehemiah uses the older terminology for the various features in the city. Here, too, a maximalist-minimalist controversy rages, for the one camp holds that Nehemiah's description encompasses both hills, while the other holds that it encompasses only the City of David and the Temple Enclosure.

In the abundant scholarly literature written on this subject, the minimalist view presently retains the upper hand. But since few traces of this wall have survived, and since the gates and towers can be identified only by surmise, no generally accepted solution for the problem of Nehemiah's wall has emerged.

Our excavations in the Jewish Quarter have contributed two points to this controversy, one minor and the other of more significance. In addition to the specifically named gates and towers in Nehemiah's wall, two other walls are mentioned: the Broad Wall and the Ophel Wall. Nehemiah 3:8 states that the builders worked "as far as the *Broad Wall*," and in Nehemiah 12:38, describing the inaugural procession along the completed walls, it is noted that the celebrants went up "to the *Broad Wall*." I think we can safely identify this Broad Wall with the unusually thick Israelite wall on the Western Hill, part of which we uncovered in our excavations. Nehemiah apparently refers to the spot where the wall encompassing the *Mishneh* joined up with the western wall of the City of David. From the biblical text, it would seem that the repairs under Nehemiah did not include the Broad Wall itself, but only the city wall tangent to it.

In the other, more significant matter, our excavations in the Jewish Quarter supplied unequivocal data, although of a completely negative nature. In all our excavations at many different spots, it has become clear beyond any doubt that the Western Hill was entirely unoccupied during the Persian period, the period of the Return from Exile. We have discovered here neither structures of this period nor pottery (except for a few isolated sherds). Further, in the excavations conducted within the Citadel, in the Armenian Quarter, and on Mount Zion, the only evidence from the Persian period which has come to light is a single *Yehud* coin of the 4th century B.C.

This conclusion is not especially surprising, and can readily be explained by the fact that the relatively few exiles returning were not capable of repopulating and restoring the extensive, desolate quarter on the Western Hill. The smaller City of David was more than sufficient for their needs. This is revealed by Nehemiah himself, when he relates that: "*The city was wide and large*, but the people within it were few and no houses had been built" (Nehemiah 7:4). "Wide and large" hardly seems appropriate in describing the City of David, and Nehemiah may have been referring here to the Upper City. If so, this verse might also be cited as evidence for the opinion that Jerusalem had occupied the Western Hill too in days long before Nehemiah.

From all the above we can conclude that the minimalist view of the settlement in Jerusalem in the period of the Return to Zion is correct — that is, that it was limited to the narrow confines of the City of David, and that the *Mishneh* on the Western Hill remained desolate and uninhabited.

What was more surprising was the discovery that this situation did not change in the Upper City during the Early Hellenistic period (late 4th-3rd centuries B.C.). No traces of buildings from that period have been found and the city was apparently still limited to the Eastern Hill. Though many studies have been written on this subject, the history of Jerusalem in this period remains very hazy. The historical sources are insufficiently clear and the archaeological evidence is mainly negative. But, as we have seen, even negative evidence can sometimes yield significant conclusions.

Early in the Hellenistic period, numerous changes and developments occurred in this country. When Alexander the Great put an end to the Persian empire in 332 B.C., Judea became a province of his empire, and Jerusalem fell under the influence of Hellenism. Alexander's heirs, the Ptolemies of Egypt and the Seleucids of Syria, soon became bitter rivals, and the province of Judea, situated between them, became a fierce battleground, passing back and forth several times from the control of the one to that of the other. At the beginning of the 3rd century B.C. the Ptolemies had the upper hand, and the province's fate was linked with that of Egypt. But then in 200 B.C. Judea fell to Antiochus III and it remained in Syrian hands until the time of the Maccabean Revolt.

maic seal impression:
ot from our excavations)

Under early Hellenistic rule the land of Judea enjoyed a degree of administrative autonomy apparently similar to that under the Persians. This is witnessed by coins recently found bearing the portrait of Ptolemy I and the Hebrew (rather than Aramaic) inscription *Yehudah*, that is, "Judea." This inscription is reminiscent of the *Yehud* coins and seal impressions from Persian times.

Under Syrian hegemony, the internal administration of Judea was based on a theocracy in which the priests were the foremost class of Jerusalem society, just as the Temple was its central institution. The High Priest, appointed on behalf of the Seleucid king, was not only chief pontiff but also ruler of the state. Hellenism was widespread among the upper classes, lending a new character to daily life. In 175 B.C. Antiochus IV Epiphanes came to the Syrian throne, and a certain Jason soon purchased the office of High Priest in Jerusalem, receiving permission to build a gymnasium and to turn the city into a Greek *polis* to be called Antiochia. This not only served to promote Hellenism in the daily life of the city, but also fanned internal strife between the Hellenizing Jews and their more conservative brethren. The Syrian army eventually intervened—needless to say, on the side of the Hellenizers.

In order to strengthen Syrian control in Jerusalem, Antiochus IV built a new fortress there in 168 B.C., calling it the "Akra" and garrisoning it with a force of Macedonians, Syrians, and extremist Jewish Hellenizers. This fortress, which overlooked and controlled the Temple Enclosure, was for many years a thorn in the side of the conservative camp of Jews. Subsequently, the Seleucids began to intervene in Jewish religious matters as well, even introducing certain pagan practices into the Temple. When Antiochus IV went so far as to ban the practice of the Jewish rites throughout Judea, in 167 B.C., the angry reaction of the Jews culminated in the Maccabean Revolt, under the leadership of Mattathias, head of the Hasmonean family. The Jews thereby regained political independence, which brought in its wake far-reaching changes in the development of Jerusalem and its topography. This introduces us to the subject of the next chapter, in which archaeology once again plays a major role.

CHAPTER THREE

THE PERIOD OF THE SECOND TEMPLE

1. The Hasmonean Resettlement of the Western Hill

With the advent of Hasmonean rule in the mid-2nd century B.C., Jerusalem blossomed forth and again spread over the Western Hill. We cannot be certain exactly when or how this resurgence began, but the fact is that in the second half of the 2nd century B.C. this hill was once again encircled by a city wall, and remains found there indicate that it was definitely settled at that time. After a lapse of more than four centuries life throbbed anew in the Upper City.

Even after Judas Maccabeus captured Jerusalem from Antiochus IV in 164 B.C., the "Akra" citadel remained in Syrian hands. The legal ruler of the city was still the High Priest, a Hellenizer who was supported by Antiochus. Judas' brother Jonathan continued the fight against the Syrians until Alexander Balas, Antiochus' successor, recognized the legitimacy of Hasmonean rule by appointing Jonathan High Priest in 152 B.C. But the fact that the Akra still remained under Syrian control was a thorn in the flesh of the Jews of the city. Simeon, the last of the sons of Mattathias the Hasmonean, finally succeeded in conquering the Akra fortress, thereby completing the liberation of Jerusalem in 141 B.C. Already the year before, the Seleucid King Demetrius II had unconditionally recognized Judean independence by canceling his demands for tribute.

THE AKRA FORTRESS

The location of the Akra fortress is one of the most enigmatic topographical problems concerning Jerusalem in the days of the Second Temple. The historical sources (the Books of Maccabees and Josephus) do not tally on this matter, and archaeological evidence is nonexistent. The question is, where exactly was this symbol of Syrian military and political authority, which overtowered the Temple and hampered free access to it, and which despite its isolation, had held out so long in the face of innumerable attacks.

Josephus is quite explicit in the matter. His statement that the Akra was located in the Lower City has led many scholars to assume that it was south of the Temple Enclosure, although there is no site there which could have been higher than the Temple itself. Other scholars suggested that the Akra was at a higher spot opposite the Temple on the west, in the area today known as the Jewish Quarter. The latter suggestion was based, among other factors, on an assumption first raised by the late Professor M. Avi-Yonah that the name "Antiochia" (as Jerusalem was then supposedly known), where the Akra stood, referred to a new city built according to the Hippodamic plan (with streets crossing one another at right angles and regular intervals, in a very unoriental manner), and that this city was located in the Upper City. But this assumption is deprived of all substance by the fact that no remains whatsoever have been found of such a town in the various excavations conducted in the Upper City. It would therefore seem that the granting of the status of a Greek polis to "Antiochia in Jerusalem" was a mere legal act, never followed up by the building of a new city.

Moreover, in our excavations in the Jewish Quarter, its assumed location, we have not found any remains which could possibly be interpreted as belonging to the Akra. Although we were unable to probe extensive areas occupied by modern houses, there seems little sense in even searching for such remains, for Josephus relates that Simeon razed the Akra down to its very foundations and lowered the hill on which it had stood in order to preclude the building of any other structure there which might again dominate the Temple. But the hill of the Jewish Quarter is still today considerably higher than the Temple Mount. Since we have reached our negative conclusions concerning the existence of "Antiochia" in the Upper city, proposals have been made anew to locate the Akra in the Lower City, south of the Temple Mount.

THE PALACE OF
THE HASMONEANS

It might be appropriate here to mention another building, though it is of less topographical significance than the Akra, for which we have also been on the lookout: the palace of the Hasmoneans which Josephus mentions several times. This palace, later used also by the Herodians, stood on a high spot, and from its reception rooms it had been possible to see into the inner court of the Temple. This apparently annoyed the priests greatly, and they built a special wall within the Temple court to block the view. The Hasmonean palace is described as standing above the bridge which connected the Upper City with the Temple Enclosure ("Wilson's Arch"). Thus, it is generally held that it must have stood at an elevated site somewhere west of the Temple Mount, that is, in the northeastern corner of the Jewish Quarter. We have found no remains in our excavations in this region which could be ascribed to such a building. Since our work there was rather sparse, there is still a chance that such remains are still hidden beneath modern structures and have not yet been revealed.

Such are the ways of topographical research in a city as problematic as Jerusalem. The pendulum swings back and forth between the literary sources and the archaeological evidence, often with no common denominator being found. Keeping in mind the lesson learned in solving the problem of the Western Hill in the Israelite period, we must not despair and hope that archaeology has yet to say its last word in the matter of the Akra and the Hasmonean palace. Further on we shall discuss other more fortunate instances where correspondence between historical sources and archaeological evidence does aid in reconstructing the topography of the ancient city.

THE NORTHERN LINE
OF THE FIRST WALL

One such example, which has been most instructive, is that of the city wall commonly known as the "first wall." This name, hardly new to the reader by now, is an essential element in the topographical investigation of the city in Second Temple times, and we have met it already in our discussion of the city wall of the period of the First Temple. The first wall is of significance to both periods and is

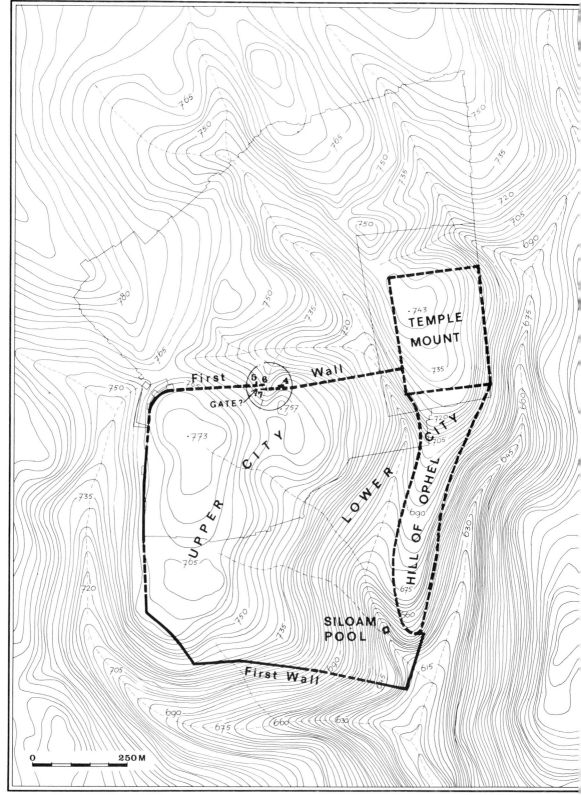

38. Plan of the First Wall of Jerusalem in Hasmonean times. The area of excavations along its northern line is circled

related to one of the most fascinating episodes in our excavations. As noted in Chapter One, the first wall was the earliest of the three walls of Jerusalem as described by Josephus in his book on *The Jewish War* against the Roman (quoted on p. 57). Josephus ascribes this wall to the period of the First Temple, but modern scholars have generally ascribed it to the period of the Hasmoneans. Our excavations have revealed that *both* these ascriptions are essentially correct. The Israelite wall has already been discussed above, and we shall now turn to the Hasmonean wall, to which the term "first wall" is most often applied.

Segments of the Hasmonean wall have been discovered on the west of the city: in the courtyard of the Citadel (by Johns, and by Amiran and Eitan); along the Turkish walls (by Broshi); and south of the summit of Mount Zion by Bliss and Dickie around the turn of the century; (Bliss, an American archaeologist, is buried on Mount Zion, in the English cemetery there!). The northern line of the wall, however, is more problematic. The assumed line along the Transversal Valley was based on Josephus' description, but no remains were found there which could be ascribed to it with any certainty. In St. Mark's Street, a wall fragment with two towers was incidentally uncovered in the last century, but the true character and dating of that find are entirely uncertain.

When we first began our search for authentic traces of the northern line of the first wall, we were full of hope, for this was the first time that we were excavating at a particular spot in accordance with assumptions based on a historical source. In Chapter One I have related our work here, in Area W (p. 32), in connection with the discovery of the Israelite tower. As we dug at a spot some 35 meters south of the Street of the Chain, more or less on the assumed line of the first wall, we were gnawed by doubts as to whether the limited area available for excavation would prove worthwhile, for it could not possibly be expanded on any flank. We have described the difficulties and disappointments which were our constant lot there at first, but our final results exceeded all expectations. Within a pit measuring a mere 10x12 meters, and at a depth of some 12-15 meters, a tower about nine meters square came to light, as if tailored to fit the pit. Bull's-eye! Deep down, I felt a great admiration for Flavius Josephus, whose topographical description had once again proved his reliability. But what of our part? We were just plain lucky, but this time according to plan.

And this was only the beginning. Between 1975 and 1978 we discovered further segments of the first wall some 50 meters west of the Hasmonean tower (4, p. 50), at the northern end of Jewish Quarter Street and south of David Street — in other words, also approximately on the assumed line of the first wall. While we were engaged in uncovering the pavement of the Byzantine *cardo maximus*, (discussed in Chapter Five), the impressive fragments of massive walls came to light beneath the latter pavement. Working in and among the dense blocks of houses, and under conditions of darkness which severely limited our activity, we uncovered as much as possible of the wall.

While we were not able to clear these important remains in their entirety, located at a key spot in the city's defenses, even the small part we did manage to uncover is of great significance. As can be seen in the plan 30 (p. 50), we found there four sections of walls: one from the Israelite period, already mentioned above (3); and

39

30

three others which can certainly be ascribed to the late Hellenistic or Hasmonean period (5-7). The foundations, which are based upon the bedrock far below, at the bottom of the ravine branching off from the Transversal Valley, are preserved to a height of 6.5 to 8 meters. We could determine the thickness of only wall 6, which is 4.6 meters.

CITY GATE

30,38

The gap between the line of this wall and that of the parallel fragment 7 suggests that a city gate may have been located here. Topographically, the ravine could have provided a suitable setting for such a gate on the north, a possibility which we have already noted in conjunction with the Israelite fortifications. If our assumption is correct, we might identify this gate with the much discussed "Gennath Gate" mentioned by Josephus as being located in the northern line of the first wall; at the point of juncture with the second wall, which enclosed a quarter of the city to the north.

We should reiterate here the fact that the lower parts of all the Hasmonean walls cut through a thick Israelite layer; this earlier layer also contains remains of walls, some seven meters below street level. Further, Hasmonean fragment 7 abuts Israelite fragment 3, a remarkable phenomenon observed as well at the Hasmonean tower (4) to the east.

he Hasmonean city wall beneath the Byzantine street pavement.
nt 6

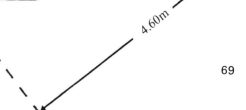

4.60m

We shall now return to the Hasmonean tower (4, p. 50) in Area W—for the solution of the history of Josephus' first wall is concealed there. Much to our surprise, we found that this tower was built adjacent to the eastern face of the imposing Israelite tower (2), of which we have already spoken so much. The Hasmonean tower juts out to the north 6 meters beyond the line of the city wall. It is 9 meters square and shaped like the Greek letter ⊓ , that is, a square open on the south, with walls 2.5 to 3 meters thick. The walls are built of medium-sized, draughted ashlars, in the style of the Hasmonean stones found in many parts of the first wall on the west and south.

30

The dating of this tower can also be fixed by stratigraphy: its foundation trenches are dug into the Israelite layer, and abutting the wall are an earth fill and a crushed limestone floor, dated by the pottery to the 2nd century B.C. A similar fill and floor, with identical associated pottery, abuts the Israelite tower on the north face, some 1.3 meters above the Israelite floor. This shows that in the 2nd century B.C. both fortifications—the Israelite and the Hasmonean—functioned as a single unit. This secondary utilization of the original Israelite tower is further demonstrated by the upper courses of stones which were added to the Israelite tower, by remains and small finds (including a typical Hellenistic arrowhead) within the tower itself, and by the fallen debris abutting the northern face of the tower, above the floor, which contained Hellenistic material.

43

This, then, is truly an amazing phenomenon: we know that the Israelite tower (and the Israelite city wall to which it had belonged) was destroyed in 586 B.C. The

42. Hellenistic arrowhead

41. The face of the Hasmonean city wall, segments 5-6

Hasmonean tower abutting the Israelite tower. Abu Ribhi, our foreman, is seen standing on the Hellenistic pavement, common to the two towers (so at the left)

ruins stood forelorn and desolate for hundreds of years (!) until the 2nd century B.C. when the Hasmoneans sought to refortify the Upper City after it had been resettled. Appreciating the value of the earlier line of defense, whose ruins were still visible, the Hasmonean builders reutilized the earlier fragments of fortifications (2-3) and integrated them into their new defensive system. This picture holds true at least along the northern line of the first wall.

The integration of parts of fortifications so widely separated in time is not a usual feature in archaeology. In the instance before us we can conclude that this locale was not settled during the more than four hundred years that elapsed between the destruction of the Israelite wall and the construction of the Hasmonean wall, at least not to an extent which left any tangible remains. This significant feature was found in every one of our excavation sites, where the Hasmonean material generally rested directly over the Israelite stratum. A similar phenomenon was encountered by those conducting excavations elsewhere in the Upper City—in the Citadel, in the Armenian Quarter, and on Mount Zion. We can account for the interval in settlement on the Western Hill in the Persian period (see above), but what of the absence of Early Hellenistic remains there? As in the Persian period, Hellenistic

Jerusalem was the capital of a minor, rather insignificant province. The local theocracy appointed by foreign overlords and deeply involved in internal strife, would hardly have been able to foster the conditions requisite for the spread of the city to the Western Hill, or for extensive, organized efforts to build a new city wall there. Further, we can reasonably assume that the Ptolemies and Seleucids were hardly interested in strengthening Jewish settlement in Jerusalem, or in bolstering and fortifying an expanded city there.

The decisive change in the city's development came about only after Jerusalem had again become the capital of an independent Jewish commonwealth. A project as extensive as the resettlement of the Upper City and its fortification could have been carried out successfully only if it were initiated by the rulers. And the successful and energetic Maccabean rulers not only had valid motives for undertaking this task, but they also possessed the power for carrying it out.

When, then, did the city begin its expansion and who fortified it? Although we cannot answer this question decisively, several educated guesses can be made. There may have been some sort of occupation on the Western Hill, perhaps by squatters, already in the 3rd century, or at least early in the 2nd century B.C. — that is, even prior to the Hasmoneans. Several Ptolemaic and Seleucid coins, as well as various Hellenistic pottery vessels and an Aramaic inscription on a sherd, may well point in this direction. But there is also evidence to show that the area was not yet included in the fortified city at that time: as for instance a pre-Hasmonean rock-cut tomb in area F which must have been *extra muros*.

EXPANSION OF THE CITY

Since the fortification of the Upper City with a defensive wall was too huge an undertaking to have been executed by a single ruler, we must then ask which Hasmonean ruler began building the city wall and who completed it. Attempts to answer this question on the basis of archaeological evidence alone have not been successful, and resorting to the historical sources alone has led to the proposal of virtually every Hasmonean ruler as a likely candidate. It would seem, however, that insufficient attention has been paid to the particular wording in the First Book of Maccabees concerning the construction work carried out by Jonathan and Simeon: "... Jonathan settled himself in Jerusalem, and *began* to build and renew the city. And he commanded the workmen to build the walls..." (10:10-11); and "So he (Simeon) then... made haste to *finish* the walls of Jerusalem, and he fortified it round about" (13:10). Only when these two passages are read in conjunction can the connection between them be seen. It could hardly be incidental that Jonathan is cited as having begun the construction, and Simeon as having completed it. Rather these passages hint that Jonathan began building and fortifying the new part of the city, but was prevented from completing his task (for he was killed by Tryphon, the Syrian usurper); and that Simeon, who assumed leadership after his brother's death, rushed to complete the fortification of the city. It seems that these passages do indeed provide a clue to the understanding of the entire question.

BUILDERS OF THE WALL

It is natural that these outstanding Maccabean leaders, so ambitious and successful, would soon turn their attention to the strengthening and embellishment of Jerusalem, their capital. Interestingly, the Seleucid King Demetrius I offered the Jews a treaty and proposed to undertake construction of the walls of Jerusalem and

44. Hellenistic storage jar with four handles, 2nd century B.C.

to fortify it round about, entirely at his own expense (I Maccabees 10:45). This clearly shows that the fortification of the city was an outstanding issue at the time. Jonathan rejected the proposal out of loyalty to his erstwhile ally, Alexander Balas.

In another passage in I Maccabees, Simeon's son John Hyrcanus I (134-104 B.C.) is also mentioned as a builder of the walls of Jerusalem: "Concerning the other acts of John, and his wars, and worthy deeds which he did, and the building of the walls which he made, and his deeds, behold, these are written in the chronicles of his priesthood, from the time which he was made high priest after his father" (I Maccabees 16:23-24). However, the stereotypic manner of this passage, in the biblical style, renders it of little value to our discussion.

Another possible candidate as builder of the city wall of Jerusalem is Alexander Janneus, the greatest of the Hasmonean kings (103-76 B.C.) and well known for his

45. Bowls in the pool

numerous conquests and other deeds. Jerusalem undoubtedly developed considerably and, though he is not specifically mentioned in this context, he certainly must also have had a part in its fortification.

The fact that very few remains of Hasmonean buildings have been uncovered can be attributed to the extensive demolition and construction work carried out in Herodian times. This is evidenced by the numerous Hasmonean cisterns, pools, and baths hewn into the rock, which have been found preserved beneath Herodian buildings while the Hasmonean superstructures themselves have completely disappeared. But even so, it still seems that the Hasmonean city was far less densely built up and developed than the Herodian city which succeeded it.

We found a considerable concentration of Hasmonean structures in our Area A, with their foundations laid upon the Israelite remains. One such building had even been built directly upon the remains of the Israelite city wall! The foundations of another building were sunk into an Israelite floor, and alongside was a plastered, stepped pool containing many Late Hellenistic pottery bowls. On a rock terrace in the south (Area T-2, p. 32), we found a Hasmonean layer containing the remains of a simple dwelling which was similar in character to the Israelite house over whose ruins it had been built. In other words, there was no intermediate stratum here, but a gap in occupation between the Israelite period (which came to an end in 586 B.C.) and the Hasmonean period (which began in 152 B.C.).

COINS
47

Our numismatic finds included several Ptolemaic (late 3rd century B.C.) and Seleucid (2nd century B.C.) coins of types which were still current even under later Hasmonean rule. The coins of Alexander Janneus (103-76 B.C.), which we found in large numbers, are inscribed "Of King Alexander" in Greek, and "Jonathan the King," or "Jonathan the High Priest and the ḥever of the Jews" in archaizing Hebrew. Jonathan was Alexander's Hebrew name; he bore the title of "High Priest," heading the ḥever of the Jews, apparently the "Great Assembly." We also uncovered a hoard of 23 coins of Mattathias Antigonus, last of the Hasmonean kings (40-37 B.C.), which bear similar legends: "Of King Antigonus" in Greek, and "Mattathias the High Priest and the ḥever of the Jews" in archaizing Hebrew. One of the most common emblems on the coins of the Hasmoneans was a pair of crossed

Some of the bowls from the pool, 1st century B.C.

47. Bronze coin of Ptolemy II, from the mint at Tyre (ca. 270 B.C.)

48. A group of coins of Antiochus IV (top), Alexander Janneus and Judah Aristobulus II (163-63 B.C.)

49. The hoard of coins as found in Area T (p. 32)

50. The hoard of coins of Mattathias Antigonus, after cleaning

al impression: *Yehud-Ṭ*

52. Clay *bulla* depicting palm tree and inscribed: "Jonathan the King" [not from our excavations; see *Israel Exploration Journal*, 25 (1975), pp. 245-246]

53. Clay *bulla* depicting palm-tree and inscribed: "Jonathan the High Priest/Jerusalem *M*" [not from our excavations; see *Israel Exploration Journal*, 25 (1975), pp. 8-12]

cornucopias, with a pomegranate between them. As we shall see later on, this same symbol appears on an ornamented stone table found in our excavation.

ADMINISTRATION

37

We can learn something about the administration of Judea in the Hellenistic period from seal impressions found on storage jar handles. We have already seen that the storage jars used in the Persian period bore sealings with the name of the province, *Yehud*, in early Aramaic script. Such impressions were found on the Eastern Hill, in the City of David, where other material from the Persian period has also been found. However, since no remains from the period of the Return from Exile have come to light, in either our excavations or those at other spots on the Western Hill, these Aramaic seal impressions are also lacking.

UD" SEAL-IMPRESSIONS

51

In contrast, a number of similar impressions have come to light in the Upper City, but they are inscribed in the archaizing Hebrew script and read "*Yehud Ṭ*." Here again, *Yehud* refers to the province of Judea; the letter *ṭet* was apparently of some official significance. The everyday Hebrew script of the Hasmonean period is the one often called "square," which had actually developed from the Aramaic form. However, the archaic Hebrew script was traditionally retained, apparently for nationalistic reasons, for official and symbolic use, such as on official seals and coins, as well as in some of the sacred writings.

EM" SEAL IMPRESSIONS

54, 56

In addition to the "*Yehud Ṭ*" impressions, there are jar handles bearing a five-pointed star, the pentagram, with the letters of the name "*Jerusalem*" in archaic Hebrew inscribed between the points. For the first time we can date impressions of this latter type (which have been known for a long time), since two examples came to light in our excavations, on the handles of jugs clearly 2nd century B.C. type. These "*Jerusalem*" stamps, apparently the last in the series of Judean official stamps on pottery vessels, seem to have been an innovation of the Hasmoneans.

All the above official seal impressions have been found at other sites in Judea as well, particularly at Ramat Raḥel south of Jerusalem. The stamped storage jars bearing the official marks obviously served some official function, possibly for taxes in kind for the royal treasury or the Temple.

STAMPED JAR HANDLES

Another type of epigraphic find from the Hellenistic period, and one most worthy of mention, consists of the handles of large storage jars or amphorae from Rhodes and other Greek islands, bearing legends in Greek. In the 3rd and 2nd

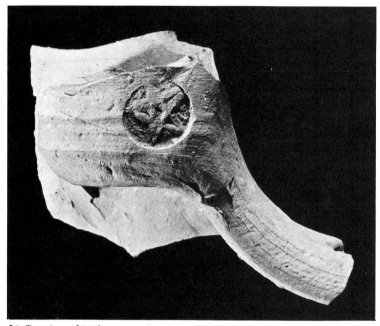

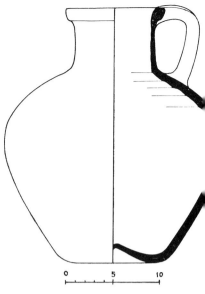

55. Complete jug from the 2nd century B.C., of the type represented in fig. 54

54. Two views of jug fragment with seal impression on handle: "Jerusalem" and pentagram

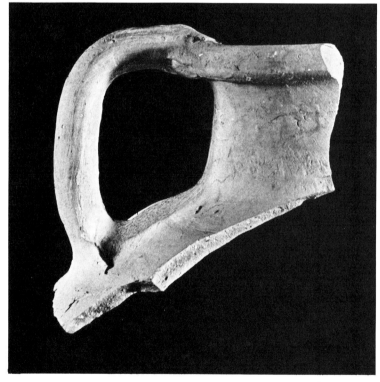

56. Seal impression: "Jerusalem" and pentagram, on storage jar handle

centuries B.C., Rhodes developed a widespread trade based on her home-grown wine which she marketed in large, long-necked amphorae having two elongated handles and a pointed base. One of the handles was stamped with the name of the chief priest or magistrate of Rhodes in whose term the jar was manufactured (the "eponym"), and the other bore the name of the manufacturer of the jar. The month and a symbol were added to one or the other of the two names.

Judea imported much wine from Rhodes, and many such stamped jar handles have been found on the sites of the various Hellenistic towns there, although the vessels themselves were almost all broken long ago. Jerusalem, too, imported wine from Rhodes, and many hundreds of handles of the Rhodian type have come to light in the Lower City on the Eastern Hill. This would tend to confirm the assumption that the Syrian center of authority, as well as the Seleucid garrison, were located in that area, for the people there would have been the primary consumers of this Greek wine. The fact that relatively few such handles have been found in the Upper City indicates that the place was but sparsely inhabited in the early Hellenistic period, and that in the Hasmonean period foreign wine was not favored there because it was regarded impure by observant Jews. We encountered a similar problem in one of the Herodian houses, where wine jars of Italian origin were found.

57. Rhodian jar handles bearing seal impressions

| 1 | 2 | 3 |

. Oil lamps: 1, 2nd century B.C.; 2, 1st century B.C.; 3, 1st century A.D.

59. Pottery of the Hasmonean period, 2nd-1st centuries B.C.

60. Storage jars of the 1st century B.C.

2. Intense Development under the Herodians

After the Romans subdued Seleucid Syria, and Pompey conquered Jerusalem, in 63 B.C., Judea became a vassal-state of Rome. A new era began in Jerusalem's history, signified by the reign of the Herodian dynasty and the rule of the Roman procurators, by the building of Herod's Temple, the rise of new concepts of living, the revolt against Rome, and the subsequent destruction of the city.

The archaeology of Herodian Jerusalem, in the Early Roman period, has always attracted scholars and laymen alike. Naturally, discoveries in the Jerusalem of the time of the Gospels have also awakened special interest among students of the New Testament. Our excavations in the Jewish Quarter have much to offer in this respect. The nature of our finds in the period of the Herodian dynasty (37 B.C.-A.D. 70) changes decidedly when compared with those of the previous periods, for here we leave behind matters of topography and city walls, and encounter human dwellings — the homes of Jerusalemites and the artifacts of their daily life. This new aspect, new insofar as the archaeology of Jerusalem is concerned, was largely unknown prior to our excavations. Indeed, we have uncovered more remains of the Herodian period in our excavations than those of any other period, and we found them in almost every spot where we dug in the Jewish Quarter. The extent to which these remains have been preserved is often most impressive. In fact, the Herodian layer is the only archaeological stratum from which we have been able to reconstruct a true picture of contemporaneous life in the city. The period is named after Herod the Great, who impressed his mark upon the city deeper than any other ruler at any time. We shall therefore look, however briefly, at the man, his character, and his deeds.

HEROD THE GREAT Herod, the son of Antipater the Idumean, dethroned Mattathias Antigonus, last of the Hasmoneans; with the support of the Romans, he assumed the throne in 37 B.C. and reigned until his death in 4 B.C. His modern appellation "the Great" is well deserved, for he was great in his deeds — both good and evil. Herod was a cautious politician who, throughout his life, was able to garner unstinting Roman support by appeasing the rulers of Rome. This enabled him to rule without serious competition and to extend his hegemony over more of the Holy Land than any of his predecessors, and even to lands far beyond. He was uncompromisingly cruel in suppressing the Hasmoneans, and relentless in the persecution of his opponents among his subjects and his own kinsfolk. Jewish enmity toward him stemmed from opposition to his foreign origin, and from his being a usurper who exterminated the Hasmoneans, the legal dynasty in Judea.

As king, Herod aspired to glorify both his kingdom and his name. He was among the most extreme admirers of Hellenistic-Roman culture, and his desire to gain a standing for Jerusalem equal to that of the foremost Hellenistic cities led him to imbue his capital with a decidedly Hellenistic flavor. This found expression in the dominant architectural style of the buildings and their monumental proportions, as well as in the current life style, which called for theaters, gymnasiums, hippodromes and "the games" — a cosmopolitan atmosphere and a luxurious court. This was neither entirely new nor unique in Jerusalem, where Hellenistic influence had already taken a hold among the Jews of the city under the Hasmoneans.

Herod's penchant for the grandiose led to one of the most important facets of his rule—especially for us today—his being undoubtedly the greatest builder Palestine had ever known. His craving for construction projects had no bounds, and Josephus dwells at length on his many building activities in this country and abroad. Indeed, his impressive monuments, including fortresses, palaces, and even whole cities, have been revealed at various sites scattered about the country. He fulfilled his wish to impress his Roman imperial patrons by building new cities according to the best of Roman standards: his port city of Caesarea, and the town of Samaria, which he renamed "Sebaste" (Greek for "Augustus"), with a Temple of Augustus at its crown. These well served to express Herod's extreme admiration for Roman urbanization, architecture, and art. In the fortresses and palaces which he built at Masada, Herodium, and Jericho, Herod gave full architectural expression to his daring eccentricity, in which he sought to combine security, luxurious living, and tranquillity with desert solitude. His winter and summer palaces established norms which deeply permeated the material aspect of the lives of the upper crust in Judea. It is noteworthy that in all these projects he strove to avoid any ornamental motifs which might give offense to the tenets of traditional Judaism—in deference to the customs of his people. This implies that even under Herod figurative art was not fostered among Jews.

In Jerusalem, Herod sought to win over the hearts of the population by rebuilding the Jewish Temple, exceeding anything previously known in the city, in its monumentality and architectural magnificence. This was his *magnum opus*, intended to glorify his name and perpetuate his memory. Indeed, even the Jewish sages — who were not particular admirers of Herod — said of his Temple: "Whoever has not seen Herod's building has never seen a beautiful edifice." From our excavations in the Upper City, we could readily look out over the Temple Mount to the east, and we feasted our eyes on the magnificent panorama daily. The beauty revealed before anyone standing there makes the heart beat faster, and still magnificently reflects one of the most ambitious building projects the ancient world ever knew. Despite the fact that much of the original splendor has long since disappeared, there are very few sites in the world anything like it. It is a spacious esplanade, surrounded by mighty ramparts, with the Western Wall, the focal point of modern Jewish devotion, prominent among them. Quite understandably, the Muslims—who adorned the site with the Dome of the Rock—call it *Haram al-Sharif*, "The Noble Enclosure."

The Herodian period was an era of general development, a time of expansion and intensive, well-planned construction. This is well reflected on the Western Hill, in the Upper City which was a residential quarter. Josephus mentions several palaces there: the Hasmonean palace, the palace of Herod the Great, and the palace of Ananias the High Priest, as well as other mansions. Of these, only Herod's palace can actually be placed, in the northwestern corner of the Upper City, from the site of the present Citadel near the Jaffa Gate and stretching southward. This palace was defended on the north by three huge towers, which Herod named after members of his family: Hippicus, Phasaelis, and Mariammne. The lower part of one of them has survived and is often identified with the Phasaelis tower, though some scholars hold it to have been Hippicus.

In our excavations we found no structures which could be ascribed to Herod's official projects, but several architectural elements did come to light which must have belonged to monumental public structures, the location and nature of which are as yet unknown. In general, we have assumed that all the actual buildings uncovered were private dwellings.

The excavations did not yield sufficient data for us to be able to restore the street system of the quarter here. Some think that the Herodian city was laid out in the typical Hellenistic, Hippodamic fashion, with a uniform network of streets set at right angles to one another. But since only parts of a single street were uncovered, the matter remains conjectural. On the basis of the orientation of the buildings, it might be assumed that the direction of the streets was not uniform, but instead was influenced by local topography. In the northern part of our excavations, the buildings were oriented almost according to the points of the compass, whereas there was a decided angle in the orientation of the houses in the southwest, where the bedrock slopes down in oblique terraces.

Construction in the Upper City was dense, with the houses built quite close together; but the individual dwelling units were extensive, and inner courtyards lent them the character of luxury villas. These homes were richly ornamented with frescoes, stucco work, and mosaic floors, and were equipped with complex bathing facilities, as well as containing the luxury goods and artistic objects which signify a high standard of living. This, then, was an upper class quarter, where the noble families of Jerusalem lived, with the High Priest at their head. Here they built their homes in accordance with the dominant fashion of the Hellenistic-Roman period. It is generally assumed that the Jerusalemite nobility was of the Sadducee faction, whose members included the Hellenizers; the lower classes tended more to the Pharisee faction, which opposed foreign influences. Thus, it can be assumed that this quarter was occupied chiefly by Sadducees. Even so, there is no specific archaeological evidence here to indicate any laxity in their upholding of the traditional precepts of the Jewish religion. On the contrary, the finds indicate that the laws of ritual purity were strictly kept, as were the injunctions against statues and graven images.

3. A Residence from the Days of Herod

It is generally difficult to date a given building and its associated finds to the specific period of the reign of Herod the Great; such dwellings, though built under that king, often continued in use long after his death. Most of these houses were destroyed during Titus' destruction of Jerusalem, and the artifacts found within them can generally be dated to the final phase of the houses' existence. Thus, we often tend to ascribe such houses together with their finds, to the general period of the Herodian dynasty, that is, the span beginning with Herod's ascent in 37 B.C. and terminating with the destruction of Jerusalem in A.D. 70. It is therefore of great significance that we can ascribe a particular building with certainty to the actual reign of Herod, possibly even slightly earlier, but definitely no later. This outstanding house was uncovered in our Area E, and we have come to denote it the "Herodian Residence." The fate of this house was quite different from that of most

61. The Herodian residence, looking northwest (Area E)

62. The "footbath"

63. Artist's view of the ritual bath

other houses in the quarter, for it did not continue until A.D. 70, nor was it sacked at that time. It contained no traces of fire, no destruction debris, and no indication of its having been ravished in war. Quite the contrary, we received the impression that it had been evacuated intentionally, in an orderly fashion. While most of the rooms and their floors were bare of any objects, two of the side rooms were full of broken pottery and other objects, as if rubbish had been gathered and left there after the house was abandoned.

Of particular importance among the small finds in this house are the large quantities of coins, mostly *perutot*, minute coins of low value. Analysis revealed

CHRONOLOGY

84

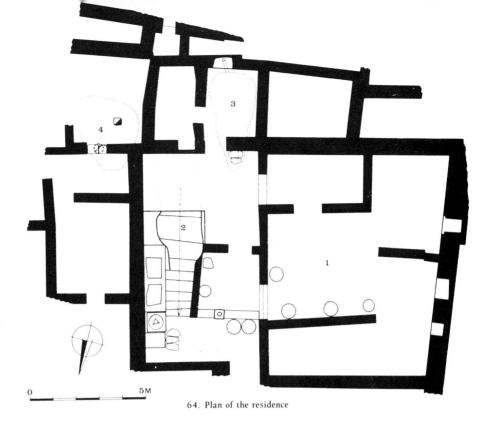

64. Plan of the residence

that a majority of these coins were of the days of Alexander Janneus and some from the time of Herod; but the *perutot* coins of Alexander Janneus are known to have remained in circulation even under Herod. We found no coins of a period later than Herod's reign, indicating that the house had gone out of use still in Herod's time or shortly after his death.

We also uncovered revealing evidence regarding the initial building of this house. When we "opened up" several of the floors to see what lay beneath them, it was discovered that the house was founded partly on bedrock and partly on the walls of an earlier building. The fill beneath the floor contained pottery of the late 2nd and 1st centuries B.C., as well as coins of Antiochus IV, Alexander Janneus, and Mattathias Antigonus—that is, all of them were of the Hasmonean period. However, there were none of Herod's coins. Furthermore, an early cistern (4, above plan) located beneath the house, which had been sealed up by the new builders, contained a group of pottery vessels of the 2nd century B.C., including jug types known to bear seal impressions with the "Jerusalem" legend. At one spot beneath the floors, we found remains of foundations and pottery from the Israelite period.

All this would point to the house having been built late in the Hasmonean period upon earlier Hasmonean remains, on a site which had been settled in First Temple times. The house flourished during the second half of the 1st century B.C. and was destroyed around the turn of the millennium or very early in the 1st century A.D. The circumstances of its destruction are discussed below.

The remains discovered in the building enable us to learn much of the nature of the house and its inhabitants. This was a rather large dwelling which spread over an area of some 200 square meters, its rooms arranged around a central courtyard (1 on plan 64). The floor of the courtyard contains four sunken ovens. To the south is a cistern for water storage (3). A prominent place is occupied by a large ritual bath

65. Pottery resting on bedrock beneath the floor of the residence

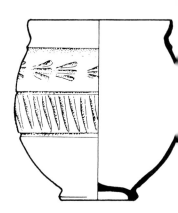

66. Thin-walled pottery beaker (imported)

(2), partly vaulted over, which was entered by a stairway. Near the entrance a peculiar stone vessel was found *in situ*, a square basin, round within with a bulge at *62* its center and its bottom pierced by three holes. This may have served as a laver for washing the feet prior to descending into the ritual bath and, if so, was a "footbath" of the type noted in the Mishnah (Yadaim 4, 1). We have found such "footbaths" in other houses as well, although smaller and not in their original position.

In the western wall of the house there are three niches, raised some 1.5 meters above the floor; they were apparently wall cupboards for storing vessels and the *76* family "china"—the finest of the household pottery. Indeed, we found here much broken pottery which, after mending, was returned to one of the niches, as can be seen in the photograph. That this was obviously the house of a well-to-do family is indicated by its very quality, and by the nature of the associated finds.

Most of the pottery vessels were found here within the fill beneath the floors, and they belonged to the final phase of the previous building on the site. Some of this pottery, contemporaneous with the construction of the new house (1st century B.C.), was identical with that found above the floors. It is thus evident that not too long a time elapsed between the building of the house and its destruction; we can therefore treat all the pottery found there as a single group.

67. Artist's view of one of the rooms in the residence

86

68. Asymmetrical flasks

69. Wine amphorae imported from Italy

A set of red pottery found here was undoubtedly the pride of the household. This type of ware, outstanding in its pleasing design and fine quality, decorated the festive tables of upper class homes. The carinated decanter is of especially rare beauty and very well preserved, as are the flat plates. This pottery, known to archaeologists as "Eastern terra sigillata ware," represents some of the finest pottery produced in Late Hellenistic times, and is generally considered to have been manufactured somewhere along the eastern littoral of the Mediterranean Sea. Many vessels of this type have been found in the Jewish Quarter, along with pottery known as "Western terra sigillata ware," produced in Italy, which is shinier and somewhat thinner. These vessels show that the upper class inhabitants of Jerusalem followed the international fashion of the day.

"TERRA SIGILLATA" WAR

75

Another group of pottery vessels worthy of mention are the amphorae — storage jars for wine, with pointed bases — inscribed in Latin with various "trademarks." These are evidence that the inhabitants of the house enjoyed wine imported from Italy. But how was "gentile" wine used here in a period when the Jews generally adhered to the precepts forbidding consumption of such foreign products? It would seem that there have always been more and less observant Jews. We can ascribe to these same wine-bibbers the asymmetrical, pot-bellied wine flasks of very odd design, an impressive number of which were found in our excavation. Indeed, as in the photograph, these peculiar jars may well have originally been hung on strings, for they are quite unstable in any other position. This type of flask was common at the time, but because of their thinness and fragility, few have survived in a condition enabling complete restoration.

69

68

An interesting archaeological problem arose in connection with the more than twenty oil lamps found in this house. They are of several different well-known types from the Hasmonean period and Herod's reign. Not even a single example of the classical, so-called "Herodian" type of oil-lamp was found, however. Made on the potter's wheel, and having a spatulate nozzle and a knife-pared bottom, this was the most common type of lamp in the 1st century A.D. Till now it has generally been accepted that this type first appeared at the beginning of Herod's reign and was thus of considerable chronological significance. On the basis of the finds from this house, however, it appears that the "Herodian" lamps had not yet come into existence during Herod's reign, and were probably introduced only at the very end of the 1st century B.C. or slightly later. The evidence on this matter must be reconsidered and final confirmation will probably present itself only after further finds of this sort have been made.

LAMPS

58 (3)

70. The types lamps found the Herodian

As mentioned above, the Herodian Residence was not destroyed in war but was the victim of the replanning of the city's street network toward the end of Herod's reign or shortly thereafter. The building was intentionally destroyed and the new street pavement was laid down directly over the ruins, running from east to west.

We uncovered a stretch of some 50 meters of this pavement, from the Herodian residence westward up to the ruins of a house north of the Hurvah Synagogue (Area J, p. 32). The flagstones were very large, reaching 2 to 2.5 meters in length and 40 to 50 centimeters in thickness. Their surfaces were not dressed and remained very rough. Apparently they were never trod by human feet and they probably served as

THE PAVED STREET

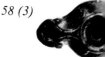

77

moval of the rubble of two destroyed synagogues ("Tiferet Israel" and the Karaite synagogue),
aration for archaeological excavations in Area E (p. 32)

ginning of excavations at the above site

73. Continuation of work in Area E, looking
north. At center left, part of the street pavement overlying remains of the building ➡

74. The Herodian residence in Area E, after clearance

75. Eastern terra sigillata pottery

76. A wall cupboard in the Herodian residence

...nent laid over demolished buildings (Area J, p. 32)

78. After dismantling of the pavement, various structures were discovered including cisterns and ritual baths

the pavement

the foundation for a layer of smoother flagstones, of which two were found in position. We do not know the width of the street, for no curbstones were found, but at one spot a width of 13 meters was preserved.

This seems to have been one of the main streets of the Upper City, leading toward "Robinson's Arch" at the corner of the Temple Enclosure. The surprisingly large stones used for the pavement may simply reflect the times — a period when the walls of the Temple Mount were built of truly enormous ashlars, some of them well over 10 meters long. In any event, the street is of great importance, for it is the only one from the period of the Second Temple which was uncovered in the course of our excavations. In this connection, Josephus relates that, after the Temple was completed, 18,000 laborers were thrown out of work. In order to ease their condition, King Agrippa II (who actually did not reign in Judea but was entrusted by Claudius Caesar with supervision of the Temple), was urged to rebuild the destroyed eastern Temple portico. The king refused all such appeals, because of the heavy financial burden it would have imposed on him. Instead, he agreed to pave the streets of the city in white stone (*Antiquities of the Jews* XX, 219-222), an interesting example of social relief work in antiquity. In this connection, Josephus notes that in this same period "even if a man worked but one hour a day, he received wages for the entire day." This exceeds even the most liberal terms of today! In our excavations, for example, we would pay our workers only half a day's wages for a solitary hour's work.

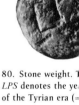

80. Stone weight. T
LPS denotes the ye
of the Tyrian era (=

In the western part of the street, the pavement overlaid the remains of earlier structures, just as it covered the Herodian house to the east. This led to the preservation of a dense series of cisterns and baths beneath the pavement. The inhabitants of Herodian Jerusalem must indeed have used very large quantities of water. Among the baths there was a variety of forms and plans, with various

81. Discovering a cistern. Ami Mazar is first to descend on a rope ladder. It's easy on the way down, but coming back up...!

arrangements of stairs leading down into them. One of these ritual baths was especially notable for the unusual discovery within it: an accumulation of waste products from a glass factory. But we shall return to this discovery later on.

4. A Palatial Mansion

At the eastern edge of the Jewish Quarter, one of its main streets, Misgav Ladakh Street, slices through the quarter from north to south. We carried out excavations here in the southern part of the street, which is located just above the eastern scarp of the Upper City, overlooking the southern part of the Temple Enclosure. Here we uncovered a row of buildings from Second Temple times, built one after the other along the street, but some seven meters below the modern street level. Judging by the quality of the finds, these buildings had all apparently belonged to upper class families. Another common feature was that they were all destroyed by fire on the day in A.D. 70 when the Upper City was conquered and Jerusalem destroyed. These buildings were on the front line of the Roman attack here, on the very edge of the quarter, and they all suffered the same bitter fate. The traces of conflagration were much more obvious in them than in the houses in the interior of the quarter.

The mansion which we shall now discuss was found in our Area P, on the eastern *8* side of Misgav Ladakh Street and south of the new flight of stairs leading down to the Western Wall Plaza. This area was in the eastern part of the "Yeshivat Hakotel," then in construction. Our excavations there will long be remembered by us, principally on three counts: first were the technical difficulties involved in cutting through the street itself in order to join up the two parts of the ancient building found on either side of it. At the time, the pipes below the modern pavement—both water and sewage—were suspended above our heads; our trench also cut off one of the major arteries within the Jewish Quarter, forcing the inhabitants to make a wide detour in order to get from one part of the street to the other. Our second memory relates to our great surprise at the unexpectedly good state of preservation of several of the buildings. Our third unforgettable point was the magnificent view toward the Temple Enclosure, the Mount of Olives, Silwan village, and the Kidron Brook. Two millennia ago, the inhabitants of these buildings here must have had a still more imposing view through their windows.

In this same area (P), the remains of two large structures came to light, one abutting the other and similar in plan. We shall concentrate upon the northern one, which is the better preserved of the two buildings. It occupies an impressive area of *84* over 600 square meters; its arrangement as a series of rooms surrounding a central courtyard indicates that it had been a single dwelling unit. While modesty has led us to call it the "Mansion," its scale would justify referring to it as a palace. Fragmentary remains of later structures, from Byzantine to Arab times, were found throughout the area. Particularly troublesome to us were chunks of gravel mixed with a very hard, limey mortar, which had been poured in the Arab period to form deep foundations; these had caused extensive damage to the Herodian stratum. In order to remove these blocks of "concrete," we resorted to air hammers, persistence, and patience. The late water cisterns here were an equally hard nut to crack through. Peeling away these later accretions was an extensive operation, but it was the only way to reach and isolate the structures of the Herodian Period.

The palatial mansion, general view looking toward
Temple Mount and the Mount of Olives

The Mansion was built on two levels—the ground floor, intended for dwelling, and a basement level built down the slope, which contained service areas, mainly water installations such as pools, baths, and cisterns.

PLAN OF THE MANSION The main floor was arranged around a square courtyard paved with flagstones (1 on plan 84, p. 98). This gave access to the various wings of the building, and it was here that water could be drawn from the cisterns beneath; stairs here also led down to the lower basement. On the west of the courtyard was a doorway leading to the only surviving wing of the ground floor, which included living and guest quarters. There are two rows of rooms interconnected by doorways. The walls, built of ashlars, have survived in some spots to a height of 3 meters. In the building to the south, the western wall has survived up to the height of the ceiling, including a row of sockets for the roofbeams. This state of preservation is most extraordinary for structures of Second Temple date here in the Jewish Quarter excavations. What led to the preservation of these walls from destruction was apparently the presence of the street which overlaid them for many centuries. Adjacent to the high walls were heaps of building stones which had fallen from the walls, probably from an upper story. The stones are covered with soot, evidence of the blaze which had raged in all the houses here. The conflagration is dated by the coins found here, which are from the second and fourth years of the First Jewish Revolt against Rome. In other parts of the houses in this area, the traces of the fire were obliterated by later building activities.

s in a house adjacent to the mansion. The plastered wall on the far (west) side is preserved to ceiling height.

84. Plan of the palatial mansion

From the courtyard of the ground floor (1), we enter the guest quarters through room 2. This room has been denoted a vestibule, for it leads to the other rooms in the wing. Judging by the fine mosaic floor, however — the only one in the wing — it undoubtedly had a more important function. At the center of the pavement there had been a colored panel, which was mostly destroyed by one of the later blocks of "concrete." From the remaining portions we can reconstruct the original pattern: the square frame, of an intertwined fret pattern, enclosed a circular frame with a guilloche pattern. In the corners between the round and square borders there were pomegranate motifs. The center was entirely destroyed, though there are indications that it had contained a large rosette pattern. The fire in this room had caused the ceiling to collapse, and we found the charred beams resting directly on the floor. (Professor A. Fahn, of the Hebrew University, has defined the wood as cypress.) The cubes of the mosaic pavement were also charred, discoloring the stones considerably. A thick layer of ash covered everything, and this, in turn was covered by the debris of the stone walls.

108

85. A comple

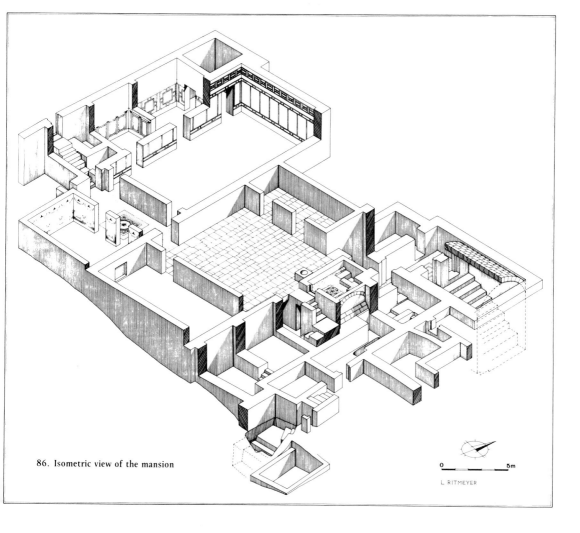

86. Isometric view of the mansion

0   5m

L. RITMEYER

This burnt layer is also found in adjacent room 3 to the south, a room notable for the fact that it contained the largest wall area of frescoes found in our excavations. The southern wall, some 2.5 meters high, is covered entirely with colored plaster painted in red and yellow panels, with imitation windows and other ornamental architectural features which are more imaginative than realistic. The fresco terminates above in a sort of cornice, above which are acroteria painted in white. The entire wall closely resembles the wall paintings at Pompeii. Especially noteworthy is the fine quality of the painting, executed in the true fresco technique; that is, with the painting being done while the plaster was still wet. The wall painting was still blackened with soot when we discovered it, but even after we had washed the surface several times, the full splendor of the colors was still intact. Such painting represents the finest technique possible, as well as the most costly (see below, p. 149).

Returning to the vestibule, there are several stairs to the west which may well have ascended to an upper story or to the roof. Instead of following them up, however, our tour now takes us through either of the two doorways on the north into a large hall (4), which measures 6.5 meters wide and 11 meters long. This seems to have been a magnificent reception hall with white stucco ornamentation arranged in broad panels and imitation courses of bossed ashlars. Large areas of plaster remained intact on the western and northern walls, and many hundreds of

87. Fallen stones in the stuccoed hall (4, p. 98). On the far (northern) wall, plastered panels were preserved almost to ceiling height

88. Imitation ashlar masonry in stucco

Molded stucco fragments from the ceiling of the hall

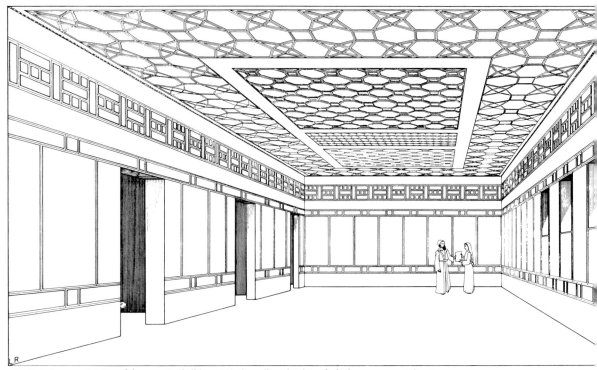

90. Artist's reconstruction of the reception hall (4, p. 98), the walls and ceiling of which are ornamented in stucco

plaster fragments were found among the debris which filled the hall. A large heap of *101* toppled stones still remains adjacent to the northern plastered wall, which was preserved to a height of some 3 meters. We thought it best to leave the pile there, to preserve the plaster safely for future restoration. Among the plaster fragments there were some bearing "egg-and-dart" motifs in relief, forming triangles, squares, *89-91* hexagons, and octagons, apparently from the ornamental ceiling. Similar geometric patterns in stucco may be seen in vaulted ceilings at Pompeii, which are from the period preceding Augustus (1st century B.C.).

The ornamental style of the interior walls, in imitation of ashlar construction, originates in Greece. Such decoration was very common in the Hellenistic cities of Asia Minor, where it was considered a mark of distinction and of good taste. Late in the Hellenistic period the style reached the West (Italy), where it remained in vogue until the 1st century B.C. (the "First Style" at Pompeii). In Israel, plaster modeled in relief has been found at the Hellenistic site of Tel Anafa in Upper Galilee.

What is puzzling here is how did such ornamentation find its way to Jerusalem, to appear in the interior decoration of a house of the 1st century A.D., at a time when the style had already become *passé* in the Hellenistic world and even in Italy. In Jerusalem there was an independent stylistic tradition imitating stone, in the rock-cut tombs of the Second Temple period, but this does not serve to explain its application in the interior decoration of this house, which combines broad panels with narrow courses of "stone." This division, which is reminiscent of the Hellenistic examples, is not derived from the local Jerusalem style. It seems that this earlier mode survived in the East much later than in its original countries. At Masada and Herodium we also find imitations of ashlar construction modeled in plaster on the walls.

Much to our surprise, we found during our work that the plaster modeled as panels and "ashlars" was not the first layer to have been applied to the walls of this

102

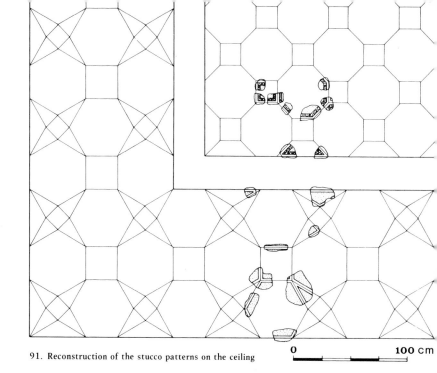

91. Reconstruction of the stucco patterns on the ceiling

0   100 cm

hall, for it was preceded by a painted plaster. Among the numerous fragments of plaster found in the hall, there were some which showed the two layers still attached to one another. As noted, the upper layer was modeled in relief while the lower one was painted in various colors; thus, initially the hall had had a painted ornamentation. From among the painted plaster fragments, we were able to restore a decorative frieze containing a repeated pattern of floral motifs in an uncommon style. This was the work of a true artist, one who did not stick to convention but sought out an original design, somewhat oriental in character. Possibly in order to keep up with changing fashion, the walls were eventually replastered, covering the paintings over with the new stucco ornamentation.

106

It is interesting to note that the opposite process has been observed at Pompeii, where early walls were ornamented in stucco-work imitating ashlars in relief (the "First Style"), whereas later colorful wall paintings came into fashion (the "Second Style"). This reversed order of fashion here in Jerusalem raises an interesting question of chronology which we shall not even attempt to solve here.

ARCHITECTURAL FRESCO

Continuing our tour, we go on to the first room (5, p. 98) in a row of three on the western side of the hall. The walls of this room were found to be plainly plastered. During our work here, however, we peeled off some of the white plaster and found a painted layer beneath. Unfortunately, it was mostly destroyed, but in one corner a section of the fresco has survived, containing the first example of an architectural painting known in Palestine. It depicts fluted Ionic columns bearing a schematic Doric frieze, clearly influenced by architectural frescoes in the "Second Style" of Pompeii. In the adjacent room (6), the plastered walls are incised with thin lines, in imitation of courses of ashlar masonry. We found traces of painted plaster beneath this plaster, too. Indeed, this was a phenomenon common to all the rooms, where the initial ornamentation had been in the fresco technique and subsequently the paintings were plastered over.

105

We made an interesting discovery beneath the floor of the third room (7): a stepped pool containing Late Hellenistic potsherds. This showed that a house had stood here already in Hasmonean times.

Leaving this wing of the house, so rich in finds and in interior decoration, we now cross over to the eastern side of the courtyard where the remains of only one room (8) of the wing have survived. This is a small bathroom paved in colored mosaics with a compass-formed rosette as its only pattern — simple and nice. A low bench in one corner is also covered in mosaics, and there is a sunken sitting-bath at the far end of the room. This was undoubtedly a very pleasant and intimate bath-room, and it seems to have been connected with one of the bedrooms in the eastern wing.

BATHROOM

97, 162

92. Artist's view of the bath-room

We now descend by way of the southern stairway to the lower level of the house, which contains a series of water installations. Once downstairs, we enter a long corridor hewn into the bedrock, with a ceiling constructed of large stone slabs. This corridor gives access to three rock-hewn pools, barrel-vaulted in ashlar masonry; their openings had been blocked with stones in a later period, when they were used as mere cisterns. The pool situated at the northern end of the corridor (9) is of special interest here, with its double, side-by-side entrances. This was a fairly large pool, measuring 3.5 x 4 meters, with steps running its entire width. In the Arab or Byzantine period, this pool was converted into a cistern, and the steps were hewn

THE BASEMENT LEVEL

93

away (leaving only traces on the walls), in order to increase its capacity. The original openings were also blocked up, and a new hole was opened in the ceiling for drawing water.

We were somewhat mystified by the double entrance. Why was it needed by anyone going down the steps to draw water? R. Reich, a member of our staff who is currently investigating the subject of the pools and cisterns, had suggested that it is related to the Jewish laws of ritual purity, and that the pool originally served as a ritual bath. The bathers would descend for immersion through the one entrance, and would ascend through the other opening after immersion. Another ritual bath *149* has been found in which the stairs are divided into two by a low "railing"—the one side for descending and the other for ascending—and this would support this interpretation (we shall return to this subject below).

Another stairway on the northern side of the courtyard takes us down to a small, THE LOWER COURTYARD lower courtyard (10), paved in white mosaics, which gives access to doorways on all sides. In the northwestern corner there is an opening to a cistern below. West of this courtyard is a large, vaulted chamber (11), possibly a storeroom, most of which was destroyed. On the east are two stepped baths, and on the south, beneath the small bathroom of the ground floor, is a vaulted chamber which had several doorways, also probably a storeroom. In time, the openings were blocked up and the room was utilized as a cistern.

On the north is a corridor paved in mosaics in a checkerboard pattern (12); two *100* doorways in its eastern wall lead to a large stepped pool, roofed over by an impressive vault built of ashlars (13). This, too, is a ritual bath with a double entrance, one for entry and the other for exit. But why should there be so many baths within a single house, several of them quite large? The phenomenon, pointing to what was virtually a cult of immersion, may well hint at the nature of the Mansion's inhabitants and their customs.

In any event, it is clear that this extensive mansion was the dwelling of a wealthy patrician family of some stature in Jerusalem society. As we have seen, of the dwelling story little more than one wing, containing several reception rooms, remains. The large, magnificent reception hall and several guest rooms were all decorated in Hellenistic-Roman fashion, and the house must also have been equipped with beautiful furnishings. The luxury these items had once imparted to the house is little in evidence now, for few objects survived the destruction of A.D. 70 and the activities of builders in later periods. But even the meager remnants discovered in the ruins have much to tell us. Let us now review some of the special objects found in the Mansion and the adjacent house.

Foremost are the stone tables, which represent a major and most interesting STONE TABLES innovation among discoveries in excavations in Jerusalem. The first such table came to light in the Burnt House (see below), and fragments of several tables of this sort were found in the Mansion and the house next door. Of particular note is a rectangular tabletop ornamented with a floral pattern on its edge. Besides these *94* rectangular tables, which had had a single central leg, there were smaller, round tables with three legs. Only the tops of this latter type have survived, for the wooden *188*

legs have long since perished. The round tables, analogous to our modern coffee-tables, were used for dining (see also below).

This variety of tables was further augmented by another small, decorative type, of which only fragments were discovered. One of these tables had a thin top of black bituminous stone ornamented with a colored stone inlay. Other fragments were found ornamented with incised floral patterns.

110

GLASSWARE Of the other luxury wares found in these houses, one of the most pleasant and costly objects was an ornamented pitcher of mold-blown glass. The fragments of this vessel came to light in the Mansion, on the floor of a niche behind the eastern wall of the large frescoed room (3, p. 98); all the pieces had been deformed by the heat of the conflagration that destroyed the house. The base bore a petal pattern, while the body was fluted and the shoulder had a frieze of palmettes. The neck and handle are missing. The beauty of the vessel is still quite apparent, despite its present state. It was certainly an object of great beauty, as can be seen in the restored drawing. The vessel bears a small frame beneath the handle, a *tabula ansata*, containing the Greek inscription: "Ennion made it." Ennion is known to have been a glassmaker in the 1st century A.D., and apparently worked in Sidon. Our vessel is one of his larger and finer products. Three other vessels of this same type are known, all made in one and the same mold. Two of them are in collections in the United States (at the Metropolitan Museum of Art in New York, and at the Corning Museum of Glass in Corning, New York). The third and most complete example, in the Glass Pavilion at the Ha'aretz Museum in Tel Aviv, is made of blue glass, whereas ours is green and now has a polychrome coating of iridescence.

95

97. The early stages of c
palatial mansion, overlo
Temple Mount and the
Olives ➔

95. Glass pitcher made by Ennion. The glass was
distorted out of shape by the heat of the fire.
The neck and handle are missing

96. Restored drawing of the pitcher (height: 20 cm)

98. The two-story palatial mansion; on right—the central courtyard and the bathroom with mosaic pavement; on left—the basement with water installations

100. Vestibule with mosaic pavement (12, p. 98) giving access to the double entrance to a vaulted bath (the second doorway is blocked with stones

99. The stairwell

101. Entrance to the stucco-paneled hall

102. Within a room of the palatial mansion (5, p. 98); in the corner, remains of a wall painting

103. A wall fresco (room 3, p. 98), depicting and architectural motifs; note traces of fire ➜

104. In the corner of room 5 (p. 98), frescoes found beneath the plain plaster

105. Detail of the fresco in fig. 104, depicting a column and entablature

106. A painted frieze with stylized floral motifs

...oms filled with fallen masonry

108. A burnt mosaic
pavement in room 2
(p. 98)

...bonized wooden beams lying on the mosaic pavement

110. An inlaid stone panel

111. Cooking pots found in a cistern

112. Fragments of a glass
pitcher made by Ennion

114. Ribbed glass bowl, imitating the bronze form

113. Ribbed bronze bowl

While our vessel was being prepared for exhibition at the Israel Museum, in 1976, Mrs. Yael Israeli noticed that the fragments which we had found included the base of a second vessel of the same type. She also brought our attention to another glass fragment from the Mansion, ornamented with an ivy wreath and a suspended jug; this was another type of vessel, with hexagonal body, and is known in Ennion's repertoire; a complete example is in the Metropolitan Museum of Art. The discovery of three or four glass vessels made by Ennion within a single house is of signal importance; most of the vessels known to have been made by him were purchased on the international antiquities market, and are of unknown provenance. Our discoveries now enable us to date Ennion's products definitely to the 1st century A.D.

A ribbed bowl of green glass, also found in the Mansion—a very fine vessel indeed—is further evidence of the status and good taste of the owner of the house. The form of the bowl imitates that of a ribbed bronze bowl of a type quite common in this period and earlier. Such a bronze bowl was found together with several bronze pitchers in one of the cisterns beneath the Mansion. The rarity of bronze vessels surviving from this period is underlined by the fact that they came to light in our excavations only in this one instance.

A PAINTED BOWL

We must not neglect the fine pottery also found in the Mansion. We were quite lucky in this realm, for, despite all the destruction on the site, one pottery vessel has survived of which we can truly be proud. This single item—indicative of what has been lost—is a bowl as thin as eggshell. It was smashed, but its fragments were cemented by lime deposits to the mosaic floor of the small bathroom east of the courtyard (8, p. 98). We labored to separate the delicate sherds from the pavement and transferred them to the laboratory of the Israel Museum. As can be seen in illustration, the results fully reveal the mending skill of Adaya, the pottery restorer.

115, 201

It must be admitted that this bowl, ornamented with a harmonious composition of floral motifs in red paint, is a most graceful and artistic piece, a fresh breeze in the otherwise bland and uninspired pottery repertoire in the Palestine of the 1st century A.D. This painted bowl is not an isolated phenomenon; it is merely the most delicate of an entire family of painted bowls lately discovered in the Jewish Quarter and in other excavations in the city.

115. Pottery bowl painted with floral motifs (restored drawing)

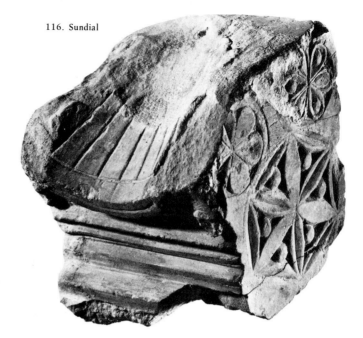

COOKING POTS   From this delicate pottery (to which we shall return later) we pass on briefly to plain everyday ware, to the lowly cooking pot. Such vessels were the most common and practical in the household, they were thin-walled and thus quite fragile. Thus, their turnover was rather rapid. An unfailing source for such pots are the cisterns which served as dumps for broken pottery. We discovered one such cistern abutting our building, filled to the brim with potsherds after it had gone out of use for storing water. In order to determine the number of cooking pots represented there, we counted the number of handles and divided the total by two (each pot having two handles). On this basis we figured that about 750 broken cooking pots had been cast into the disused cistern, in addition to a large number that were found intact. While this ceramic "cemetery" can readily be explained, it is more difficult to account for

111   the 35 intact cooking pots which came to light on the floor of a cistern beneath the central courtyard. Many of these pots had been pierced with small holes and it has been suggested that these were made intentionally, to render the pots unfit for use after they had become ritually unclean. But this matter requires further thought.

A SUNDIAL   We bring our review of the special finds from the Mansion to a close with a most unusual find, an object which embellished the house and added to it another dimension, that of time. This is a sundial made of soft limestone, measuring 12 centimeters long, 10 centimeters wide and 11.5 centimeters high. It is of the conical type, common in this period, with a molded base; the concave dial is divided by incised lines into twelve radial segments. At the top there had been a horizontal rod of metal, called a gnomon, which cast its shadow on the concave dial. The stub of the rod is still stuck in the stone. Such rods were known as the "point of the sundial" in the Mishnah (Kelim 12, 5; 'Eduyot 3, 8). Our sundial is ornamented on one side with a series of rosettes carved in bas-relief. The style and "woodcarving" technique of the rosettes are identical with the ornamentation commonly found on the Jewish ossuaries of the Second Temple period. This small, portable sundial is unique in its ornamentation and rare in its size. It must have been kept in the house and taken out into the courtyard and placed in a fixed position, in the sun, to tell the time of

119

day. Much more common were larger sundials, permanently fixed to exterior walls. Two small sundials have previously been discovered in Jerusalem — one in the recent excavations adjacent to the Temple Mount, and another long ago, in excavations on the Ophel Hill.

Dealing with our time-measuring instrument brings to my mind that it is about END OF THE TOUR time to end our tour of the Mansion. It is my hope that this tour has enabled the reader to imagine himself wandering through the rooms and corridors of this splendid dwelling when it was still a flourishing household, to gaze at the colorfully frescoed and vividly stuccoed walls, and at the delicate furniture and artifacts. The wealthy owners, belonging to the aristocracy of Jerusalem, could have imagined themselves sitting amidst their luxury in a villa at Pompeii or Herculaneum, were it not for the fine view of Mount Moriah through the window, rather than of Mount Vesuvius.

The pursuit of things Hellenistic was then not uncommon in Jerusalem, particularly among the Hellenistic nobility. That this in no way prevented them from maintaining the Jewish precepts, particularly the requirement of immersion which the Jews of Jerusalem observed so devotedly, is indicated by the many ritual baths uncovered in our excavations. In the Mansion the baths seem to have received especial attention, both in number and in total area, as well as in design. This raises the possibility that there was some connection here with the occupation of the owner. Might this have been the home of one of the High Priests, who were known to have lived in this quarter? In the next section we shall see that the Burnt House, in the same close neighborhood, can most probably be ascribed to a member of one of the High priestly families.

5. The "Burnt House"

The incidents surrounding the discovery and uncovering of this house have earned it a very special place in the story of our excavations. Not only was it an emotional experience of great depth for our team as its discoverers, but it aroused such general interest that it has also become ingrained in the consciousness of a broad public. Even today, some ten years after its initial discovery, I cannot help but feel guilty when tourists whom I meet wandering through the Jewish Quarter, groping their way through the confusion of construction and tumult, ask where they can find the "Burnt House" mentioned in their guidebooks. In the first place, we cannot guide them to the remains of this building because the site is temporarily inaccessible and has not yet been prepared for visitors. Additionally, I am well aware that we shall never be able to present the site and its finds in a manner that will enable visitors to envisage even a fraction of the excitement and emotion it aroused in those who had the good fortune to view it while it was being excavated.

From the vantage point of hindsight, it seems that we excavators would probably not have been so overawed by the discovery of the Burnt House had we not come upon it so suddenly, in the very first year of our project. At that time we had not yet come across any house that had witnessed the catastrophe of A.D. 70, and we were still emotionally unprepared for the impressions and associations raised by the prospect laid bare before us. In subsequent years, after several other such burnt houses had been discovered, our emotions were already somewhat blunted to the sight of such stark violence. But this Burnt House was not only the first such discovery, but it also exceeded all the others in the quantity of objects found and in the preservation of the traces of destruction and fire. It was a good thing that the Burnt House was the first of its type to be found, for it caught us while we were still open to impression.

117. The Burnt House, bird's-eye view

In January 1970, work began in preparation for construction at 36 Misgav- THE DISCOVERY
Ladakh Street, near the modern stairway leading down to the Western Wall Plaza
(our Area B, p. 32). After the heaps of rubble and refuse had been cleared away,
initially by mechanical means, there was a rather thick layer of fill and refuse
containing nothing ancient. Then stone walls suddenly began sprouting out of the
earth. As we leveled off the area in order to lay out a grid of squares in preparation
for our systematic archaeological excavations, we saw immediately that these were
the walls of actual rooms. As a first step in stratigraphic excavation, we dug a trench
the breadth of one of the rooms, in order to determine the sequence of the layers. At
a depth of about a meter we encountered a floor of beaten earth. Already, the sides
of the trench provided a clear and impressive cross-section, which we were able to
read like an open book.

The upper layer contained fallen building stones which had changed color as the
result of a fire. The layer beneath was a mixture of earth, ashes, soot and charred
wood; at the bottom of the cross-section, overlying the floor, were pottery fragments and parts of scorched stone vessels. The plastered walls were also black with
soot. The picture was clear to any trained eye. There was only one phase of
occupation, and its composition was unambiguous: the building had been destroyed by fire, and the walls and ceiling had collapsed along with the burning
beams, sealing over the various objects in the rooms. When did this occur? The
pottery indicated that it was sometime in the 1st century A.D.

This stirred our imagination. Was the destruction of this building, so close to the
Temple Enclosure, connected with the Roman destruction of Jerusalem in A.D. 70?
We seemed to have before us a unique picture — of a house sacked by the Roman
legions, burying all the household effects and leaving everything just as it had been,
undisturbed by later activities. I could not call to mind any similar discovery in
earlier excavations in Jerusalem.

In the excavation diary, I wrote: "On the same day (13 January 1970) I was THE EXCITEMENT
somewhat excited." But after the initial excitement came moments of doubt. My
initial impression might merely have been wishful thinking, and the facts might not
lend themselves to such far-reaching conclusions. My chief assistant at the time,
Ami Mazar was away and Ronny Reich, the area supervisor, was as carried away as
I was. I therefore invited several of my fellow Jerusalem archaeologists to visit the
site, each one separately, to see their reactions to the cross-section. All of them
arrived at the same conclusion as ours.

Systematic excavation of the entire area only served to increase our tension, as
well as our expectations. The salient question was whether the same phenomenon
was found in the other rooms as well. As we cleared each room, an identical picture
emerged. First we would come across stone debris from the collapsed walls, which
filled the rooms. The dressed blocks were of the soft, local *nari* limestone, which had
been baked to various colors by the great heat of the fire. Some had become
lime-white, while others were grey, red, and yellow, and mostly very crumbly.

Among the debris filling the rooms was a mixture of ash and soot, and large quantities of charred wood.

A HUGE FIRE Soot reigned over all, clinging to everything. It covered the plastered walls, and even the faces of our workmen turned black. There was no doubt that the fire had rampaged here, apparently fed by some highly inflammable material contained in the rooms. It may well have been some oil, which would account for the abundance of soot. The traces were so vivid that one could almost feel the heat and the smell of the fire. So at least some of our visitors maintained.

When we reached the floor level, objects began appearing, scattered about or in heaps: pottery, stone vessels, broken glass, iron nails, and the like. The known types of pottery gave us a general dating in the 1st century A.D. for the destruction of the building. But the many coins strewn over the floors — partly of the Roman Procurators of Judea and mostly from the First Jewish Revolt against Rome — permitted a more precise dating. The coins of the revolt bear the legends "Year Two/The Freedom of Zion," "Year Three/The Freedom of Zion," and "Year Four/Of the Redemption of Zion." The latest of them, of the fourth year of the revolt, are from A.D. 69.

THE BURNING OF THE CITY It was now quite clear that this building was razed by the Romans in 70 CE, during the destruction of Jerusalem. For the first time in the history of excavations in the city, vivid and clear archaeological evidence of the burning of the city had come to light. We refrained from publicizing this fact immediately, in order to keep from being disturbed in our work by visitors. But word of the discovery soon spread and people began thronging to the site to see the finds on the spot. The already considerable excitement upon seeing the scorched objects being recovered from the ashes increased with the discovery of a spear leaning against the corner of a room, and it reached a crescendo when the bones of a human arm were revealed.

Beyond the image of the destruction, each of us pictured in his mind the scene so vividly described by Josephus: the Roman soldiers spreading out over the Upper City, looting and setting the houses ablaze as they slaughtered all in their path. The owner of this house, or one of its inhabitants, had managed to prepare his spear; another member of the household did not manage to escape from the house, and died in the flames. The tangible evidence, surprising in its freshness and shocking in its realism, gave us the feeling that it had all happened only yesterday.

Something amazing occurred in the hearts of all who witnessed the progress of excavations here. The burning of the Temple and the destruction of Jerusalem — fateful events in the history of the Jewish People — suddenly took on a new and horrible significance. Persons who had previously regarded this catastrophe as stirring but abstract and remote, having occurred two millennia ago, were so visibly moved by the sight that they occasionally would beg permission to take a fistful of soil or a bit of charred wood "in memory of the destruction." Others volunteered to take part in uncovering the remains, regarding such labor as sacred. The latent sentiment released — by people normally quite composed and immune to showing their emotions — was unbelievable.

118. Heap of broken stone vessels in the Burnt House. In the corner of the room is a round oven, with a stone roller for tamping the earth floor

119. Clearing the finds in fig. 118

The international news media took considerable interest in the discovery of the Burnt House, far beyond our expectations. Visits by journalists and by radio and television teams, most of them from abroad, brought our work almost to a standstill for several days. The extent of the broad coverage throughout the Western world is reflected in the fact that *The New York Times* published four reports on our excavations on four consecutive days (16-19 January 1970).

This deep international interest in ancient Jerusalem was revealed again and again during the years of excavating in the Jewish Quarter.

THE FINDS   Let us now turn to a brief description of the finds from the Burnt House which caused all of this excitement. Our work in Area B was continuously plagued by two phenomena: a sewer and the weather. The sewer, a faulty one left over from Turkish times, ran beneath Misgav-Ladakh Street which bordered our excavations. It was most unpleasant, to say the least, when the products of this channel occasionally spilled into our trenches. Circumstances also forced us to conduct our work here in the rainy season, when even a mere drizzle presented an almost unbearable hazard in combination with the soot which contaminated everything. We sought refuge from the rain beneath sheets of plastic, but the wind soon blew these away and we were forced to build a roof of corrugated iron sheeting. Fortunately, we were so engrossed in uncovering the finds that we were usually able to forget our tribulations.

THE BUILDING   The series of rooms uncovered is from the basement level of a large house whose continuation lies beneath Misgav-Ladakh Street on the east and a new dwelling on the north—areas which could not be excavated. On the west, the building is abutted by an earth fill and building remains from the Israelite period. This is a good example of how a house from the days of the Second Temple was built over a site from the First Temple period, necessitating the removal of earlier remains in order to make room for the new structure.

120   The plan of the Burnt House (p. 126), as far as it could be recovered, encompassed a small courtyard paved with stones (1), three medium-sized rooms (2-4), a small room (5) which was the only one not burnt and which contained no finds, a small kitchen (6), and a small, stepped ritual bath (7). The walls of the rooms were generally preserved to the height of about one meter; they were coated with a thin white lime plaster, while the floors were of beaten earth. The ovens sunk into the floors of these rooms are evidence that these were not dwelling quarters. Although a variety of small objects was scattered in disarray throughout the rooms, the outstanding feature in each room was a heap of broken objects, including stone vessels, stone tables, and pottery. Before the building collapsed, the violent hand of man had cast unwanted belongings into heaps on the floor, recalling Josephus' description of the Roman soldiers looting the houses after the city had been conquered. We found the iron spear leaning against one corner of room 3; this may have been the personal weapon of one of the household, who had put it in a readily accessible place but never managed to use it.

THE FIRST STONE TABLE   Many surprises emerged when we began piecing together the various fragments, and vessels and other objects began to take shape. The first artifact to be mended was a stone table composed of a central leg in the form of a column and an ornamented rectangular top measuring 50x80 centimeters. This table, of ordinary

141   height, is of particular interest because no similar object had previously been found in Israel. It was shown as the Exhibit of the Month at the Israel Museum in November 1970, and this new object of daily life in antiquity whetted the museum visitors' interest for more. Our excavations indeed were able to provide other objects from this sphere of life in ancient Jerusalem.

125

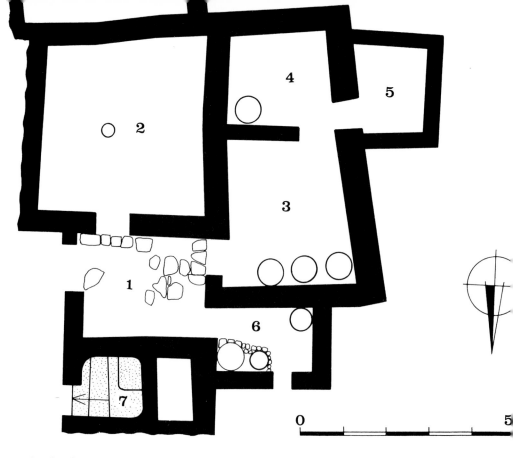

120. Plan of the Burnt House

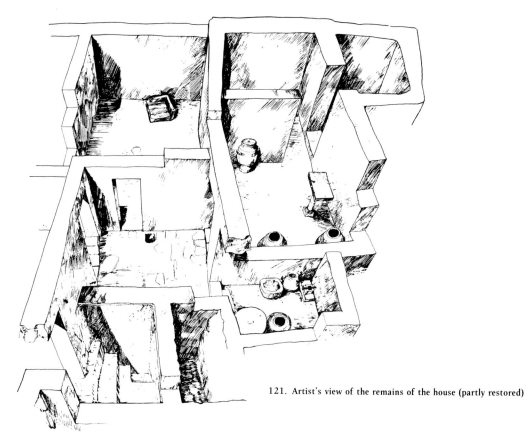

121. Artist's view of the remains of the house (partly restored)

122. Pottery inkwell

123. Mortars and pestles

The Burnt House, and the other houses such as the Mansion described above, yielded several more tables of varying design. These represent merely the most outstanding and unusual class of stone objects found in the Burnt House, and there were many other types of stone vessels as well. In fact, the abundance of stone objects was so great here that their manufacture must have been a well-developed and widespread industry in Jerusalem. Since we discuss this topic separately, in Section 10 below, let us now review the other finds from this house.

STONEWARE We found a great many large and small vessels made of soft stone, both hand-carved and turned on a lathe. Of the latter type, mention should first be made of the large jars (60-70 centimeters high) in the form of huge goblets. We found six of these which could be mended, and fragments of several others. Despite their size and *125* material, these impressive vessels are precisely made. The widespread use of such costly vessels is quite surprising. Only two similar jars were known previous to the recent excavations in Jerusalem, one from Jerusalem itself and the other from Ain Feshkha on the Dead Sea, a settlement of the Essene sect. Two pottery inkwells *122* found in our excavations resemble those found at Khirbet Qumran, the center of the Essenes; they were used there for penning the famous Dead Sea Scrolls. The link between these finds was one of the first aids in establishing the cultural milieu to which the Burnt House was to be ascribed.

Another group of stone vessels turned on a lathe are the bowls, plates, and cups, also of fine form and workmanship. Certain deeper or square bowls, as well as rectangular trays, were carved out of the stone by hand. The largest group of *125, 209 (1)* hand-carved vessels were the single or double-handled cups whose outer surface was pared vertically with a knife. These are the "measuring cups," so-called because they are often found in graduated sets. The wealth of stone vessels on this one limited site is quite astonishing, for stoneware was much more costly than pottery. The reasons for undertaking this expense should be sought in the laws of ritual purity to which the Jews of Jerusalem adhered so strictly, and which are particularly evident in the household of the Burnt House. We shall return to this point in section 10 below.

123 The basalt mortars standing on three stubby feet, together with basalt pestles, were used in every household; but again, their use was much more prolific in this particular house. No less common, and possibly more prominent here, are the *127* many stone weights. Of a squat, slightly bulging cylindrical form, they are graduated in weight from small to large.

OTHER FINDS The pottery finds in the Burnt House were not abundant. They included jars, cooking pots, bowls, juglets, and many small "perfume bottles." Miraculously, *124* several glass "perfume bottles" survived the fire intact. A common find in all the

127

124. "Perfume bottles" of pottery and glass

125. Stone jars and measuring cups

126. Stone mold for casting coin blanks

rooms were iron nails, many of which were large and bent over at the tip. They should be ascribed mainly to the wooden ceiling beams and partly to wooden furniture. In room 2, there was a burnt wooden box with nails still stuck in the corners; these nails were small and very thin. Among the special finds we must include a part of a stone mold used for casting blanks for coins. The presence of a coin mold obviously raises the question of what the finds here tell us concerning the use of the rooms uncovered.

A WORKSHOP   The fact that the rooms were on the basement level, and that there were ovens in several of them, indicates that they were not dwelling quarters. The ovens, cooking pots, mortars, "measuring cups," and numerous weights found all point to the fact that materials were ground, weighed, measured, and cooked here on a scale much larger than that required by any ordinary household. At the time of the discovery we suggested that this had been a laboratory or a workshop for some sort of "preparation" (not in the modern pharmaceutical sense). Of course, other suggestions also come to mind. Fortune again came to our assistance and provided us with a bit of epigraphic evidence which seems to reveal the name of the family owning or running the workshop.

BAR KATHROS   One fine day in January 1970, while we were still excavating the Burnt House, our registrar of finds, Sara Hofri, came running over from our expedition office with a stone weight in her hands, shouting: "Inscription!"—a word which electrifies any

128   archaeologist working on a dig. This weight, one of the many found in the Burnt House, had been washed and was then found to bear letters incised with thin lines. The inscription was not in the Greek script so often found on such weights, but rather in Hebrew (to be more precise, in the "square" Aramaic script). Except for the first letter in the upper line, of which only the tip remained, and the first letter in the lower line, which was partly blurred, the inscription was intact and could clearly be read: "(of) Bar Kathros," or "(of) the son of Kathros."

Stone weights

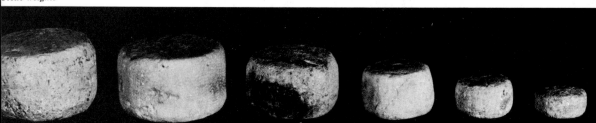

128. Stone weight, inscribed: "[Of] Bar Kathros"

Brief inscriptions of this sort, which lend a personal touch to the silent finds, are invaluable to the excavator. They bring bone-dry discoveries to life by adding the historical dimension to the material itself. This inscription opened up the possibility of identifying the owner of the house and ascertaining the sort of people who lived there. Did the name Bar Kathros fit into the picture of the period, the locale and the events being revealed before us through the archaeological discoveries? Indeed it did! Kathros, a Greek name, appears as a noun in the Book of Daniel (3:5), where it denotes a musical instrument; and the Greek word *kithara* is often used in the Greek translation of the Bible as the equivalent for the Hebrew word *kinnor*, "lyre." The "House of Kathros" is known as one of the families of High Priests who, in practical terms, ruled the Jews of Palestine in the days of the Roman Procurators. They had taken over important offices in the Temple and abused their position there through nepotism and oppression. A folksong preserved in talmudic literature relates the corruption of these priests:

> Woe is me because of the House of Boethus,
>   woe is me because of their slaves.
> Woe is me because of the House of Hanan,
>   woe is me because of their incantations.
> Woe is me because of the *House of Kathros*,
>   woe is me because of their pens.
> Woe is me because of the House of Ishmael, son of Phiabi,
>   woe is me because of their fists.
> For they are the High Priests, and their sons are treasurers,
>   and their sons-in law are trustees, and their servants beat
>   the people with staves.

(Babylonian Talmud, Pesaḥim 57, 1 = Tosefta, Minḥot 13, 21).

This refrain gives vent to the groanings of a people under the oligarchic rule of a priesthood which used any means to further its own interests. Apparently, each of the priestly families mentioned here practiced its own form of oppression: the one

through a sharp tongue, the next through a sharp pen, and most of them through simple brute force. The members of the "House of Kathros," who are accused of misusing the written word, were infamous for their libelous slander.

It can be assumed that our Bar Kathros was a scion of this same Kathros family. He lived in the same period, and his name — not a common one — was unknown outside that family. (The word *bar*, literally "son of," without a personal name before it, indicates that the name here is a family name rather than that of an actual father.) The house in which this inscription was found is situated opposite the Temple Enclosure, in a neighborhood that was populated by the nobility of Jerusalem. Moreover, in the light of the above folksong, we might assume that the workshop of our Bar Kathros engaged in manufacturing some product for the Temple, probably spices, incense, or the like. To this end, large stone vessels were required for holding quantities of ritually pure water. Furnishing products to the Temple was probably one of the "privileges" which had been usurped by this family for its own gain.

THE KITCHEN   Returning to the workshop in the Burnt House, there is a small room at its northern edge (6) which we have defined as a kitchen; it suits the kitchen of a workshop better than that of an upper class home. This room, too, was entirely

137   burnt out during the fire. Near its northern wall was a crude hearth of small fieldstones, built in two parts. The left-hand section contains a round pottery oven, while the right-hand one, also an oven, had gone out of use at some time and was reutilized as a worktable by placing a round stone slab over it. After further examination, we realized that this slab was actually the top of a round stone table which had had a central leg, and was reused here secondarily.

An oven sunk into the floor in another corner of the kitchen contained light-colored ashes. Among the few finds here was a pair of square basalt grinding stones and a portable stove of stone with inner knobs to support a cooking pot. This stove allowed a pot to be heated over a small fire of coals. There was almost no pottery found in this kitchen,

129. Pottery storage jar

130. Artist's view of the kitchen

131. An assemblage of stone vessels from the Burnt House

133. One of the burnt rooms, with heaps of broken stone vessels and

134-136. Within the burnt rooms

137. The burnt kitchen

141. A stone table with stone vessels, from the Burnt House

A unique find came to light near the doorway on the east, where the wall was destroyed more than at any other spot. Leaning against the preserved fragment of the wall were the skeletal remains of the lower arm and hand of a human being, with the fingers still attached. The hand was spread out, grasping at a step. Dr. B. Ahrensburg, who examined these remains, determined that they were of a woman in her early twenties. The associations conjured up by this spectacle were rather frightful. We could visualize a young woman working in the kitchen when the Roman soldiers burst into the house and put it to the torch. She tried to flee, but collapsed near the doorway to perish in the flames. This arm seems to be the first and only human remains discovered so far which can definitely be associated with the great human tragedy which accompanied the destruction of Jerusalem in A.D. 70.

THE CONQUEST OF
THE UPPER CITY

We are well aware of the events of this tragedy: the Romans captured the Temple and burnt it on the 9th of Ab (28 August), taking the Lower City at the same time. But the Upper City on the Western Hill, above the scarp facing the Temple Mount, held out stubbornly. On the 8th of Elul, a month after the Temple had been burnt, they attacked the Upper City with full fury, taking it, setting the houses afire and slaughtering the inhabitants. Josephus describes the fighting in detail:

> Caesar, finding it impracticable to reduce the upper city without earthworks, owing to the precipitous nature of the site, on the twentieth of the month Lous (Ab) apportioned the task among his forces. The conveyance of timber was, however, arduous, all the environs of the city to a distance of a hundred furlongs having, as I said, been stripped bare... The earthworks having now been completed after eighteen days' labor, on the seventh of the month Gorpiaeus (Elul) the Romans brought up the engines. Of the rebels, some already despairing of the city retired from the ramparts to the citadel, others slunk down into the tunnels. Pouring into the alleys, sword in hand, they (the Romans) massacred indiscriminately all whom they met, *and burnt the houses with all who had taken refuge within.* Often in the course of their raids, on entering the houses for loot, they would find whole families dead and the rooms filled with the victims of the famine... Running everyone through who fell in their way, they choked the alleys with corpses and deluged the whole city with blood, insomuch that many of the fires were extinguished by the gory stream. Towards evening they ceased slaughtering, but when night fell the fire gained the mastery, *and the dawn of the eighth day of the month Gorpiaeus (Elul) broke upon Jerusalem in flames*—a city which had suffered such calamities... The Romans now set fire to the outlying quarters of the town and razed the walls to the ground. Thus was Jerusalem taken in the second year of the reign of Vespasian, on the eighth of the month Gorpiaeus (20 September, A.D. 70). (*Wars* VI, 8-10).

2000 YEARS LATER

The story of the Burnt House, which so dramatically and vividly illustrates a most tragic and fateful chapter in the history of Jerusalem, thus comes to an end. But although the house met its end, the story itself is actually not yet complete, for in our own days, two thousand years later, when the descendants of the slaughtered returned to the site, they uncovered the physical traces of the destruction, and rebuilt their homes over the ruins. Now they too, like Bar Kathros, can look out

Rebuilding the Jewish Quarter stage by stage: fore-
d — the archaeological excavations; middle — construction
already excavated area; background — newly completed
ngs

through their windows and see the Temple Enclosure, where the "previous tenant"
had apparently worshiped. History has repeated itself. Hopefully, no other folksong beginning with the refrain "Woe is me" will ever be heard here again.

6. Jewish Ritual Baths

The excavator in Jerusalem often is amazed by the sight of so many water
installations — cisterns, baths, and pools — that have come to light among the
remains of the buildings of the Second Temple period. Water cisterns were essential
in a city like Jerusalem, where the populace depended mainly upon the storage of
rainwater to ensure their water supply; therefore, the more cisterns, the better.
These cisterns were hewn into the bedrock and then plastered with a grey mortar
containing organic matter such as soot and ash. This grey plaster is typical in all the
water installations of this period. Although not very strong, it was apparently an
efficient sealing agent.

With at least one immersion bath (*miqveh*), and sometimes more, to be found in
each house, besides a bath-pool and a bath-room, we cannot help but be surprised
by the seemingly casual attitude of the inhabitants in their use of precious water.
But since this is not an isolated instance, but a general phenomenon in the Upper
City, we must conclude that the inhabitants here could well afford this luxury. It
appears that these great quantities of water were needed to comply with the current
religious precepts. These precepts of ritual purity were all the more incumbent upon
those associated directly with the Temple, that is, the priesthood and those eating
sacred offerings. According to *halakhah*, the Jewish religious law, a ritual bath must
hold no less than forty *seahs* (about 750 liters) of spring water or rainwater, drawn
directly into the bath. Since this was not always practicable, impure water could be
made suitable by bringing it into contact with ritually pure water. For this purpose,
a special "store pool" of at least forty *seahs*' capacity was often installed adjacent to
the ritual bath, to hold pure rainwater. The wall between the two pools contained a
connecting pipe, through which the waters could come into contact, thus making
the bath water suitable for ritual immersion.

COMPLETE RITUAL BATH   Only one of the many ritual baths uncovered in the Jewish Quarter (in Area T-4,
p. 32) was found to have the complete arrangement noted above. A vestibule paved
with mosaics leads to this ritual bath, in which five steps run its full width. The bath,
145, 175   3.15 meters long and 2.2 meters wide, holds much more than the required forty
seahs (about 750 liters). Alongside the bath, to the east of its entrance, is the much
smaller "store pool," measuring only 1.4 meters long, 1 meter wide and 1.6 meters
deep; it, too, contains several steps. The wall between the two pools contains the
pipe through which the ritually pure water comes into contact with the waters of the
actual bath. The vestibule here also led to a smaller bathroom with a bathtub built
adjacent to the wall and paved in mosaics. This is surely the most complete ritual
bathing complex yet discovered in Jerusalem.

143-144. Ritual baths in Area J (p. 32)

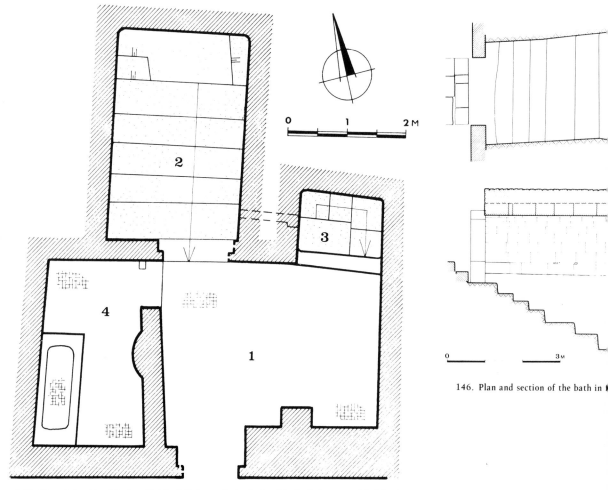

145. Plan of ritual bath in Area T-4 (p. 32): 1, vestibule; 2, ritual bath; 3, "store pool"; 4, bathroom

146. Plan and section of the bath in

147. Stepped and vaulted
ritual bath in Area F-3 (p

As already noted, ritual baths with accompanying "store pools" are most rare. They have been found elsewhere in Jerusalem, as well as in Herod's palace at Masada and in the Hasmonean palace at Jericho. The absence of "store pools" in the many other baths discovered in the Jewish Quarter is a matter which remains to be studied. In any event, it is clear that the installation of a ritual bath in a private house was a technically complex and costly matter. One could, of course, immerse oneself in a public ritual bath, but the inhabitants of the Upper City would hardly have resorted to such plebian means. They had at least one ritual bath, and sometimes even more, in the privacy of their own homes.

From the ritual baths found in almost every house in this quarter, it is possible to discern differences in attitude toward the precepts on immersion. Some households sufficed with small open pools, which met the minimal requirements of *halakhah* *143-144* with a capacity of forty *seahs* and a depth of 1.2 meters. At the other extreme were the "ambitious" patricians who built spacious ritual baths impressively vaulted in *147* fine stonework and having broad, stepped entrances. These luxurious baths were no more ritually pure than their less pretentious counterparts, but they undoubtedly bolstered the pride of the noble owners.

We have seen that some of the ritual baths were arranged so that the bather could DESCENDING AND ASCEND descend into the pool by one path and emerge ritually purified by another path. This was seen in two especially large baths in the Palatial Mansion, each of which had two separate doorways, side by side. Separate entrances and exits for ritual pools are mentioned in the Mishnah (Shekalim 8, 2), and Rashi has interpreted the Babylonian Talmud (Pesahim 19b) in an identical vein: "Through the one (entrance) they would descend to the house of immersion, and they would ascend through the other one." Such an arrangement is to be seen also in a ritual bath found in our Area J, where the steps are divided down the middle by a sort of very *149* low partition somewhat like the white line of a modern highway. Partitions between the descending and ascending paths are found in other ritual baths in Jerusalem, as well as at Khirbet Qumran on the Dead Sea. Our archaeological finds thus give substance to the literary sources and demonstrate the importance of the ritual bath in the daily life of the Jews of Jerusalem in Second Temple times.

I should remind the reader that these baths were used only for ritual immersion, and not for bathing as such, which took place in other pools or in bathtubs. Bathrooms were one of the characteristic features of the wealthier homes here, and of a high standard of living. Their presence in so many houses in the Upper City testifies to a cleanliness exceeding that of the ritual immersion required by *halakhah*. Several private buildings were even equipped with steam baths, besides the ordinary bathrooms. These were a Roman innovation, and had hypocausts (heating chambers) beneath their mosaic floors. The floors here were supported by pottery pipes rather than by the small brick columns generally found in such hypocausts.

The bathrooms, ritual baths, and cisterns were generally centered around a common vestibule, forming a single unit within the house. Often this is the only part of a building to have survived, and its size and quality are occasionally the only indication of the standard of the house itself.

148. Niche in wall for an oil lamp

The only element lacking in these installations to render them truly modern is a water closet. It was the lack of running water in the city in that period which precluded the presence of this convenience within the house, relegating it to the courtyard or beyond. We have often been asked if any "toilet" facilities were found in our excavations, and the answer has remained a firm "No." This brings to mind a suggestion raised by Professor Yigael Yadin, that the members of the extreme Essene sect would go out far beyond the walls of Jerusalem in order to relieve themselves, so as to preserve the sanctity of the city.

...ual bath, showing traces of the "partition" running down the steps. The refuse from ...orkshop was discovered here (beneath the pavement of the street in Area J, p. 32)

7. Early Mosaic Pavements

A primary measure of a domestic culture is its artistic standard. In the Hellenistic-Roman world, the high artistic standard in the home found expression chiefly through wall paintings and decorative floors — that is, frescoes and mosaics. The mosaic pavements discovered in the Jewish Quarter are among the earliest found in Jerusalem and the first which can be ascribed to the days of the Second Temple. It is still difficult to say much of their distribution, for in the buildings which we have uncovered most of the floors had been destroyed, often making it impossible to determine how they had been paved. It would seem, however, that mosaic pavements became widespread in this upper class quarter soon after they were introduced into Jerusalem. We have uncovered ten ornamental mosaic pavements so far, as well as numerous plainer ones. Contemporaneous mosaics have been discovered in Herod's palace at Masada, as well.

One feature which is quite obvious is that mosaic pavements are often present in bath-rooms and their vestibules, where water was utilized. Fortunately, a relatively large number of such bathing units has been preserved, among them the small bath-room of the Mansion mentioned above, where the floor bears a compass-drawn rosette motif, with six bichrome petals in black and red. Another mosaic *162* floor in a vestibule in the basement of the Mansion has a checkerboard pattern in black and white within a red frame. A three-petaled rosette pattern appears in a mosaic found in a bathroom situated west of the Mansion (in Area F-4, p. 32). The *163* rosette pattern is well known in Jewish art, and is especially dominant in the ornamentation of ossuaries from the same general period as these mosaics. As the central motif of these floors, it conveys a particular though simple charm.

A bathing complex preserved in one of the structures south of the ruined Tiferet-Israel Synagogue, beneath the Yeshivat Hakotel (Area F-3, p. 32), was especially impressive. This stepped ritual bath, measuring 2.6 x 4 meters, and which *147* is 3.75 meters deep, was preserved in its entirety including its barrel-vaulted ceiling. The bathroom itself had an ornamental floor with a "wave-crest" border motif. *160* The bottom of the tub, too, was paved in mosaics, as was the floor of the vestibule which had a square frame of "wave-crest" pattern enclosing a circle (mostly *161* destroyed) with a central multicolored rosette of numerous petals. In the corners, between the square frame and the circle, were depictions of two palmettes and a spindle bottle. The use of this latter vessel as an ornamental motif in a mosaic pavement is an entirely new feature, and one of considerable chronological significance: this type of bottle was widely used in Hellenistic times and went out of use early in the first century A.D.; thus, we can date the mosaic pavement here to the time of Herod the Great, at the latest.

Only three mosaic pavements have survived in living rooms, and of these, the rosette appears in two (both very fragmentary) as the central decorative motif (see mosaic in room 2 of the Mansion described on p. 50). The third floor (in Area F, p. 32, beneath the new Yeshivat Hakotel) is quite different: its frame contains triangu- *165* lar "crowsteps," a guilloche, and the "wave-crest" pattern in black and red. What is especially characteristic here is the central part of the panel, which is laid out like a carpet with intertwined meanders forming complex "swastika" patterns. This floor

150. Cleaning the mosaic pavement

...e mosaic pavement *in situ* within the remains of the building in Area F (p. 32)

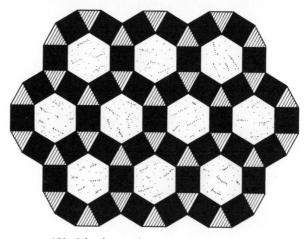

152. Colored stone tiles, reconstruction of pattern

is the largest and most pleasing of all the mosaics uncovered in the Jewish Quarter excavations. It apparently belonged to the central room of its house, of which little else has survived. In dating this pavement, we were aided by a bronze coin from the First Jewish Revolt ("Year Two"), which was stuck to the mosaic stones by the burnt material overlying the floor.

Another multicolored mosaic pavement was discovered in 1978, in Area O-2 (p. 32). This small pavement (partly destroyed) has a central complex rosette within a square frame. The corners between the roundel and the square frame bear angled *164* patterns with denticulated ends, resembling the Greek letter *gamma*. A similar arrangement of rosette with "gammas" appears on a contemporaneous ossuary from Jerusalem. These are the earliest examples of this design. The interesting history of the "gamma" motif is outlined by Professor Yadin in his book on Bar Kokhba, the leader of the Second Jewish Revolt against Rome, for it has also been found on the outer garments of the women who perished in the Judean Desert Caves. This motif seems to have become fashionable on certain textiles in the Roman-Byzantine period, and these robes became known as "gammadia." The "gamma" pattern can also be seen on women's garments in wall paintings in the synagogue at Dura-Europos, as well as on men's robes in the Christian mosaics at Ravenna, Rome, and other places.

Many of the decorative elements in these early mosaics found in Jerusalem have their counterparts at Masada, where they may appear in different combinations. Another feature common to the mosaics at these two sites is the total lack of animate motifs. The care generally taken by the Jews of this period in avoiding contravention of the biblical injunction against graven images led them to design their mosaic floors in their own fashion, though Hellenistic-Roman motifs and techniques were utilized to the full.

Another sort of flooring was made up of colored stone tiles rather than small cubes. Traces of one such floor were found in one of the rooms in Area M. The pavement itself has disappeared, but its bedding made of a greyish mortar still preserves the impression of the tiles making up the design. A few isolated tiles were still scattered about, and these, together with the impressions, enabled us to reconstruct the pattern of the "carpet" on this floor. It comprised interlocking circles made up of alternating black squares and red triangles. The Romans called this technique of flooring *opus sectile*, and examples have also been found in Herod's palaces at Jericho and Masada.

146

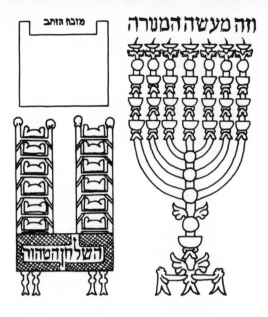

זה מעשה המנורה

מזבח הזהב

השלחן הטהור

153. Ritual objects from the Temple, according to an illuminated Bible of 1299. (Their order has been modified to match that of the *menorah* graffito in Jerusalem.)

8. The Menorah Graffito and Fresco Fragments

In archaeological excavations it occasionally occurs that a fill beneath a floor proves to be an important source for interesting finds, particularly when the earth of the fill was taken from the ruins of other, usually earlier buildings. We had such a case in our Area A, where a fill between two floors of the Herodian period contained several hundred fragments of colored plaster, originally from some other building. This earlier building had apparently been a splendid structure in the days of Herod the Great (37-4 B.C.), a dating revealed by the coins found in the fill, which were of Alexander Janneus and Herod himself.

154

Among these plaster fragments, two were especially interesting; though not painted, they bear the graffito of a seven-branched candelabrum — the *menorah*. At first we found only the lower fragment, with the thin lines of the triangular foot, the low stem, and the very beginning of the two last branches. Even this stirred great interest, for depictions of the *menorah* from the Second Temple times are few and far between. This was still in the first season of excavations, before we had found anything of particular significance and the public was anxious for "news." My team tried to convince me that this discovery must be publicized at once, but I decided to wait in the hope that more of the graffito would turn up, completing the *menorah* design.

One day three weeks later, between lectures at the Hebrew University, I received a phone call from Ami Mazar in the Jewish Quarter, telling me that a second fragment had been found. The design was not yet complete, for the three left-hand branches were still missing, though all the details of the *menorah* were now clear. It was 20 centimeters high, with a triangular base, low stem, and rather tall branches. All parts of the *menorah* bear an ornamentation of ovoids alternating with pairs of lines, a schematic astragal pattern. With the flames atop the branches, it was a most impressive depiction, despite the fact that parts were missing.

155 Depictions of *menorot* from Second Temple times are very rare. One on the coins of Mattathias Antigonus, last of the Hasmonean rulers (40-37 B.C.), although

147

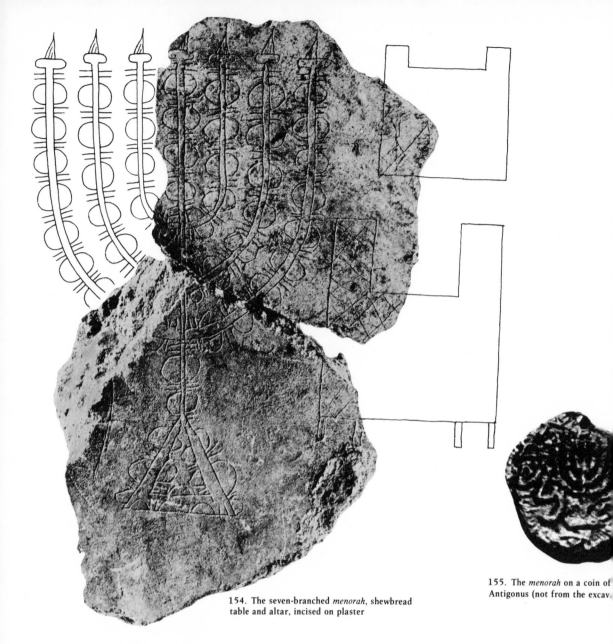

154. The seven-branched *menorah*, shewbread
table and altar, incised on plaster

155. The *menorah* on a coin of
Antigonus (not from the excav...

minute and very schematic, closely resembles our example in its general proportions and triangular base. Another, the splendid representation of the *menorah* on
the Arch of Titus in Rome, was carved but a short time after the destruction of the
Second Temple. Many scholars consider that the stepped base, with its ornamentation of animal forms, is not an original Jewish component, but the *menorah* itself
also closely resembles our depiction in general proportions and in the treatment of
the branches.

It therefore seems that the graffito from the Jewish Quarter is the earliest detailed
depiction of the *menorah* which had stood in the Temple. It was incised in the
plaster as a symbolic ornamentation at a time when the original *menorah* was still in
use in the Temple, only some 270 meters away. Although we may assume that
whoever scratched the design into the wall may have actually seen the *menorah* in
the Temple, this mere sketch is too brief and schematic in execution for us to assess

148

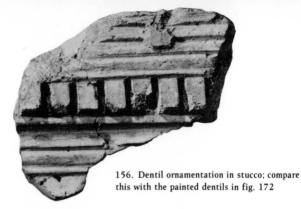

156. Dentil ornamentation in stucco; compare this with the painted dentils in fig. 172

its accuracy in reflecting the original, or how much artistic license was taken. In any event, the artist's product does confirm our general idea of the form of the *menorah* in the Temple and provides further food for thought on this subject.

To the right of the *menorah* depiction there are traces of two additional schematic designs which may very well represent other objects associated with the Temple ritual. Professor Bezalel Narkiss has suggested that the upper pattern represents the altar, and the one below the table for the shewbread. The parallels which he cites are *153* from an illuminated Bible manuscript of the 13th century, and one does not usually seek later analogues for earlier objects; but the resemblance is great and the possibility of a lengthy artistic tradition here should not be ignored.

FRAGMENTS OF PAINTED PLASTER The fragments of colored plaster also found in the fill are from wall paintings which had adorned the original building and are amazing in their variety of color and patterns. We have already discussed the wall paintings discovered in the Mansion, and similar fragments were found scattered in other houses in the Jewish Quarter as well. But even the mere fragments from within the fill reveal a wealth of information on wall paintings in this period. Dr. A. Poseq, of the Hebrew University, who initially examined the plaster fragments, distinguished two paintings techniques on them. The one method was fresco, described above; this type of painting is done on a very thin layer of fresh, wet plaster, to which powdered marble is sometimes added for whiteness. The pigment is actually absorbed into the smooth surface and cannot peel off; nor can it be erased merely through touch or washing. Such true fresco is thus a damp method. Most of our fragments were painted in this technique, the most common tints being red, yellow, green, brown and black.

Other fragments were painted in a second technique, dry or "**secco**," which is simpler in execution and thus less costly. Here, paint is applied directly to dry plaster. The surface is thus less even and the pigment has not been absorbed and tends to peel off, being readily effaced by touching. Sometimes the two techniques are combined; that is, various details in white, light blue, and purple are added onto a fresco, using the secco technique.

The most common layout of the wall paintings is a division of the dado, the lower portion of the wall, into panels of alternating or differing colors, Many such panels *168-171* were painted in imitation of marble, with various wavy lines and markings, often in bright and bold colors, imitating the striations of marble stone to give the illusion of the wall being overlaid with slabs of colored marble. Complete panels of this sort have survived at Masada, and similar examples have been found in Herod's constructions at Jericho, Herodium, Samaria, and Caesarea. As Professor Yadin has noted, these wall paintings are hardly in the best of *modern* taste, but they are certainly representative of the style fashionable throughout the Roman Empire two thousand years ago.

The innovation in the wall paintings in Jerusalem lies in their including floral and architectural motifs, which have not hitherto been known in Israel. The notable motifs here include bunches of apples and pomegranates among a tangle of leaves, *166, 167* apparently part of a garland motif, a well-known pattern in Hellenistic-Roman art. What is surprising here is the high quality of execution and the artistic standard of the painting. The plastic effect attained in the highlights on the fruit and leaves is fully in keeping with the impressionistic naturalism typical of Hellenistic paint- ing — the same source which nurtured the early wall paintings at Pompeii. Another such motif is the three-dimensional depiction of dentils, as well as the architectural *172* motifs depicted in the Mansion. As with the architectural remains found in the Jewish Quarter, the Jerusalem frescoes also far exceed the standards usually encountered in Israel.

Wall paintings were fashionable in Jerusalem in that period just as they were throughout the Hellenistic-Roman world. But the frescoes in Jerusalem, Masada, and Jericho differ in one respect from those abroad: in their almost complete lack of animate motifs. As we have noted, the Jews of that period — even the Hellenizers among them — strictly adhered to the biblical injunctions against graven images. But every rule has exceptions and, as if to prove this, fresco fragments bearing fine depictions of birds were found in the excavations directed by M. Broshi on Mount Zion. This instance is so exceptional in the local Jewish art of the days of the Second Temple that an equally exceptional explanation for it must be sought. While it is possible that the building in which these depictions were found was the home of a Jewish family which was less strict in observance, it might also be conjectured that it did not belong to a Jewish household. In the period of the Talmud, several centuries later, even synagogues and tombs were decorated with figurative depictions, but by then the attitude of the Rabbis had changed considerably.

9. Remnants of Monumental Architecture

One of the most fascinating chapters in our excavations (how often have I repeated that phrase already?) is related to the finding of architectural fragments of a type which has opened new vistas for our comprehension of the architecture of ancient Jerusalem. Generally, the structures which we have been uncovering in the Upper City were private dwellings, some of them quite magnificent but, except for one instance, they had none of the decided traits of monumental architecture, in particular that definitive feature, the column. But exceptionally, we did find parts of columns, indicating that there had been some monumental architecture in the Upper City. Indeed, the quality and dimensions of these finds were entirely unanticipated.

157. The Corinthian capital with carved lily scrolls at center

A CORINTHIAN CAPITAL   Our first discovery of importance was made near the Byzantine bathhouse in Area C (p. 32), under very clear stratigraphic and chronological conditions. The Herodian stratum here contained three successive floor levels. On the uppermost floor, dated by coins to the First Revolt (that is, to the destruction of Jerusalem in A.D. 70), we found a capital and two drums from a column. The column, some 40

200   centimeters in diameter, is of normal proportions. The capital is made of the hard local limestone known in Arabic as *mizzi ḥilu*. Though slightly damaged, it is generally in so fine a condition that it might have just left the workshop. It was as if time had not touched it at all. This is a capital of the Corinthian order, slightly differing from the usual pattern in that the acanthus leaves are smooth and stylized.

157   And by adding lily scrolls to one side of the body of the capital, the stonemason gave it a particular Jerusalemite flavor. Delicate and attractive, it is a masterpiece of ornamental stonecarving, similar in style to, but of finer and more sophisticated workmanship than the capitals found in the 1st century A.D. "Tombs of the Kings" (actually the Tomb of Queen Helene of Adiabene) in northern Jerusalem.

THE HUGE BASE   Beneath the floor on which the Corinthian capital was found there were two other floors, the lower one of which is dated by coins to the days of Herod the Great. Upon removing this floor, we found the huge base of a column made of the

151

local *meleke* limestone, turned upside-down. The foundations of the Herodian building had been built over it. The earth-fill here contained late Hellenistic pottery of the 2nd-1st centuries B.C., dating the huge base to late Hasmonean times. When the round surface of this stone, some 1.8 meters in diameter, first began to emerge from the soil, our curiosity was aroused. And when it turned out to be the base of a *199* column, there was general joking about so large a column being found in so small a country. To capture the moment for posterity, five of the expedition staff climbed atop it and were photographed, and there was still ample room left for the two staff members who were not present at the time. The surprising thing about this base,

158. Proud staff members standing on the column base

160. Bath complex in Area F-3 (p. 32); on right — entrance to the ritual bath; on left — vestibule to the bathroom

161. Mosaic pavement in the vestibule

The mosaic pavement in the bathroom of the palatial mansion

163. The mosaic-paved bathroom in Area F-4 (p. 32)

Mosaic pavement in Area O-2 (p. 32)

66. Fresco fragment depicting pomegranates and foliage

Mosaic pavement with meander fret-pattern in area F (p. 32)

167. Fresco fragments with apples and foliage

170

Fresco fragments, including some imitating marble

172. Three-dimensional dentils depicted on a fresco fragment

resco fragments: lotus blossom and dentils

174. Fresco fragment: "running wave" pattern

175. Ritual bath complex in Area T-4 (p. 32): ritual bath, "store pool" and bathtub; see fig. 145

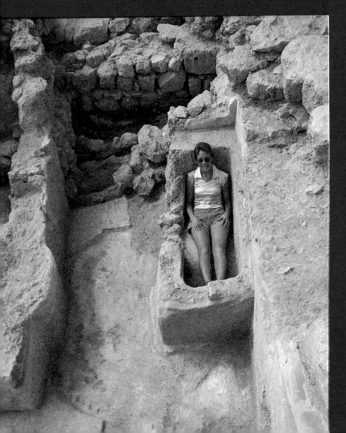

176. Within the bathroom

177. A volute of a large, finely executed Ionic capital

177   besides its size, was the perfect execution of the Attic molding, which calls to mind the fine workmanship of some volutes of Ionic capitals which we had found on an adjacent site. Those, too, are larger than commonly found in Israel, and are outstanding in the perfect form of their spirals. These discoveries led us to believe that we might be on the track of some monumental piece of Hellenistic architecture, the likes of which had not hitherto been known in Jerusalem or, for that matter, anywhere else in Israel.

THE IONIC CAPITALS   In the following year, while digging in the area between the Bethel and Rambam Synagogues, we made another significant discovery of monumental architecture. *178* First we found an Ionic capital whose magnificent size and form were stunning, for we had never seen anything quite like it in Israel. And then we came across another base, similar to the one mentioned above, and almost as large (1.56 meters in diameter), together with several drums from its column (1.06 meters in diameter). All these elements were found in a stratigraphically undefined layer of debris. Nearby, in Area Q (p. 32), we later found a second capital of the same type, broken into pieces and reused as building material in a Byzantine structure.

179-181   This group of architectural elements are of the Ionic order, and the columns would have stood about 10 meters high. The Ionic capitals are outstanding in the fine carving of their details and in the purity of the Hellenistic forms. Particularly noteworthy is the scale pattern with florets, ornamenting the center of the *pulvinus* (the "cushion" connecting the two volutes on the sides of the capital), as well as the row of "niches" around the stump of the column attached to the capital. These "niches" are actually the beginning of the fluting which usually runs down the entire length of the column shaft, but which here was intentionally left uncarved lower down, resulting in an unusual ornament at the top. This rare feature can be seen in two Hellenistic temples, at Sardis and at Didyma in Asia Minor. In Jerusalem itself the pattern is found in imitation on the pilasters carved on the *182* façade of "Zechariah's Tomb" in the Kidron Valley. Long ago, I put forth the suggestion that the architect of this tomb copied this rare architectural feature from some building standing in Jerusalem at that time. As chance would have it, we were now able to confirm this suggestion.

    These new finds have revealed a monumental and ornamental architecture different in chracter from that hitherto familiar to us in Jerusalem. Except for Herod's Temple, which in itself represents a blank chapter, the ornamental archi-

178. The Ionic capital and a column drum, as found

tecture of this period in Palestine is characterized by its provincial stamp. Here for the first time, we have found the combination of monumental proportions and excellent workmanship, representative of the highest international standard of that day. Something of the style of the cosmopolitan metropolis had finally made its appearance in Jerusalem.

Parallel examples for our capitals are found in the large centers of Hellenistic architecture, mainly in the Hellenistic temples in Asia Minor. We would not, of course, encounter such large columns, unusual even in royal palaces, in ordinary dwellings. Capitals of such dimensions have been found in Palestine in the Temple of Augustus at Samaria-Sebaste built by Herod the Great, but there the execution of the details on the capitals is inferior, and can certainly be defined as provincial.

This brings us face to face with the problem of identifying the building in the Upper City of Jerusalem which could have included such large columns, for there could not have been any temple there. This complex and fascinating problem has so far defied solution. Since our capitals and column drums were not found in any actual building context, any number of suggestions might be put forth as to the building's identity.

After the first large base was discovered beneath the Herodian floor, the late A TEMPLE? Professor Michael Avi-Yonah raised the possibility that it had been intended for a temple which Antiochus IV Epiphanes intended to build in "Antiochia" in Jerusalem and dedicate to the Olympian Zeus, but which he never managed to execute beyond certain preparatory work. This was in keeping with the accepted assumption that such columns are to be associated with temples. However, since we have come to doubt the very existence of "Antiochia," this suggestion, too, can hardly be considered reasonable.

The other columns were not found in clear stratigraphical contexts and their date is uncertain. It has been suggested that they were from Herod's Temple, and that several such columns were brought to the Upper City after the destruction of the Temple, either for some symbolic reason or for secondary use (for instance, in some structure as the Nea Church; see below). Although this theory cannot be proved, it is a tempting one which should not be rejected out of hand. Is there any evidence for

VIIII

179. The Ionic capital and column base. Note the number "VIIII" on the drum

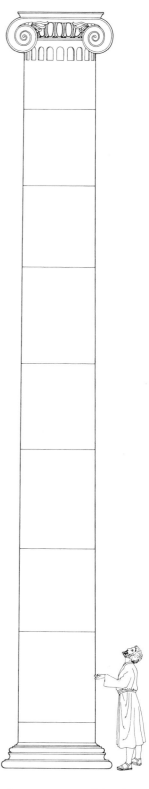

180. Reconstruction of the column

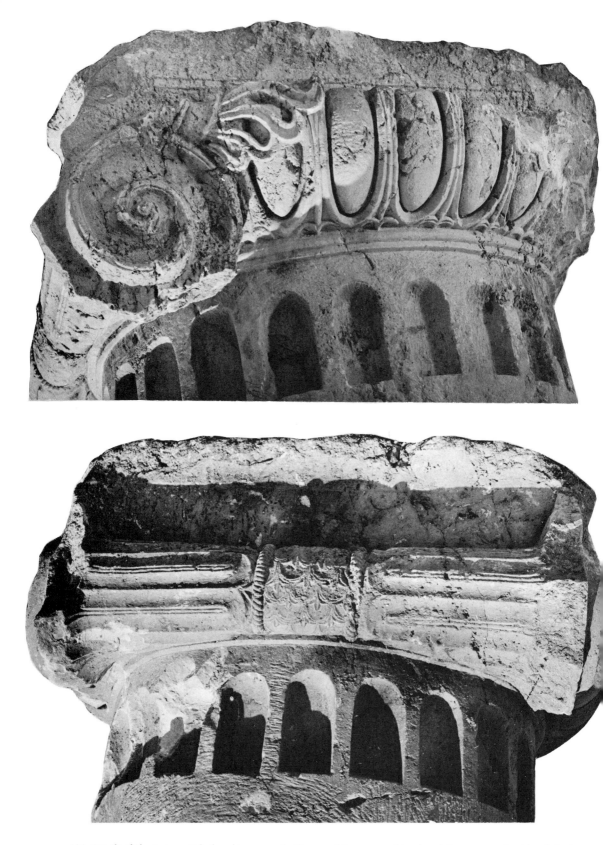

181. Details of the Ionic capital: the echinus, carved with egg-and-dart pattern (above), and the ornamented *pulvinus* (below)

179 dating these columns besides their Hellenistic-Roman style? On the column drum attached to the preserved capital, the Roman numeral VIIII is incised, indicating that it was the ninth drum of the column. This use of Roman numerals here is of considerable chronological significance for it is inconceivable that such numerals would have been used in Jerusalem prior to the days of Herod. This eliminates the possibility of ascribing the capital to the Hasmonean period, as we initially tended to do. Greek letters were generally used as numerals in Judea during this period; and a Greek letter *delta* is incised on the first large column base mentioned above, signifying that it was fourth in its row of columns. (Interestingly, the column drums at Masada are marked with Hebrew letters, indicating that the builders there were Jewish.) Stylistically, these capitals are surely no later than the days of Herod.

Josephus relates that the capitals in the royal portico of the Temple were of the Corinthian order, and that the columns were so thick that three persons could just join hands around them. In contrast, our columns are Ionian, and two persons are sufficient to reach around them. But the Temple Enclosure had other porticoes surrounding it as well, and they may have had such columns. It should also be noted that several fragments of an Ionic capital resembling ours (including the "niches") have been found in the excavations adjacent to the Temple Mount. In any event, this is an interesting and provoking problem: could the large columns have been taken from the Temple Mount? And, regardless of their origin, what building in the Upper City did they serve?

10. The Crafts of Jerusalem — Stone, Pottery, Glass

There are several crafts which were quite common in Jerusalem, and some of them were specific to the city, for which it was well known. Foremost among these were crafts utilizing the common raw material naturally available locally — stone. The art of working stone was well developed here, as is especially well evidenced by the tombs of the Second Temple period, scattered around the city. The architectural carvings and ornamentation found in the rock-hewn tombs, and on carved stone sarcophagi and ossuaries (which are found in such large quantities in Jerusalem), are witness to the local skill in this craft, which eventually evolved a typical Jewish style. This subject as such is outside our scope here, for no sepulchral discoveries

184. Ornamented stone from a monumental building

183 have been made in the Upper City. But in order to demonstrate the high standard attained by the Jerusalem artisans in stonecarving, we illustrate here one of the finest of the sarcophagi from the necropolis of the city, discovered on the campus of the Hebrew University on Mount Scopus.

Excavations in Jerusalem over the last decade have immeasurably increased our knowledge of the city's stonework in the period of the Second Temple. In the realm of artistic stonecarving, the ornamented stones with geometric and floral patterns discovered near the Southern Wall of the Temple Mount fully display the ornamental richness and variety which typified the Royal Portico in the Temple Enclosure. *184* One stone ornamented in a similar style was found in our excavations, and it, too, was apparently from a monumental building somewhere in the Upper City. The stone capitals described above attest to the quality of architectural carving in Jerusalem as well.

Our excavations have shown that other types of stonework were done in the city, too, including the production of such practical wares as tables and household vessels. In other words, Jerusalem had a flourishing and variegated stone industry, employing many artisans and craftsmen. The major features of this production have already been touched upon briefly in the previous sections of this chapter. However, since these were typically Jerusalemite crafts—the extent and nature of which we are only now learning—they deserve a more detailed discussion. Two other crafts will also be treated—pottery and glassware—both of which display features specific to Jerusalem.

THE STONE TABLES Until we discovered the first stone tables in our excavations, the furniture of the period of the Second Temple in Israel had been an absolutely unknown entity insofar as the archaeologist was concerned. Even now this is the only type of furniture actually found in this country and period. The ordinary tables in the Jerusalemite home were, of course, made of wood; but they have long ago disintegrated under local climatic conditions. We now know that there were also stone tables, decorative in nature and quite expensive, which had specific functions within the house.

We have already described our discovery of the first stone table in the Burnt House, and of our general wonder concerning it. Later in our excavations we found more of these tables, and it turned out that they were to be found in many houses in the Upper City. Moreover, fragments of such tables had been discovered in other excavations in Jerusalem — some of them long ago — but they were not recognized as such, and fragments of the small columns which form the legs of these tables had long puzzled excavators here.

Two types of stone tables were found in our excavations, one rectangular and high, and the other round and low. The rectangular tables have a single central leg and a rectangular top. A projection on the under side of the top slab fitted into a corresponding depression in the top of the leg, joining the two together. The leg is fashioned in the form of a column, with all the usual elements including base, shaft, and capital. These tables were of the same height as modern tables, 70 to 80 centimeters, and the tops measure about 45x85 centimeters. They are not entirely uniform in all details: some vary in the design of the central leg, and others in the ornamentation of the top. One unusually elegant table has a thin top and a foot in the form of a tall, well-designed column; it is made of a hard, polished stone which was shattered into dozens of fragments and splinters by the fire in the house where it had come to light. Our search for its pieces continued over two seasons, during which we carefully sifted all the earth removed from rooms of the house. Unfortunately, a new construction stood on the edge of our site, overlying part of the ancient building, and we could not continue our search in that direction. Another table shown here bears more typical proportions — a thick top and stubby central leg. The fore-edge of the top bears a stylized leaf pattern, also found on the Jewish ossuaries from Jerusalem; its leg has a capital in Doric style. The top and leg of the table as illustrated were found in different buildings and did not originally comprise a single table. They do, however, go together quite admirably, as can be seen in the photograph.

The edges of these tables are generally ornamented on three sides with geometrical and floral patterns, while the fourth side is most often left plain. This would suggest that they were originally stood up against the wall. On the edge of one fragment there is an unusual motif — two crossed cornucopias with a pomegranate between them. Until recently, this motif was known only from Hasmonean coins, and this is the first instance that the Hasmonean emblem was found on an object other than a coin. An unusual motif on another tabletop, a fish, is particularly noteworthy because it is the only animal figure to have been found in ornamental use.

The smaller round tables are about 50 centimeters in diameter. Their tops are usually of soft limestone, though some fragments are of a hard, reddish Jerusalem stone, a blackish bituminous stone, or imported black granite. On the bottom of these smaller tabletops are three depressions, where they had been affixed to wooden legs. Nothing survives of the legs, but on the basis of Hellenistic and Roman paintings and reliefs, we can suggest that they were in the form of animal

RECTANGULAR TABLES

185 (1)

230

94

186

185 (4)

ROUND TABLES

188

1) Stylized wreath frieze. The projection on the bottom was intended to fit into a depression in the top of the table leg

2) Meander fret-pattern with flanking rosettes — the most common motifs on the tabletops

3) Laurel sprig (?)

4) A fish, the only faunal motif on the tabletops

186. Tabletop fragment with carved pair of cornucopiae and a pomegranate between

187. Hasmonean coin with pair of cornucopiae and a pomegranate between (Hebrew University Collection)

legs, sometimes with bronze fittings at the bottom. A round table of this sort appears in a wall painting in a Hellenistic tomb at Marisa, some 35 kilometers southwest of Jerusalem, as well as on several of Herod's coins.

The group of tables from the Jewish Quarter thus reveals a hitherto unknown aspect of home furnishing in ancient Jerusalem. Hellenistic and Roman paintings

189. Three-legged table in wall painting, in a Hel tomb at Marissa (southern Judea)

188. Round tabletop (wooden legs restored)

190. Animal's paw, a bronze fitting from a wooden table leg

o groups of reclining diners. Between them is a serving table with a single, central leg; flanking are round, three-legged tables (Roman relief from Italy)

rvants at a single-legged serving table; on and beneath the table, wine vessels relief from Trier in Germany)

193. Roman depiction of a serving table with vessels on and beneath it (after Daremberg-Saglio)

and reliefs depicting rectangular tables with a single leg show that they were used as serving tables to hold drinking vessels; the round variety of table with three legs is shown being used for meals, surrounded by guests reclining on couches. The single-leg tables are mentioned in Talmudic literature (Tosefta, Kelim, Baba Bathra 3, 4), as are those with three legs (Mishnah, Kelim 22, 2).

Stone tables of these types were widespread throughout the Roman Empire, although they originated in the Hellenistic East. The Roman historian Livy, who lived in Herod's day, mentions "tables with one leg" among the booty brought from Asia Minor in the 2nd century B.C., when they were apparently still considered a novelty in Rome. The Roman scholar Varro (1st century B.C.) describes "a stone table for vessels, square and elongated, on a single small column...: many placed it in the house alongside the central pool. On and near it, when I was a lad, they would put bronze vessels." A graphic representation of such a group is also found on a *193* Roman pottery oil lamp. Even today, the visitor to Pompeii will find such decorative tables in the dining rooms and patios of the luxurious villas there. In Jerusalem, too, these attractive stone tables added beauty and culture to the home. The basic technique of the Jerusalem stonecarvers who made these tables, as well as the style of their ornamental motifs, was deeply rooted in the local tradition of stoneworking and, although their work was patterned after foreign models, it had a decided, local flavor.

An ornamented fragment of a stone tabletop was recently purchased from an antiquities dealer in Jerusalem by Dr. L.Y. Rahmani on behalf of the Israel Department of Antiquities and Museums. The dealer claimed that it had been found at Turmus-Aya near Samaria. Dr. Rahmani showed this fragment to me prior to its purchase by his Department, and asked if I thought that it might have been stolen from our excavations, for we had just found the first such tables in the Burnt House. Moreover, the stone offered for sale bore the typical traces of soot, as did ours. I was in an embarrassing position, for we had carried out the excavation of the burnt rooms under strict supervision, employing only staff members and volunteers, and the site was guarded after working hours and at night by a special guard. Since a heavy fragment of a stone table was no mean item to put in your pocket and smuggle away, I told Rahmani that I didn't think it was ours. I began having second thoughts, however, for one of the day workmen, in cahoots with the night watchman (who also worked for us during the day), could explain the manner in which such a bulky item could be removed. It might have been placed to one side during the day and been removed at night, to be sold to a waiting antiquities dealer. Several other factors also seemed unexplainable; for instance that, at the very time when we were uncovering the first such rare objects in the Jewish Quarter, a similar fragment of a Jerusalem table should come to light at a site far away in Samaria, where no excavations were currently known to be in progress; and that this fragment, too, bore traces of fire. Thus, there may after all have been good reason to think that this fragment was indeed taken from the Burnt House in the Jewish Quarter.

According to Rahmani's published description, various motifs are incised on the edge of the tabletop: on the long side is a ship, while on the shorter side there is a table with a single leg, bearing various vessels and flanked by two large jars with *194* high bases. This latter depiction appears to be a precise graphic counterpart of Varro's description, noted above, and is also in surprising agreement with the depiction on the Roman oil lamp, also mentioned above. In ornamenting this

194. Ornamented edge of stone tabletop purchased in Jerusalem. At center, a depiction of a serving table with bronze vessels, and two large jars beneath

195. Table with vessels discovered in the Jewish Quarter excavations, arranged as in fig. 194

tabletop, the Jerusalem artisan had simply chosen the motif of the table itself, with all the vessels usually associated with it; in other words, a page straight out of the book of the everyday life of his period. On the basis of these depictions, both literary and pictorial, we have been able to restore such a grouping, using finds from our excavations: one of our tables with four bronze vessels from the Mansion and two stone jars — essentially an authentic view of the corner of a house in Jerusalem in the Herodian period.

The discovery of stone vessels became a routine matter in our work, for whenever we approached a stratum of the Second Temple period, and a building which was burnt during the destruction of the city in A.D. 70 began revealing itself, they invariably made their appearance as well. Thus, even in the absence of other specific chronological clues, we were often able to date a structure as Herodian solely on the basis of the presence of even a single stone vessel — or even mere fragments. Generally, these vessels are accompanied by traces of fire, obviously from the destruction of A.D. 70.

Our initial discovery of stone vessels, in the Burnt House, came not as a surprise, for their existence in Jerusalem had long been known from previous excavations. What did surprise us was their great number and variety. Previously regarded as isolated luxury items, our discovery of them in almost every house soon led us to realize that their use was much more widespread. Some of them served in the same functions as their pottery counterparts, while others were of special shapes and special uses. In general, the stone vessels are a rich and variegated addition to the types of utensils known to have been in use in the Jerusalem household in antiquity.

The production of stone wares in Jerusalem reached a pinnacle in both technical ability and design. Stone vessels were produced in other lands, as well; for example numerous stone vessels have been found in the Hellenistic city of Delos in Asia Minor, some of them quite similar to ours. The Jerusalem artisans undoubtedly learned much from others, but the peculiar and specific need for stone wares in the city (see below) led them to outstanding achievements, such as the manufacture of very large, well-designed jars. The products of Jerusalem were undoubtedly famous, and were apparently unrivaled within Palestine. The one large stone jar found at Ain Feshkha, and the several stone vessels found at Masada and other sites, were surely made in Jerusalem.

The stone vessels are generally made of a soft, readily carved limestone, found in abundance in the vicinity of Jerusalem. Among the smaller vessels found in our excavations, a few are made of other types of stone such as alabaster or marble. On the basis of form and finish, it is possible to distinguish between vessels made on a lathe and those carved by hand. In either case, the craftsmen would use chisels to give the vessels their general form, and then usually drills to extract the material from the interior.

The lathe-turned vessels have open and cylindrical shapes, as is dictated by that technique of manufacture; among them are the very impressive large jars of goblet form, standing on a high foot. The rim has a molded profile, as does the high base; and the surface is well smoothed and often ornamented with horizontal bands or *125* vertical ribbing. Where ledge handles are present, the strips between the two handles are rougher, lending them an ornamental effect. It is possible that these jars are to be identified with the stone "jar" (*kallal*) mentioned in the Mishnah (Parah 3, 3), a large stone or pottery vessel which was used for holding the ashes of the Sin Offering. Long ago, the late J. Brand described the *kallal* of the Mishnah as a goblet-shaped vessel with a broad rim, straight sides, curved bottom, and a high base — a description which fits our vessels perfectly.

The blocks of stone from which these jars were fashioned must have weighed several times as much as the finished products, which were 65-80 centimeters tall. This makes it all the more surprising that the ancient lathes could support such a mass, and we can only ponder how they were powered. Most of the lathe-turned vessels, however, are much smaller: plates, bowls, and handleless cups, which are also rather attractive, some of the forms clearly imitating pottery vessels. These smaller vessels were readily made on a bow-powered lathe, somewhat resembling a primitive drill. Small stone vessels are still produced in Bethlehem for decorative purposes, although larger shapes are no longer manufactured.

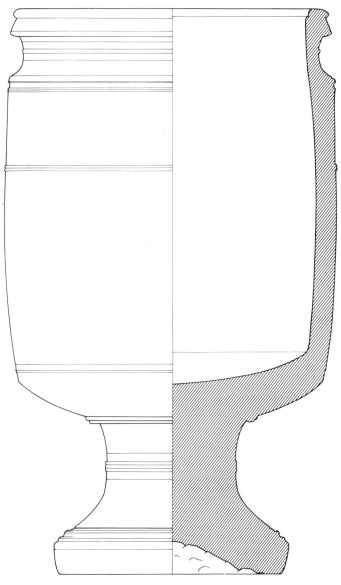

196. A stone jar of goblet form

ne bowls, lathe-turned

198. Stone "coffee cup"

Hand-carving was employed for special forms of stone vessels, where a lathe **HANDWORK** could not be used—as in the case of vessels with a vertical handle (which would interfere with the turning of the lathe) or of vessels which were not round. Of the types with handles inconvenient for turning, we may note two examples: a cup of fine form, resembling a modern coffee cup, has a delicate handle apparently imitating some pottery form, of foreign origin. Ordinary cups of the period are in the form of a deep bowl; indeed bowls were generally used for drinking in antiquity. Another sort of stoneware cup was cylindrical with a pierced, vertical handle; its surface was not smoothed but rather pared vertically with a knife or an adze. These latter cups often have a short spout at the rim, not opposite the handle but at a right angle to it. These two types of cup were the most common stone vessel found, and we meet them often outside Jerusalem as well. The fact that they were made in various sizes, from large (15 centimeters high) to small (5 centimeters high) has led archaeologists to consider them to be "measuring cups" for liquids and dry *209 (1)* measures, and one opinion holds that their standard corresponds with that mentioned in the Mishnah, but the matter requires further investigation.

Handwork is, of course, also necessary on vessels which are not round, as is especially obvious on deep, square bowls—a shape not found in pottery but one apparently considered very convenient for kitchen use. Another noteworthy vessel has multiple compartments, with two, three, or four divisions; one such vessel is reminiscent of a salt and pepper shaker, while another resembles an army "mess *208* tin," or a serving dish for a selection of relishes. Round or elongated serving trays with ornamental handles have also been found. Such trays are depicted in Roman *204, 205* mosaics loaded with food. In one depiction, a tray of our type bears a large fish. Another handcarved vessel worthy of note is a stone oil lamp, the only example known to us. Additional stone objects were found, the original function of which cannot even be guessed.

All in all, we were astonished by the rich and attractive variety of the stone vessels. Neither the local abundance of their raw materials nor the attractiveness of their shapes would alone serve to explain this phenomenon. And not only is their manufacture much more costly than that of pottery, but they are more restricted and less convenient in use, because of their weight and the softness of their material. Why, then, did they appear so suddenly and in such quantities in the Jerusalem household?

199. Discovery of the huge column base

The first glimpse

Transferring the base to a safe location

The base and our staff

The base and R. Reich

Jerusalem painted bowls

0. The Corinthian capital as displayed at the Israel Museum

202. An abundance of finds in a pool

203. Washing potsherds

204. Restored stone tray

206. Fragment of a marble tray with ornamental handle

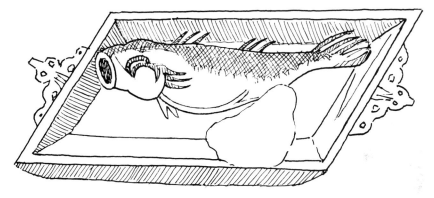

205. Fish served on a tray (from a Roman mosaic at Antioch)

207. Rectangular stone bowl

208. Stone vessel with three divisions

1) Measuring cup

2) Goblet

209. Various stone vessels

3) Square vessel with "windows," of unknown use

4) Mortar and finger-shaped pestle

5) Alabastron-shaped green serpentine vessel, unusually large (36 cm tall); found in a Herodian context but of earlier date (5th-4th centuries B.C.), and apparently kept in the house as a precious "antique"

210. The discovery of stone vessels in Area F-4 (p. 32)

STONE UNSUSCEPTIBLE
TO UNCLEANNESS

The answer to this lies in the realm of *halakhah*, in the Jewish laws of ritual purity. The Mishnah includes stone vessels among those objects which are not susceptible to uncleanness (Kelim 10, 1; Parah 3, 2), but no details are given there. Stone was simply not susceptible to ritual contamination. When a pottery vessel, however, became ritually unclean through contact with an unclean substance or object, it had to be broken and withdrawn from use. In contrast, a stone vessel would preserve its purity and thus its usability, even if it had come into contact with uncleanness. Curiously, one of the clearest literary witnesses to the Jewish ritual of purity of stone vessels is preserved in the New Testament, in the episode of the wedding at Cana in Galilee, during which Jesus performed the miracle of changing water into wine. The text reads: "Now six stone jars were standing there, for the Jewish rites of purification, each holding two or three gallons" (John 2:6). These were most probably jars of the very type we have been discussing.

With the destruction of Jerusalem in A.D. 70, the flourishing production of stone vessels and tables came to an end, and the tradition of their manufacture was not revived in subsequent generations. Our excavations in Jerusalem have lifted the veil of centuries from these fine objects, revealing them in a rich variety.

POTTERY

The most common sort of article in any household in antiquity was, of course, its pottery. The corpus of pottery in Palestine during the Herodian period is not especially rich, but in the light of the recent excavations in Jerusalem, it turns out to have been more variegated than previously believed. The most common vessels were those most used in the house: cooking pots and storage jars. Most of these vessels were not found in the kitchens and storerooms which, at least in our excavations, were mostly looted and destroyed; rather, they came to light in the cisterns and pools of the houses, which had been turned into refuse dumps. We have already told the story of the cooking pots in the Mansion, which illustrates this vividly.

The cooking pots are almost invariably blackened with soot — evidence of their daily use. We would expect, in keeping with the large number of cooking pots in which food was prepared, that there would be a correspondingly large number of bowls or plates for serving. But the pottery of this period includes few locally made bowls or plates, types which are generally found in large quantities in other periods. In this particular period, only small, thin bowls are found here, suitable only for small portions. This raises an interesting gastronomical question, for from what we know from other sources of that period, people generally enjoyed not inexcessive meals.

211. A group of pottery from Area E (p. 32); late 1st century B.C.

212. A group of storage jars from the 1st century A.D.

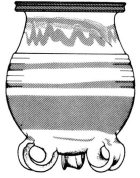

213. A deep bowl with three ring-feet

214. A painted krater with three ring-feet

212　　Most of the storage jars used for keeping water, wine, or oil have elongated bodies; fewer of the more globular, sack-shaped form were found in our excavations. Another basic vessel-type, in this as in all periods, is the jug in its various forms. Such smaller types of pottery were quite common in the Jewish Quarter: *211* juglets and small bottles for minor quantities of oil or perfume. Equally common *68* were the thin-walled asymmetrical flasks discussed above. Fragments of these flasks have been found in large quantities among finds from the 1st century A.D.

PAINTED BOWLS　　In addition to these common vessels, we have found several types of pottery which augment the repertoire of the period. Foremost are the painted bowls sometimes known as "Pseudo-Nabatean"; curiously, this type of bowl was entirely unknown during the first hundred years of excavations in Jerusalem, and only since 1968, with the commencement of excavations near the Temple Mount, have these painted bowls made their appearance. They have since become a regular feature in the excavations in the Upper City as well, among the finds of the 1st century A.D. These bowls are very fragile, and they are seldom found intact; but even so we have been able to mend and restore an impressive group.

201　　These thin-walled bowls, which measure about 12-15 centimeters in diameter, are of very fine quality, and are painted on the inside in stylized floral patterns in red and, sometimes, in brown or black. Two styles of painting are evident. The one employs symmetrical compositions taking up the entire area of the bowl; the motifs are usually arranged radially, but sometimes they are in concentric circles, as on one example found in the Mansion. In the second, more carefree style, the painter often sufficed with a few quick strokes of the brush, much in the manner of abstract artists today.

When these painted bowls were first found, they were called "Pseudo-Nabatean," for they superficially resemble the Nabatean bowls, famous for their thinness and painted motifs. But the bowls from Jerusalem are different in the form of their motifs, in their composition and even in the quality of the ware itself. They seem to be a sort of Jewish alternative to the fine Nabatean bowls, which simply did not reach the Jerusalem market in significant quantities. Since these locally produced bowls have been found so far only in Jerusalem, it would be most appropriate to recognize them as a class in themselves, and to denote them "Painted Jerusalem Bowls."

201, 214　　Among the local pottery of this period there is one painted vessel which is outstanding—the attractive krater standing on three looped feet and ornamented around with red bands. This peculiar type of ring-feet is found also on unpainted hemispherical bowls, and both type of vessel are quite rare within the pottery repertoire of Palestine. Similar in concept is a hemispherical bowl also having three *231* feet, but here in the form of knucklebones. This type of bowl and others like it are

185

216. Lumps of glass ➡
217. Fragments of molded bo
218. Glass rods and tubes ➡

noteworthy for their hard ware and metallic glaze. Scholarly opinion is divided as to the origin of this pottery, some scholars ascribing it to the Nabateans while others — preferably, it would seem — regard it as an import from abroad.

Jerusalem is famous for many things, but who would have thought that it also held an important place in the technological history of ancient glass? This came to light through one of our most unusual discoveries — the refuse from a glass factory, found in the Jewish Quarter, in our Area J (p. 32).   REFUSE FROM A GLASS FACTORY

Now the reader might ask what value scrap glass could have for us, preferring complete vessels to broken discards. But scientific research is not a treasure hunt for finished products in perfect condition, and the archaeologist prefers any material which can provide an insight into methods of manufacture and their development. These, of course, could best be learnt from the recovery of a complete workshop, with all its various installations, tools, and products in various stages of manufacture, but no such glass factory has ever been found, and the next best thing is the waste materials which derive from one. But even such refuse is infrequently found, and its rare instance of discovery in our excavations can thus be considered a blessing in disguise. And if the composition of such material is optimal, that is, if it contains raw materials, spoiled pieces, unfinished pieces and the like, a wealth of information can be gleaned from it on methods and techniques of production.

We should remind the reader here of the paved street covering the Herodian Residence, dating from the 1st century B.C. In providing a proper foundation for the roadway there, the builders filled in all the pools and baths with earth and rubbish, brought from nearby locations. Of particular interest here is one of the ritual baths (Area J), the westernmost of the group, for the earth filling contained a   *149*
pile of refuse from a glass factory which had operated somewhere in the vicinity. This waste material included a rich variety of glass fragments, some of them distorted by heat, unfinished products, hunks of raw glass, and lumps of slag.

Among the vessel fragments, we could distinguish two major types of glass products, each based on a different mode of manufacture. The one type was made by forming vessels in molds, while the other type was made by blowing the hot glass into the desired shape through a tube. Chronologically, the molding process is the earlier of the two. We found hundreds of fragments of thick glass bowls, hemispherical or conical in shape, all of the molded type. The glass itself is greenish, but the surface is now generally covered with a layer of thick, black patina. These bowls, attractive in their simplicity, were very common in the Late Hellenistic period, and similar examples have been found in many places in Palestine. Alongside these fragments were a small number of fragments from another type of bowl, also molded; they are of thinner material, and are either rounded or carinated, with rims that are modeled and bodies that are ribbed — a very common mode of decoration in the Hellenistic period.   MODES OF PRODUCTION   *217, 220*

The fragments of the second type are of closed vessels, such as small bottles of the "perfume bottle" type. This is the simplest shape to obtain in the glass blowing technique, and it was probably the first shape ever produced by this process.   *221*

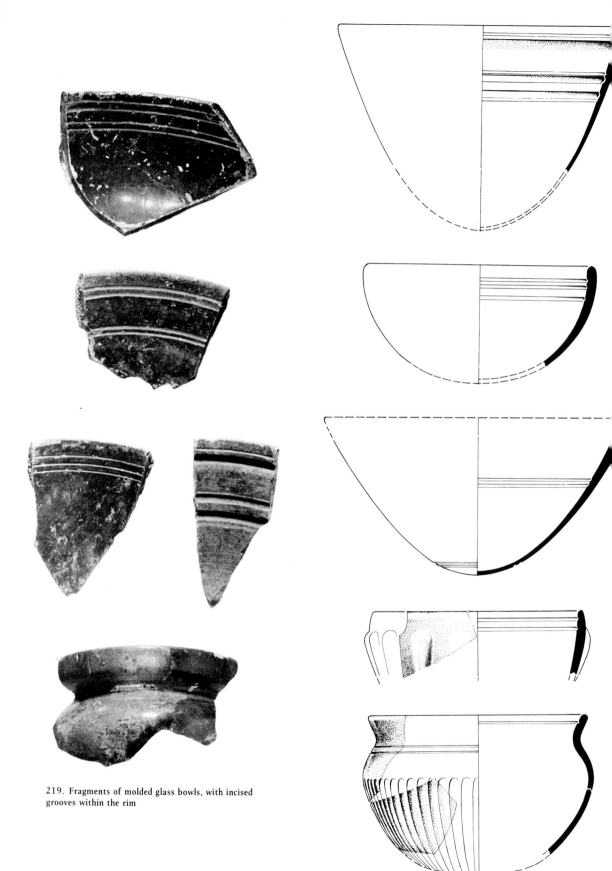

219. Fragments of molded glass bowls, with incised grooves within the rim

220. Drawings of restored molded bowls

221. Glass bottles made by glassblowing; that on the left was blown from a two-colored tube

This mixed find of molded and blown glass is especially interesting, for we see here a single factory using two different techniques side-by-side. Despite the numerous excavations in Israel and abroad on sites rich in glass finds, never before has such clear-cut evidence for the initial stage of glass blowing come to light. This process revolutionized the production of glass vessels and facilitated their "mass production," relatively speaking. Its invention could be compared to that of the potter's wheel in ceramic production. In our glass finds we can see at least a partial explanation for the actual beginning of glass blowing. Scholars have long believed that, since the initial invention of glass blowing, vessels have been blown from a gob of hot, plastic glass stuck on the end of a metal tube or pipe, as is still the practice today. But the finds from Jerusalem now indicate that the earliest glass blowing was done with glass tubes. These are perhaps the very first stages of experimentation at glass blowing, followed later by the use of the blow-pipe.

222

Our pile of glass refuse included many thin glass tubes, some of them with the beginning of a swelling at one end, though the continuation was broken off. There were also bulbs of glass the size of a bird's egg, which had clearly been blown from a glass tube. In other words, both the pipes and the bulbs of glass comprised a single element, the initial phase of blowing a glass vessel. For one reason or another, the blowing ceased on these pieces, and the vessels were never completed; however, fragments of completed blown bottles were found. It is not quite clear yet how blowing with a glass pipe was accomplished, in the heat of an open hearth, and the matter requires further specialized study.

Dr. Gladys Weinberg and Professor Dan Barag, well-known experts on ancient glass, examined the glass refuse soon after its discovery, and they tell me that no evidence of this sort has been found at any other site in the world, and that this find of the earliest phase of glass blowing is of revolutionary significance for technological research. In their opinion, Jerusalem is the first site at which the meeting of the two techniques, glass molding and glass blowing, has been encountered. This discovery, then, represents a transitional phase in which the production of glass continued in the older molding technique alongside the newly introduced technique of glass blowing.

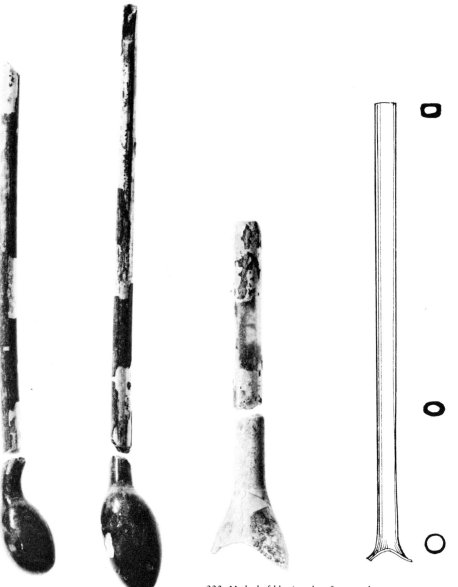

222. Method of blowing glass from a tube

When did this occur? It has generally been assumed that glass blowing was introduced toward the beginning of the Roman period, that is, around the middle of the 1st century B.C. In Israel, the earliest blown glass vessels are found in Herodian contexts of the late 1st century B.C. A single blown glass bottle was found in 1961 in a burial of late Hasmonean times in Naḥal David in the Judean Desert—by an expedition under my direction. At that time it was considered to be surprising, for it was "too early" for blown glass. In Professor Saul Weinberg's excavations at the Hellenistic site of Tel Anafa in Upper Galilee, in 1969, many molded glass vessels were found in the Hellenistic stratum, but not even one fragment among them was of blown glass. Since Tel Anafa was abandoned in 75 B.C., and was not resettled for an extensive period, the glass artisans represented there did not yet know about the technique of glass blowing early in the 1st century B.C.

The Tel Anafa discoveries in 1969 led to the conclusion that the transition period of the two techniques should be sought somewhere between the abandonment of Tel Anafa in 75 B.C. and the beginning of Herod's reign in 37 B.C. And then, in 1971, our excavations provided the key for a more precise dating when the glass refuse was found in a clearly stratified context together with Late Hellenistic pottery and about a hundred coins of Alexander Janneus. On this basis, we could date the glass finds to the first half of the 1st century B.C. To be on the safe side, since we know that the coins of Alexander Janneus had a lengthy "lifetime," and taking into account the evidence from Tel Anafa, our entire glass find can certainly be ascribed to around the middle of the 1st century B.C.

TWISTED GLASS RODS Another glass product demonstrating the process of manufacture are thin, twisted rods, most of them found broken but originally about 15 centimeters long with one end rounded and the other pointed. Generally known as "kohl sticks," and probably used for cosmetics, they are rarely found in excavations but can be seen in some museums. Here we suddenly uncovered an abundance of them, as well as of the smooth rods which were the raw material employed in their manufacture. The many hundreds of these smooth rods were certainly used for other purposes as
223 well. We can follow the process of their manufacture into twisted sticks, from smooth rods, through the phase of twisting, and to their actual finishing. The marks of the pincers used to hold the hot, plastic rods are still clearly visible. Other glass objects discovered among the refuse included spinning whorls, conical gaming pieces, discs, inlay plaques, and other less definable items.

USALEM ON THE MAP OF Despite the abundance of ancient glass found in various lands, there are few
SS PRODUCTION examples which are truly indicative of their mode of manufacture. It is odd that we should find such significant remains in this sphere specifically in Jerusalem, for scholars have generally assumed that the centers of glass production were located close to sites rich in silica sand, the principal raw material of glass. However, the production of glass vessels, like that of pottery or metal wares, was not restricted to a single zone. Chunks of raw glass could readily be transported from place to place, and glass artisans in various locales, however remote, could use them in whatever manner they desired.

The significance of our unanticipated discoveries in the excavations in the Jewish Quarter, both insofar as the site and the potential scientific data concealed within it, are still to be evaluated fully. After deeper research into this material, the glass experts no doubt will be able to clear up many of the longstanding problems relating to the earliest history of blown glass. One of these questions concerns the part of the Jews in the production of glass in antiquity, for it is commonly held that their role was a major one. Though this has not been proved conclusively, our finds from Jerusalem may well be a valuable contribution to that discussion, since they were most probably manufactured by Jews.

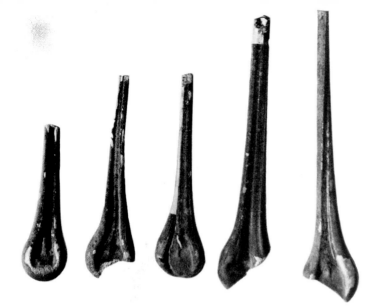

1) Rods of glass with traces of pincers which held them while hot

223. Phases of manufacture of twisted cosmetic rods

3) Finish

2) Rods twisted while held with pincers

224. A bone die

11. Odds and Ends—"Theater Tokens," Coins, and Inscriptions

Nothing among the small finds in our excavations aroused so much curiosity as two bone discs of a type long known in professional literature as Roman "theater tokens." Our staff's amused reaction to this discovery was: "Now that we have the tickets, all we have to do is find the theater!" Needless to say, we have not found the theater, but I think that we have also lost the tickets: after studying the matter, it appears that the identification of these discs as theater tokens is not only controversial but highly doubtful.

"THEATER TOKENS"   The discs, found in a Herodian building in Area M, are very handsome examples of fine ivory or bone carving. One of them, three centimeters in diameter, bears the relief of a monumental gate in the form of an Egyptian pylon on one side, and is incised on the other side with the inscription *PTERA*, "wings (of a building)," in Greek, and the number 14 in both Greek and Roman numerals. The second disc, 2.6 centimeters in diameter, bears a human hand with the fingers held in a particular pose, carved in relief; it, too, has the number 14 on the back, but only in Roman numerals.

239   These are the first such bone tesserae found in Israel, but the type was known throughout the Roman world and has been discovered at such sites as Rome itself, Pompeii, Alexandria, etc. They were a popular collector's item in the 19th century, and can be seen today in many museums. Their ornamentation generally includes typical classical motifs from the realms of mythology, literature, philosophy, theater and athletics, and depictions of buildings in Alexandria. There are also various animate and inanimate motifs such as the hand found on one of our discs. The numbers incised on the discs range from 1 to 15, and the inscriptions generally give the name of the figure or building which appears on the other side. The word *PTERA*, "wings," on our first disc may be interpreted as a gate with flanking wings or towers. The hand on the second disc shows the fingers in the process of counting, with the thumb holding the bent index finger and only the little finger upright. Such discs have been found bearing various numbers, and the position of the fingers varies accordingly. This would point to the existence of a method of counting with the fingers; indeed, certain medieval manuscripts teach a system whereby calculations even in the thousands can be reckoned on the fingers.

Since most of the ornamental patterns on the discs could be related in one way or another to the theater, they have sometimes been interpreted as entrance tokens. Accordingly, the inscriptions were thought to denote the section of the theater, and the number, the row of seats. Such an expensive "ticket" surely would not have been a one-time "throwaway," and was thought to have been a sort of "subscription ticket." It was argued that this was the reason that they had not been found in actual theaters. (This interpretation is to be found even in such an authoritative work as M.M. Bieber's *The History of the Greek and Roman Theater*, published in 1961.)

226. Impression on a blob of clay (not a *bulla*), depicting motifs similar to those found on coins (goblet, pomegranates)

Already in 1903, however, fifteen bone tesserae of this same type were discovered in a tomb from the 1st-2nd centuries A.D. in Kerch in the Crimea; there, each one bore a number from 1 to 15, thus forming a set. M. Rostovtzeff, the famous historian of the Classical world, interpreted this collection as a complete set of gaming-pieces, and regarded them as of Alexandrian origin. This reasonable identification has generally been accepted by scholars, despite the fact that the game itself is entirely unknown. In a more recent study, E. Alföldi has sought the significance of these tesserae not only in their artistic aspect but in their being a further contribution of Alexandria to the formation of Imperial Roman culture. In our context, the fact that Hellenistic cultural influence did not bypass Jerusalem, even in the realm of pastimes, is significant in itself, regardless of the precise interpretation of the discs.

Our numismatic finds from the Herodian period include many coins of Herod the Great (37-4 B.C.) and of his son Herod Archelaus (4 B.C.- A.D. 6), as well as of all the Roman Procurators of Judea (A.D. 6-59), of Agrippa I (A.D. 37-44) and, of

COINS

225. Coins of the Roman procurators and of the Great War against Rome

227. Bronze coin of Herod (year 3)   228. Silver coin of Nero, from the mint of Antioch (year 112 = A.D. 63); obverse and reverse

course, a rich and varied selection from the First Jewish Revolt against Rome (A.D. 66-70).

There are also various Roman coins, some of them notable for their fine state of preservation; one of these is a fine silver tetradrachm of Nero. During our decade of excavation in the Jewish Quarter we found only two gold coins, one Roman and the other Byzantine. The Roman coin, of the young Nero prior to his rise to the throne, was minted under Claudius (A.D. 51-54).

Of especial significance are the coins relating to the destruction of Jerusalem in A.D. 70, particularly when found in buildings in Jerusalem. For they often show that these houses were in use right up to the time of the destruction, and aid in confirming the date of the destruction in each case. We have already seen an example of this in the Burnt House. The coins referred to here are the bronzes issued by the Jewish insurgents in the second, third, and fourth years of the war against Rome (A.D. 67-69), as well as those of the Roman Procurators and of Agrippa I, which were still in circulation in A.D. 70. These were generally found scattered on the floors of the burnt-out houses, but occasionally they came to light in hoards or caches.

The most outstanding hoard—thirteen silver shekels from the First Revolt —was found in a small pool of a building which met its end during the destruction of the city. In contrast to the hundreds of bronze coins which came to light, we did not find even one silver shekel during our first six years of work in the Jewish Quarter. This did not surprise us, for people would have been more careful with silver than with bronze "small change," and the Roman looters, too, would have been much more attracted to the silver. Moreover, silver coins are of great value on the modern antiquities market, and there was always the possibility that workmen had been hiding them at the time of discovery and selling them later, after work.

229. Silver shekel coins of the Great War against Rome, years 1-4; obverse and reverse

Such instances have been known in excavations, and they are very difficult to prevent when hired labor is employed rather than volunteers. We would often sift all the earth from a room, but even then not a single shekel would turn up among the coins remaining in the sieves. For determining dates, it is entirely irrelevant, scientifically speaking, whether a coin is a bronze of the fourth year of the revolt or a silver shekel of the same year. Nevertheless, it is always very satisfying to come across a truly "valuable" coin like a shekel. Not only are they bright and "expensive," but are also very attractive to the eye and are of historical sentiment.

And then one summer day in 1975, I was sitting on the edge of a small pool (in Area F-4, p. 32) along with Zvi Maoz, our area supervisor, watching the clearance of the pool. It was yielding pottery from the 1st century A.D., and we seemed to be approaching the floor. While in the middle of discussing whether to start sifting the earth in order to prevent any possible coins from slipping through our fingers, Zvi suddenly jumped down into the pool and took over the digging from the workman. After a few minutes he came back up holding a cardboard box containing a clod of earth. Here and there we could see the edges of coins sticking out of the lump. The first coin removed was heavily encrusted, but we could just make out that it was a silver shekel. We removed two more coins which were stuck together, and then a glob of seven coins, also stuck together. All in all, there were thirteen coins. After they had been separated by expert hands, and cleaned of their encrustation, it was found that all were in a fine state of preservation. They were shekels and half-shekels of the first, second, third, and fourth years of the First Revolt against the Romans, bearing the inscription: "Shekel (or "Half-Shekel") of Israel/Jerusalem the Holy," followed by the year. (In the fifth year of the revolt—the year of the destruction of the Temple and of all Jerusalem—only a few shekels were struck, and these are the rarest of all.) Interestingly, this is only the second time such shekel coins have been discovered in controlled archaeological excavations where they could clearly be ascribed to the First Jewish Revolt against the Romans. Prior to the excavations at Masada in the mid-1960s, a few scholars still held that these coins were from the Maccabean Revolt, some 130 years earlier.

So at one fell swoop we had thirteen shekels of the first four years of the Revolt. Luck had indeed favored us. Along with the shekels were twelve bronze coins, also from the days of the Revolt, and the pool also yielded a nice goblet of white stone, a sort of miniature of the large stone jars discussed above. It is not clear how our hoard came to be within the pool, but it most probably was not hidden there. It may well have been thrown in unwittingly, along with rubbish from the destroyed house, during later preparations for rebuilding on the site.

209 (2)

The epigraphic material from the Second Temple period discovered in the Jewish Quarter excavations is mainly short inscriptions written on potsherds, mostly in Aramaic and Greek, with a few in Latin. The group of Aramaic inscriptions includes two ostraca (inscribed potsherds) as well as fragments of vessels bearing merely the names of their owners.

INSCRIPTIONS

One of the ostraca, bearing a five-line inscription written in ink, concerns some "bad" happening involving a person named Mattathias. The nature of this matter is unclear, for the script is blurred and several words are illegible. The letter ends with

231. Bowl with three feet in form of knucklebones

232. An imported "Megara" ware bowl (1st century B.C.)

233. Red bowls

234. Bronze vessels after removal from a cistern in the palatial mansion

. Bronze spoons

236. Bone objects: cosmetic spoons, spindle-whorls, handles

237. Oil lamps, including an "Ephesus" type lamp
of unusual size (1st century B.C.)

238. Shekel coins, before and after cleaning

239. Two bone "theater tickets," obverse and reverse

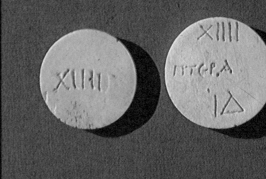

240. A gold coin of the youthful Nero, obverse and reverse

241. Inscription on storage jar fragment: "Jehezekiah the son of Shema'iah"

242. Inscription: "Shim'on"

243. Inscription on storage jar: "Shallum"

244. Incised inscription on ring-stand: *bnysn*

greetings to a woman named Salome (an abbreviated form of Shelomzion, a common name in the days of the Second Temple).

Another sherd bears the ink inscription: "Jehezekiah the son of Shemaʻiah"; this is of interest mainly because of the archaic form of the script (especially the letters *mem and ʻayin*), which dates it to the 3rd century B.C., at the latest. Significantly, this is a period in which we assume that settlement in Jerusalem was confined solely to the Eastern Hill.

Other inscribed sherds bear such names as Simeon, Judah, and Shallum. Two pottery stands of the type used to support round-bottomed vessels were of special interest, for each of them was skillfully incised in a cursive and very clear script with the Hebrew letters *bnysn*. While this would seem to mean "in (the month) of Nisan," its significance here is obscure. One would rather expect it to be some personal name, such as "ben Jason"—which is equally problematic and requires further study.

Greek and Latin inscriptions were found mostly on imported vessels. Occasionally the owner of a vessel would inscribe it with his name in Greek, as we found on red bowls of the terra sigillata type: "Of Leopeis (son of) Theodosios," "Of Aphrodisios," "Antas," and the like. Western terra sigillata plates were often stamped with the names of their potters; and we have already noted the stamped wine amphorae from Rhodes, from the 2nd century B.C., as well as those from Italy, of the 1st century B.C. Wine continued to be imported from Italy in the 1st century A.D., as evidenced by the handles of amphorae stamped with Latin inscriptions; one unusual stamp bears the inscription: EX FIGLIN(IS) CAESARIS, "From the Imperial Potteries." All of these stamps are evidence of strong commercial ties with lands across the Mediterranean Sea.

245. Inscription, apparently beginning with the name "J

246. Stone weight, inscribed in Greek: "Year 5 of the King (Agrippa?)"

247. Greek inscription: "Antas," incised on the base of a terra sigillata bowl

249. Amphora handle bearing Latin stamp: "From the Imperial Potteries"

203

248. Greek inscription: "Of Leopeis (son of) Theodosios," on a terra sigillata bowl

250. Roman pottery figurine of a woman

251. Handle of a Roman oil lamp in the form of human head

253. Roman gem with depiction of Hermes

254. Roman gem with depiction of a scorpion

252. Roman oil lamp with chariot motif (1st century A.D.)

CHAPTER FOUR
AFTER THE DESTRUCTION OF THE SECOND TEMPLE

The Roman City—A Second Interlude on the Western Hill

·After Titus had destroyed Jerusalem in A.D. 70, the city became the base of a permanent Roman garrison force. The Tenth Legion "Fretensis," which had participated in the conquest of the city, was now given the task of guarding over it. The legion's camp lay in the western part of the city and is generally thought to have spread over the ruins of Herod's palace and the area now comprising the Armenian Quarter.

The Second Revolt against Rome, commonly known as the Bar-Kokhba Revolt, broke out in Judea in the days of Hadrian and was surpressed with a heavy hand (in A.D. 135). In order to eradicate the restiveness of the Jews once and for all, Hadrian demolished Jewish Jerusalem down to its foundations and over its ruins built a new city, which he named "Colonia Aelia Capitolina," in his own honor (his full name was Publius *Aelius* Hadrianus) and in honor of the Capitoline Jupiter, divine patron of the new colony.

AELIA CAPITOLINA It is commonly held that the new Roman colony was built on the pattern of a Roman city, with a regular network of streets. There were generally two major thoroughfares at the center of the Roman city-plan, one crossing the other at right angles: the *cardo maximus*, or "main axis," which ran from north to south, and the *decumanus*, which ran from east to west. The general outlines of this plan are still reflected in the map of the Old City of Jerusalem, with one major thoroughfare running in a straight line from the Damascus gate southward, crossed at right angles by another major artery running eastward from the Jaffa Gate to the Temple Mount. We shall return to this subject in the next chapter, when we discuss the plan of Byzantine Jerusalem in the Madaba mosaic pavement.

Our knowledge of the city called Aelia Capitolina is very scanty. The ancient sources tell of its foundation by Hadrian (the event was even commemorated by the striking of a special coin), record that the Jews were prohibited from living there, and mention some of the buildings of the city. The main concentration of public buildings was apparently in the area of the later Church of the Holy Sepulcher; the city's forum seems to have been there, as was the Temple of Jupiter. However, the theory that Hadrian built the Temple of Jupiter over the ruins of the Jewish Temple seems to be unfounded; according to one early source the only thing set up on that site were two imperial statues.

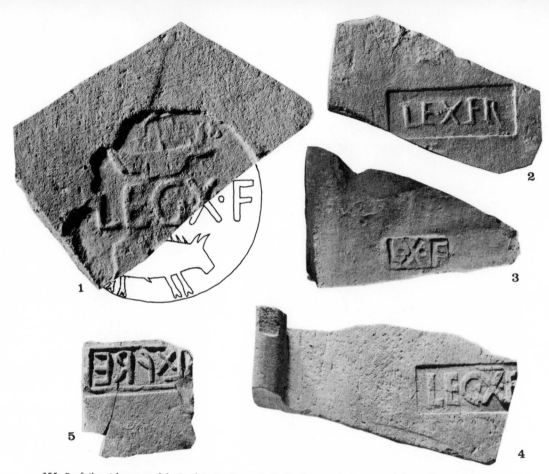

255. Roof tiles with stamps of the Tenth Legion Fretensis. On No. 1 are two legionary symbols: a galley and a boar

Of prime importance among the archaeological remains of Aelia Capitolina are two monumental triple gates. One, flanked by two towers, was unearthed underneath the present Damascus gate. The eastern entrance of the gate is completely preserved. Above the keystone of the arch there is a (displaced?) stone with a mutilated inscription mentioning the name of the city COL(ONIA) AEL(IA) CAP(ITOLINA). In the Via Dolorosa were found the substantial remains of a triumphal arch popularly denoted "Ecce Homo," and the nearby "Lithostratos" pavement. Remains of a street pavement probably belonging to the Roman *cardo* have been found at the northern gate mentioned above, and beneath the *Souq Khan ez-Zeit*. A monumental pavement from late Roman times, recently cleared by S. Margalit beneath Christian Quarter Road, is now incorporated into the modern street pavement there.

All these remains are located in the northern part of the Old City, that is north of the supposed line of the *decumanus* represented today by David Street and the Street of the Chain. The area south of this line was occupied by the camp of the Tenth Roman Legion; its main headquarter was in the west, on the site of the present-day Citadel and the Armenian Quarter. Actually, only scanty building remains which can be related to the period of Aelia Capitolina have been found there. We may note in particular pipelines built of pottery pipe segments stamped with the name of the Tenth Legion, which were found intact in the Citadel, as well as many roof tiles also bearing the stamp of the legion. The site of our excavation, the modern Jewish Quarter, lies east of the above area. We were able to ascertain quite conclusively that there are no building remains stemming from the Roman city almost in this area. The only finds from that period were many broken tiles bearing the stamp of the Tenth Legion: LEG(IO). X. FRETEN(SIS), and some sporadic Roman pottery. The Tenth Legion is long known to have manufactured such roof tiles, pottery pipes, and bricks for use in public works. This production ceased at the end of the 3rd century A.D. From the above it would seem that the main legionary camp in the west was augmented by secondary barracks scattered over the slopes to the east, in the area of our excavations.

A GAP IN SETTLEMENT Our stratigraphic excavations throughout the Jewish Quarter revealed that the remains from the Byzantine period always lay directly over the layer of the destruction of Jerusalem (A.D. 70) with no Roman stratum intervening. In other words, except for the few finds just noted, the two and a half centuries of the Roman period in Jerusalem are almost entirely unrepresented in our excavations.

The built-up area of Aelia Capitolina was restricted to the northern part of the town, while the Tenth Legion camped in the south. The Roman city was much smaller than the previous Jewish metropolis. For lack of evidence the question of the defense wall of Aelia Capitolina is still controversial. With no potential enemies in sight, the defenses of this new colony were apparently based solely on the legionary camp. At the end of the third century the legion was transferred from Jerusalem to Elath on the Red Sea, after a sojourn of two centuries in the city. Only with the departure of the legion does the city seem to have been surrounded again by a wall. Roman Aelia was an insignificant provincial town—the capital of Palestine was Caesarea. Jerusalem was to rise to prominence only with the decline of pagan rule and the advent of Christianity as the official religion of the Roman Empire.

CHAPTER FIVE

BYZANTINE JERUSALEM

1. The Flowering of a Byzantine City

With the victory of Constantine the Great over his enemies in the East, in A.D. 324, Christianity rose to greatness—and to official status throughout the Roman Empire. The Holy Land, heretofore a remote district within the province of Syria-Palestine, suddenly assumed a new importance to the ruling element of the empire, and Jerusalem, whose past splendor had long since tarnished, once again emerged as a religious center—this time Christian, the goal of pilgrims and the object of lavish building projects: churches, monasteries, and hostels. At the very outset of this period, Constantine built the large Church of the Holy Sepulcher as well as another huge edifice on Mount Zion, the Church of St. Sion, "Mother of All Churches."

The prohibition against Jews residing in Jerusalem still stood in Constantine's day, and thus the unique episode of the Emperor Julian "the Apostate" (A.D. 361-363) was all the more outstanding, for this Byzantine ruler sought not only to rebuild the Temple, but to restore it to the Jews (albeit out of anti-Christian feelings rather than any pro-Jewish sentiments). After this abortive attempt, the Temple Enclosure remained desolate until the days of the Arab Conquest.

Eudocia, wife of the Emperor Theodosius II, who settled in Jerusalem (A.D. 443-460), did much to develop the city. She built several churches, including one near the Siloam Pool, and ordered the rebuilding of the city wall around Mount Zion. It was apparently in her day that the Jews were once again permitted to live in the city. In the 5th century A.D., Jerusalem was raised by the Church to the status of a Patriarchate. The flowering of Byzantine Jerusalem reached its peak under Justinian (A.D. 527-565). He was famous for his enormous construction efforts throughout the empire, but his largest project in Jerusalem was the "New Church of St. Mary," known simply as the Nea ("new" in Greek), of which we shall speak later.

The conquest of Jerusalem by invading Sassanians from Persia, in A.D. 614, was accompanied by much destruction within the city and by the cruel slaughter of a great many of the Christian population. The Jews generally cooperated with the conquerors, in hope of restoring Jerusalem to Jewish rule, but the city was returned to the Byzantine Emperor Heraclius in A.D. 628. Christian Jerusalem met its end a decade later, in A.D. 638, when the armies of Islam captured the city, which surrendered without a fight, preventing further destruction.

BUILDING REMAINS   Many remains of the Byzantine period have been unearthed in Jerusalem, but they are mostly fragmentary and are scattered about the city. They include mosaic floors from churches and other public structures or more modest buildings, which have often come to light during modern construction work.

One of the manifestations of the development of Jerusalem in this period is the expansion of the city into a new quarter on Mount Zion, where several large churches were erected and a new section of city wall was built. The archaeological finds in the Jewish Quarter, despite their very fragmentary and disconnected nature, also point to this as a period of renewed splendor, in an area which had not

6. Byzantine mosaic pavement in Area M (p. 32)

257. Sitting-bath lined with marble, in the bathhouse

258. The hypocaust of the Byzantine bathhouse in Area C (p. 32)

been inhabited for two and a half centuries. Here and there were remains of dwellings and of mosaic pavements: in present-day Ararat ("Assyrian Convent") Street, in Area R, we discovered a long wall built of ashlars, which contained a monumental gateway; and in the northwestern corner of the Jewish Quarter (Area *258* C), we exposed a public bathhouse. The latter was heated by means of a hypocaust (subterranean fire chamber) built of brick arches; it heated the caldarium (hot chamber) above it by means of hot air passing through square pottery flues which *257* faced the walls. This hot chamber contained a sitting-bath lined with tiles of white marble.

But it is especially the remains of two monumental building projects which evoke the force behind the building and development activities which raised Byzantine Jerusalem to new heights—the southern part of the *cardo maximus*, and the Nea Church. Since both of these are depicted graphically in the famous Madaba mosaic map, a look at this interesting source may aid in revealing their true significance.

THE MADABA MAP   It is not uncommon for archaeological excavations to be prompted and guided by information revealed in an ancient literary source. In such instances, the excavations are intended to reveal a site or structure mentioned in the Bible, in Josephus, or in some other ancient source. But it happens only rarely that the ancient source guiding the excavator is not a literary document, but a graphic one. Our experience of this sort was possibly unique when we purposefully and knowingly sought the *cardo maximus* of Jerusalem, that is, the main north-south street of the city. The *cardo*, an urban architectural project of the first order, was assumed to have enhanced both Roman and Byzantine Jerusalem. Though not among the imperial building projects mentioned in the literary sources, it was commemorated in the contemporaneous mosaic map at Madaba in Trans-Jordan. This same map also assisted us in identifying the remains of the Nea church.

264   The mosaic pavement containing the map belonged to a Byzantine church discovered in 1884. The map itself depicts the Holy Land and its various towns and villages, with Jerusalem at its center shown larger and in more detail than the other cities. The depiction is "three-dimensional" and the artist sought to achieve a certain realism. Despite its schematic execution, stereotypic buildings, and the selectivity of the structures shown, what we have before us is a reliable representation of Jerusalem and its various outstanding features as they were in the 6th century A.D. This is the oldest known pictorial map of Jerusalem; and there are few ancient cities with such precious records of their visual aspect. It is a first-rate source for the study of Jerusalem's town plan and topography, facilitating identification of monumental buildings unearthed in archaeological excavations. It is this latter aspect which serves here as a guideline.

259   The map (p. 212) shows Jerusalem from a bird's-eye view, as an elongated oval (measuring 54 x 93 centimeters in the original pavement). In an attempt at perspective, the city is shown looking eastward, as was the general practice in ancient maps. It is surrounded by a wall with towers and gates. On the left (north) we see the Damascus Gate, the main gate of the city (A). In the far (eastern) wall is St.

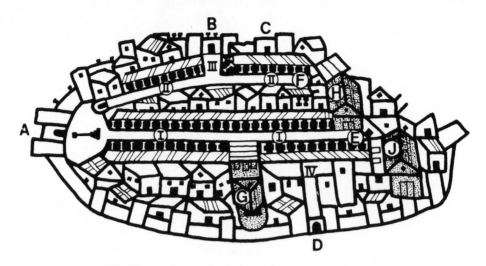

259. Schematic drawing of Jerusalem in the mosaic map at Madaba

Stephen's Gate or Lion Gate (B), and south of it, to the right, is the "Golden Gate" (C), open in Byzantine times but now blocked up. In the near (western) wall is a small gate (D), the modern Jaffa Gate, and a small street stemming from it (IV), the equivalent of the modern David Street.

Entering the city through the Damascus Gate from the north, one would find oneself in a plaza with a large column bearing probably the statue of the emperor. The Arabic name of the gate—*Bab el-Amud*, "the Gate of the Column"—is derived from this column. Two streets branch out from the plaza; one (I), flanked by porticos, crossed the city in a straight line from north to south and terminated near an inner gate (E), which may have been called the Nea Gate. South of this gate was Mt. Zion, with its buildings, including the outstanding Church of St. Sion (J), surrounded by the new city wall. The course of this street is identical to that of the series of modern streets stemming from the Damascus Gate southward: Souq Khan ez-Zeit, the three parallel markets and, finally, the two parallel streets today called Jewish Quarter Street and Habad Street.

The second north-south street (II), bordered by one portico, stems off the plaza obliquely and then continues on a parallel course southward, terminating at a structure of unknown nature (F). This bent street corresponds with the course of modern el-Wad ("Valley") Street and its course conforms with local topography. At its middle is a street (III) branching off toward St. Stephen's Gate on the east; although foreshortened because of the perspective, it includes part of the Via Dolorosa.

Thus we can see how the map of Byzantine Jerusalem, as depicted in the Madaba mosaic, still suits the city of today, with almost the same main streets still functioning. After the discovery of this ancient map a century ago, it was suggested that the present-day streets of the Old City conceal the town plan of the Roman city which, over the centuries, became clogged and narrow, and gradually took on the oriental character now prevailing there. This town plan was commonly ascribed to the Roman city of Aelia Capitolina, and it was assumed that the Madaba map reflected the Roman plan, with various elements added during the Byzantine period.

260. Dismantling late structures covering the Cardo

2. Tracing the Cardo Maximus

In the light of the foregoing, the major street (I) of Jerusalem in the Madaba map is generally held to depict the *cardo maximus* which crossed the city from north to south. The artist of this mosaic map, in his endeavor to emphasize the magnificence of the double porticos with their red tile roofs, naively depicted them in an open perspective, a sort of fish-eye view that allows one to see both sides of the street at the same time. There is a large, domed structure representing the Church of the Holy Sepulchre (G) midway along this street, on its western side. At the southern end of the street, on its eastern side, there is another large building, identified by scholars as the Nea Church (H), to which we shall return later on.

261. Arab structures overlying the Cardo pavement, with the columns in secondary use.
In the photograph: Shlomo Margalit

263. Excavations on the eastern side
Quarter Street (visible on the right). To
the street, a row of pillars of the Cardo
stones. To the left of the pillars, sparse
the Israelite city wall cut by the Car
foreground, below, building remains ea
the city wall ➡

262. Uncovering the pavement of the Cardo beneath the arches of the bazaar

Scholars have long held that such a magnificent *cardo* did indeed exist in Jerusalem, and this conjecture has been supported materially by the very numerous fragments of columns found scattered in secondary use in later buildings, most of them in shops along the assumed route of this avenue. Where could so many columns have come from if not from a colonnaded street which existed here previously? Thus, although the likelihood of the *cardo*'s existence was great, only archaeological excavations could prove the matter. But, here again, how could an archaeologist even dream of excavating in so crowded and bustling an area of oriental bazaars, narrow streets, and densely built houses? Would it ever be possible to reveal the *cardo maximus* of Jerusalem? Would the tantalizing depiction in the Madaba map, which has attracted the attention of scholars and laymen for almost a century, ever be confirmed in fact? Unanticipated as it was, the opportunity did indeed present itself.

Row of pillars

In 1975 the Jewish Quarter Reconstruction and Development Company began renovating the bazaar along Jewish Quarter Street. The Company sponsored a competition among architects for the planning of the project. And the proponents of the winning proposal appropriately named their plan "The Cardo." Well aware of the possibility that an ancient street existed beneath the modern pavement, the planners—Architects Peter Bugod and Esther Niv-Krendel—sought to integrate old and new. They had certainly not foreseen the extent to which the remains later uncovered would force them to alter their plan in order to accommodate the antiquities and ensure their preservation. The final decision to preserve the ancient structures greatly complicated their task, for the remains were scattered over a wide area—not only between the existing buildings, but within them and beneath them as well. Since plans on paper are quite different from work on the spot, we can only hope that optimal care will be taken in bringing these plans to a successful conclusion.

Our "Operation *Cardo*" involved so far the strip of land bordered by Jewish Quarter Street on the east, Habad Street on the west, extending from St. Mark *271* Street on the north to Hamalakh Street in the south. This entire area was built up, crowded with stores, workshops and houses, forming a mass of Crusader, Mameluk, Ottoman, and recent structures. Over the years many spaces within this tangle were gradually filled up with earth and remained so, undetected for centuries. Those buildings which the renewal project survey found to be in a sound structural condition were scheduled for renovation and incorporation into the overall scheme; in these houses our staff was forced to dig within dark cellars and cavities, well beneath the level of the street. Where buildings were slated for *262* demolition, we were afforded the opportunity of working in daylight, often under open skies. Our work has progressed slowly, during both summer and winter over the last few years, and is still going on. Construction projects and archaeological excavations are being carried out side by side, and we, the archaeologists, are trying to keep apace with or even ahead of the builders. Naturally, conflicts of interest arise, but when they do, compromise guides both parties. However, concessions have never impaired the scientific integrity of our work, and the architects have often had to alter their plans in order to accommodate significant features revealed by our spades.

All in all it has been an exhausting and somewhat nerve-wracking task—an experience seldom encountered by archaeological expeditions. The amount of labor ultimately invested in the excavations along the *cardo* (which were ably supervised by Hillel Geva) has certainly proved worthwhile, for our hopes have been fully realized. In view of the difficulties imposed upon us, those sections of the *cardo* which have been uncovered have rewarded us with results which surpass all expectations. Indeed, the abundant remains have enabled us to reconstruct the plan of this major avenue in detail.

ΑΓΙΑΠΟΛΙCΙΕΡΟΥCA

CΤΑΡ

ΙΟΕΝΝΑ ΒΕΘΩΡΩΝ

ΚΑΙ ΕΡΧΤΑ

ΑΚΕΛ
ΔΑΜΑ
ΘΑΜΝΑΕΝΘΑΕΚCΙP
ΤΟΥΔΑΕΤΑΔΥΤΟΥΠ

salem in the Madaba mosaic map, with the *cardo maximus* running across the town

266. Excavations on the steep southern slope; below, part of the Crusader building ➡

of the *cardo maximus* as discovered in Jewish Quarter St.; area X-5 (p. 32), looking east

269. Column bases

RIPTION OF THE CARDO

We have been able to trace the line of the *cardo maximus*, with several interruptions, over a stretch of some 180 meters. Its flagstone pavement lies about two and a half meters below the modern street level and slopes downward from south to north. The southern parts of the paved street rest on bedrock, and the pavement is preserved intact in many places. The farther north we proceed, however, the lower the level of bedrock. The pavement was laid over a thick earth fill in the northern parts, and was therefore more prone to damage in subsequent ages. Here, later construction has left little more than scattered patches of pavement. Only the northernmost part uncovered (Area X-2, p. 222), although it rests upon a thick *271* earth fill, is again fairly well preserved. In addition to the pavement itself, our excavations have revealed a large wall, pillars, drainage channels, foundations to support the colonnades, and individual columns (the bases, capitals, and shafts of which were used as construction materials in later buildings). These extensive finds have led us to reconstruct the *cardo maximus* and its several components as follows:

The long street, about 22.5 meters wide, was bordered on the west (X-5, p. 223) by a wall of large, dressed stones and on the east by an arcade, the arches of which rested on square pillars (X-4, p. 222). Two rows of columns ran down its length, dividing the avenue into three parts: a 12 meters wide road in the center, flanked by two colonnaded and roofed porticos, one on either side. A row of sockets has been preserved in the top course of the western wall (X-5) some 5 meters above the pavement; these had accommodated the ends of the roof rafters. The coping of the colonnade foundations is built of large slabs, some of which have square depressions to receive the column bases. The slabs were covered by the pavement. The molded bases, of which only very few were found in their original place, are of the Attic type and are not entirely uniform in size and profile. The column shafts are monolithic, made from single stones. Three Corinthian capitals in Byzantine style have been found as well, each one of a different pattern. The reconstructed height of the columns, including base, shaft, and capital, is about 5 meters. The only architectural element which has not yet been found here is the architrave (the beam which rests directly above the column capitals). This may well have been made of wood in the *cardo*; if that were the case, no trace of it would have survived. On either side of the street along the colonnades there are drainage channels beneath the

Stratigraphic excavations in Area T-4 (p. 32) near the city wall; remains from usader period down to Israelite times. The lower, darker stained part city wall shows the surface level prior to excavations

221

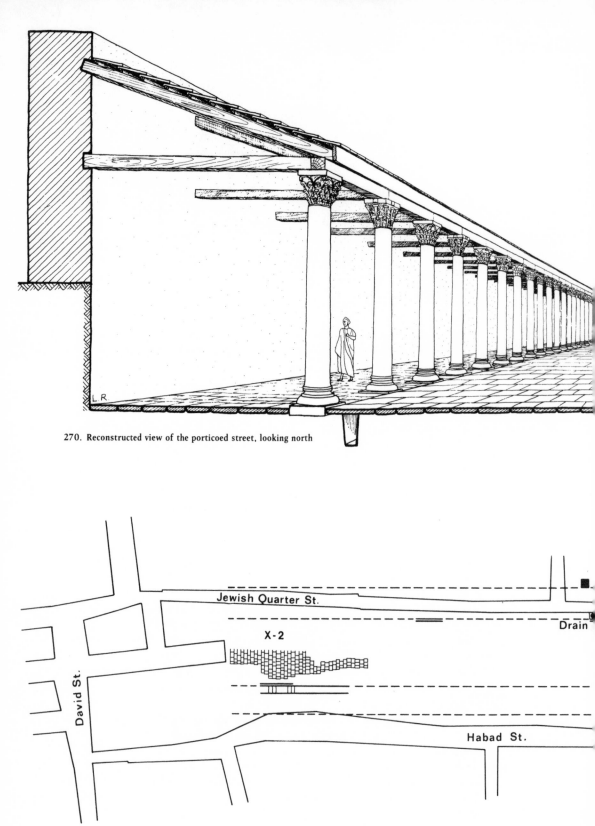

270. Reconstructed view of the porticoed street, looking north

271. Plan of the excavations along the Cardo

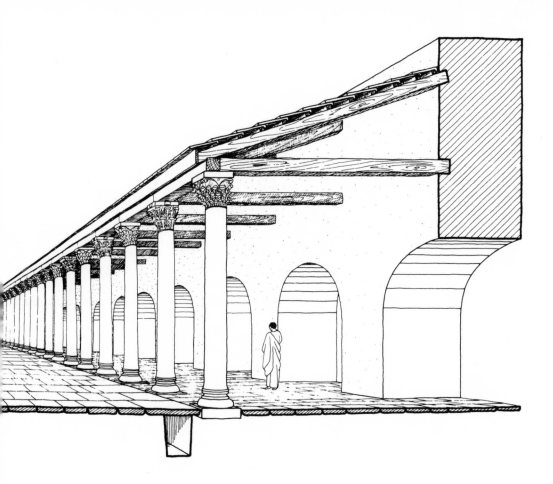

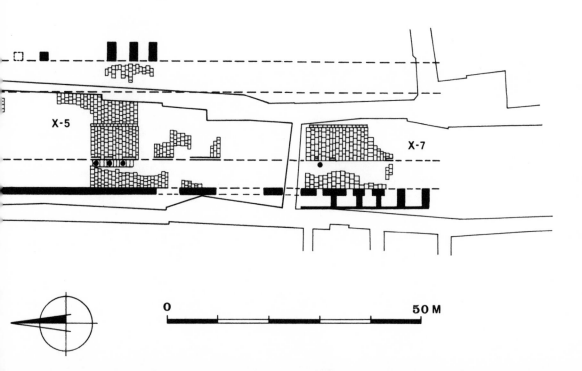

X-5

X-7

0   50 M

wo Byzantine capitals

flagstone pavement. The flagstones themselves had been worn smooth by long use and were mostly broken into pieces.

A most interesting new feature has been revealed in the southernmost section of the *cardo* (X-7, p. 223) which was excavated in 1981. It has on the west a row of chambers hewn in a rock-cliff, apparently serving as shops along the western portico.

270   This broad avenue, with its colonnades and shaded sidewalks, was the main thoroughfare of Jerusalem, like the *cardo* of any major Roman city. In striking contrast to the boldness of the plan is its poor execution in detail; but this is a common feature in Byzantine architecture, which deviated greatly from the standards set and upheld by classical Roman architecture, even in the provinces.

DATE   The task of dating the *cardo maximus* of Jerusalem represents a special challenge, for it is at once significant and problematic. When we began to excavate the avenue we had little doubt of its date: we all "knew" that, if there was indeed a *cardo* here, it would be the main north-south axis of the Roman city, designed as part and parcel of Colonia Aelia Capitolina, though it would have continued in use in Byzantine times as well (as is shown by the Madaba map). This "general knowledge" was an unchallenged axiom.

274   After we uncovered the *cardo* in the Jewish Quarter we were certain, from the pottery and coins found in the drains, that the street was last used in the Byzantine period. But what is astonishing is that we became convinced that the street was also initially constructed in the Byzantine period. This most significant conclusion was based not only on the architectural style, but even more so on Byzantine pottery found beneath the pavement. There was absolutely nothing in our findings to indicate that this was a Byzantine renovation of an earlier Roman street. Furthermore, the street was not built according to the Roman foot of 29.6 centimeters, but rather to the measure of the Byzantine foot of about 32 centimeters (as was established by architect Doron Chen). Thus, our conclusions on this matter are quite clear and definite.

The *cardo* of Jerusalem, in the section which we uncovered in the southern part of the Old City, was not a component of Roman Aelia Capitolina, but belonged exclusively to the Byzantine city. This fits in well with our previous general conclusion that the built-up part of the Roman city did not extend into the southern part of the Old City, the area of the present-day Jewish Quarter. There was no reason for the Romans to have constructed such a monumental avenue through an unpopulated quarter of the city and leading to nothing in particular. But in Byzantine times, when construction here was renewed and major edifices were being erected, the *cardo maximus* of the northern part of the city (presumably built by the Romans) was extended southward, leading into the new quarter. This magnificent avenue would then have served several important structures in the quarter, and there would thus have been every reason to build a southward extension of the existing *cardo* to the north.

THE BYZANTINE CARDO

Though we could suffice in determining that the *cardo maximus* uncovered here is Byzantine and not Roman, we had hoped that we might also be able to find who actually built it. The natural candidate for such a huge enterprise would be Constantine the Great, who raised Jerusalem to new heights as a religious center of universal significance. But the archaeological evidence, both architectural and ceramic, shows that it was built at a later date. Another builder in Jerusalem, under whom the city reached even greater heights, was Justinian (A.D. 527-565), who is known primarily as the builder of the famous Nea Church. Indeed, comparative examination of the pottery found beneath the pavement of the *cardo* with that found beneath the pavement of the Nea Church has revealed that the two projects were contemporaneous. We can thus regard Justinian, who is known to have built the church, as the builder of the southern part of the *cardo maximus* as well.

WHO BUILT THE SOUTH CARDO?

One of the apparent motives behind its construction was the desire to connect the new church with the Church of the Holy Sepulcher, at the middle of the northern section of the *cardo*. It was an imposing avenue, intended mainly for festive

274. Byzantine sherds discovered beneath the Cardo pavement, which determine the dating of the street to the Byzantine period

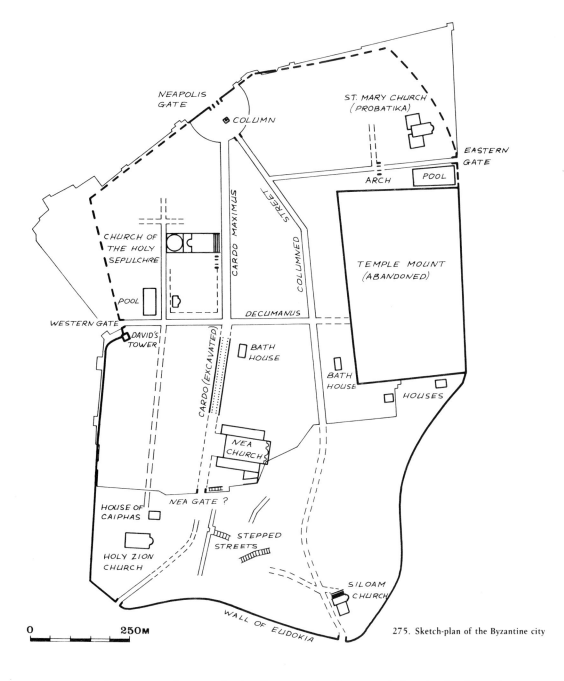

religious processions, undoubtedly a regular feature of the city in those days. Interestingly, these two major churches, the Church of the Holy Sepulcher and the Nea Church, are the only two structures specifically depicted in the Madaba map as lying on the *cardo maximus* itself. If our assumption is correct, the artist of the Madaba mosaic sought to commemorate this new architectural project in his impressive depiction of Jerusalem; this major addition to the city, built during his lifetime, achieved fame throughout Christendom.

I am well aware that our suggestion to distinguish chronologically between the two parts of the *cardo*, ascribing the southern portion to Justinian, will be frowned upon by certain scholars. The concept identifying the *cardo maximus* with Roman Aelia Capitolina is so deeply engrained in the minds of many scholars that some of them have formed the opinion that the avenue which we have uncovered is merely a Byzantine renovation of the earlier Roman *cardo*, and that it was not Byzantine practice to build such colonnaded streets. On the contrary, we are witness in the Byzantine period to a process of narrowing of colonnaded streets in Roman-built cities (as at Samaria and Gerasa), through the construction of shops in the colonnades. But I think Jerusalem should be exempted from this generalization: the narrowing of the streets in the Old City did not occur in Byzantine times, but only after the Arab Conquest. In the Byzantine period Jerusalem was the site of much ostentatious imperial building, and the emperors used the city as a means of glorifying their names, turning it into an international focal point of pilgrimage. Under such circumstances it would hardly be surprising to find that Justinian, one of Byzantium's greatest builders, should see fit to continue the Roman *cardo* *275* southward, into the newly-built quarter, where he was also erecting one of the most magnificent churches Jerusalem was ever to know.

We may note here that the Byzantines continued to utilize colonnaded Roman streets in many cities of the Eastern Mediterranean, and even built new avenues of this type in some cities. Moreover, Justinian — to whom we ascribe the construction of the southern *cardo* in Jerusalem — embellished at least one other city in this manner — Justiniana Prima, which he built and named in his own honor (modern Tsaritchin Grad in southern Serbia).

If Justinian did indeed build the southern part of the *cardo* in Jerusalem, as we hold, why is the fact not mentioned along with the other building projects ascribed to him in the literary sources? But, then, neither is mention made of the *cardo* which must have been built by Hadrian in Jerusalem and should, therefore, have appeared among the works ascribed to him in the *Chronicon Paschale*. Apparently the construction of such an avenue, no matter how splendid, was not always mentioned among other public works.

Our *cardo*, and especially our conclusions regarding it, have become controversial because they undermine the prevalent theories. But even accepted views must make way in the light of new evidence. My colleagues and I, having long trudged the road leading to the rediscovery of the *cardo*, believe that our conclusions are based on clear, checked data, and that they are exact insofar as modern archaeological methods can be considered exact.

But still, we are far from saying that the entire problem of the *cardo maximus* of Jerusalem has been solved. New findings may either confirm or correct our conclusions concerning the chronological distinction between the two halves of this splendid avenue. Such evidence must, of course, now be sought in the northern portion of the street, for the investigation of that section is still in its infancy, its precise dating not yet having been confirmed. Columns have also been found built into shops there, in secondary use. From time to time, with municipal sewage improvements in the streets of the sector (as in the *Souq Khan ez-Zeit*), fragments of early pavements have come to light; the flagstones there are much larger than those to the south, and they are grooved and often laid in oblique rows. In 1981 Menahem Magen laid bare what seems to be the beginning of the Roman *cardo* at the arched gate underneath the Damascus Gate.

What was the final fate of the *cardo maximus*? After the Byzantine period it no longer served its primary function and it underwent far-reaching changes. The columns in the western portico were replaced by pillars (X-5), and the sloping tiled roof by cross-vaulting. In the Middle Ages and under the Turks, the space of the *cardo* gradually came to be filled by stores and workshops incorporating various architectural fragments from the Byzantine structure. Through this continual process of encroachment upon the broad avenue, the narrow, still-flourishing bazaars eventually evolved, all the way from the Damascus Gate down to Jewish Quarter Street.

261

How far did the *cardo maximus* originally extend? In the Madaba map this street passes the Nea Church and reaches a gate (E, p. 212) located apparently in an internal wall, one which preceded the city wall built by the Empress Eudocia. We do not know what the Byzantines called this gate, but in the 10th century A.D. it was apparently called the "Niah Gate" in Arabic (as we shall explain below). This name surely preserves a tradition from the time when the Nea Church still stood nearby. In Crusader times the gate was known as "Zion Gate" (not to be confused with the modern Zion Gate, some 120 meters farther west).

In our excavations, we found that the southern end of the *cardo* was entirely destroyed; nothing whatsoever survived of either it or a gate here. But close to the modern city wall, east of the probable site of the gate, we did find a stepped street leading up from the east, alongside a Byzantine wall and parallel to the Turkish city wall. This street (marked 5 in fig. 278) was apparently one of the arteries of the Byzantine city and probably belonged to the network of stepped streets leading from the Tyropoeon Valley to the Upper City. We assume that this street joined the *cardo* near the gate, but the spot of the actual junction was obliterated by the construction of a tower (8) in medieval times (see below).

3. In Quest of the Great Nea Church

We have already mentioned the Nea Church several times in this volume, and now we shall turn to the detailed discussion it truly deserves. The Nea Church was famous in the annals of Byzantine Jerusalem, for it was one of the largest and most magnificent churches in the city, built by one of the greatest Byzantine emperors. Its construction is described and lauded by the contemporaneous historian Procopius, in his book on Justinian's building projects.

Although all trace of the Nea Church had disappeared as if it had never been, it was captured in art and its memory survived in literature. Modern scholarly imagination was also stirred by its supposed immensity, splendor, and beauty. For us, the excavators, the discovery of the Nea Church was a unique experience. Not only did we successfully bring a long-standing quest to a close, but—even more exciting to the archaeologist—we were able to piece together fragment after fragment and clue after clue, over a period of several years, and eventually prove that this was indeed the building we were seeking. As a sort of congratulatory gift from heaven, our conclusions were then confirmed by an epigraphic find which served to identify the structure almost by name. Such integration of all possible documentary factors—literary, pictorial, architectural, and epigraphic—is the dream of every excavator, and only rarely, very rarely, is such a constellation realized.

"Nea" is the abbreviated name for the "New Church of St. Mary, Mother of God (*Theotokos*)," the church built by Justinian and inaugurated in A.D. 543. One of the most magnificent buildings of its age, it is described in detail by Procopius, who hailed from Caesarea on the coast of Palestine. In his "biography" of Justinian's buildings, Procopius begins his description of this building as follows: "And in Jerusalem he (Justinian) has dedicated to the Mother of God a shrine with which no other can be compared. It is called by the natives 'New Church'" (*Buildings*, V, 6).

Procopius praises the huge building, noting that the stones for its construction had to be brought by special means and that its enormous columns were wrought by miracle. He also relates that the building site had to be expanded artificially, for it was too narrow to accommodate the entire structure, which included a monastery, a hostel, a hospital and, according to other sources, also a library.

The conjectured location of the Nea Church had long been based on two sources. Early Christian pilgrims related that the Nea Church stood at a high spot opposite the southwestern corner of the Temple Mount—in other words, somewhere in the modern Jewish Quarter. The second source was the depiction of Jerusalem in the Madaba map (described on p. 212), which shows a large structure (H) on the *cardo maximus* in the area of today's Jewish Quarter. On the basis of the pilgrims' descriptions, this structure has generally been identified with the Nea Church. While this led general opinion to locate the Nea Church somewhere within the Jewish Quarter, no one seriously considered that there would ever be an opportunity of looking for it there.

When we began excavating in the Jewish Quarter, we too viewed the Nea Church as an abstract, legendary edifice, and that only by some odd chance we might come across traces of it. But chance had been kind to us before, and it favored us again in our second season. In June 1970, preparations were being made for the construction of a dwelling in the court of the Batei Maḥse, near the Rothschild House (Area D, p. 32). This complex, founded in the previous century by Jews from Germany, centered around a large courtyard popularly called "Der Deutscher Platz." A Hebrew newspaper of over a century ago (*Hamagid*, 1862) relates how an ancient wall was discovered during the digging of the foundation for the Batei Maḥse. The wall, built of very large stones, was discovered together with a marble pavement. Conrad Schick, the Swiss architect who resided in Jerusalem at that time, also reported this find.

We seem to have encountered the continuation of this same wall, running from north to south. We uncovered a stretch 13 meters long and 6.5 meters thick, with foundations descending to bedrock at a depth of 8 meters. Its outer face is built of large, dressed stones with irregular margins and rough central bosses. Within this thick wall was an inscribed apse, 5 meters in diameter, oriented to the east. The direction of the apse would indicate that it belonged to a church, and that it was not the main apse but a smaller, lateral one. The extreme thickness of the wall points to a structure of huge dimensions. It is clear that a church of such size, at this particular location, could only be the famed Nea Church. This identification, which was supported by our entire staff, came as such a surprise that we hesitated at first to make it known. But fellow archaeologists who visited the site accepted the identification quite readily, and our Christian colleagues (particularly the Dominican Father P. Benoit) were most enthusiastic. Thus, the legendary Nea Church had become a tangible reality.

The fact that we had discovered the site of the Nea Church, and had uncovered a part of it, was greatly satisfying. But it also stirred in us the desire to uncover more of the building. We now had a concrete point of reference for searching out further remains of the building, whenever the opportunity should provide itself. Such an opportunity did arise in the summer of 1973, when a large open space some 100 meters west of the apse (Area T-1, p. 32) became available for excavation. After digging down through five or six meters of rubble and debris, as well as modern foundations, we reached an archaeological stratum containing Byzantine pottery. Here we found the thick, deeply set foundations of a building, with the threshold of

e eastern wall of the Nea Church with the northern lateral apse

a doorway whose original width was 5.4 meters. The door leads east, toward a large space paved with white marble flagstones. All these were the remains of a very large structure, the major part of which lay to the east; they lay opposite the wall with the apse and parallel to it. Since the building with the apse stretched to the west, and these latter remains were oriented to the east, it was obvious that both parts belonged to one and the same building, and a huge one at that—apparently the Nea Church, which would thus have been about 116 meters long (including the narthex).

What tipped the scales in favor of this identification was the fact that our assumed Nea Church reached the edge of the *cardo maximus* passing on the west—exactly as depicted on the Madaba mosaic map!

Further details of the Nea Church were revealed in a discovery made in 1973, south of the Batei Mahse, outside the city walls at a spot where the Jerusalem Foundation was preparing a public park (later to become known as the Beth Shalom Garden) along the city wall. During preparatory work there, a clearance directed by Meir Ben-Dov revealed the corner of a massive structure below the corner of the city wall, where it juts out north of Burj Kibrit. It was built of large, drafted stones resembling those of the wall containing the apse, in the courtyard of the Batei Mahse; the corner was exactly in line with the wall of the apse some 35 meters to the north. This was certainly the southeastern corner of the Nea Church.

The discovery of this corner was an important step in revealing the extent of the church proper. The restoration by M. Ben-Dov of an exterior apse near the corner is totally arbitrary and in contradiction of the extant remains. The northern lateral

277. The southeastern corner of the Nea Church (the upper course is restored)

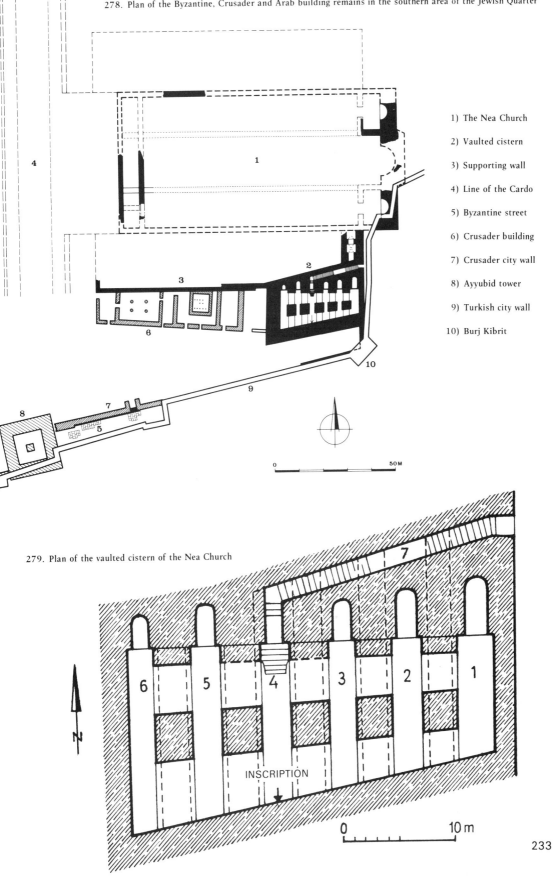

278. Plan of the Byzantine, Crusader and Arab building remains in the southern area of the Jewish Quarter

1) The Nea Church
2) Vaulted cistern
3) Supporting wall
4) Line of the Cardo
5) Byzantine street
6) Crusader building
7) Crusader city wall
8) Ayyubid tower
9) Turkish city wall
10) Burj Kibrit

0   50 M

279. Plan of the vaulted cistern of the Nea Church

INSCRIPTION

0   10 m

apse described above is known to be internal. Furthermore, by a lucky strike the southern internal apse near the said corner was also uncovered in January 1982 during construction work near the Turkish city wall performed by the East Jerusalem Development Corporation.

The shape of the central apse has not yet been determined, since it is partly destroyed and partly hidden underneath modern structures. The preserved remains of the wall seem to indicate that it was an internal apse of approximately 12 meters in diameter with a minor projection beyond the eastern line of the wall.

Procopius describes the Nea Church as a basilica surrounded by porticoes on all flanks except the eastern one; before the entrance were two huge columns. A narrow corridor led from the basilica to an atrium, also surrounded within by a row of columns; before the atrium was a round courtyard, connected with the gate structure.

The scanty archaeological remains are as yet insufficient to indicate the precise plan of the church, but in general terms it can be assumed that it was a basilical church with two rows of columns, a central nave and two aisles. The nave terminated with a large apse and each of the aisles terminated with a chamber which has a smaller apse in its eastern wall. The interior of the church was about 100 meters long and 52 meters wide, making it the largest known basilica in Palestine. A possible subdivision of this huge space should, however, also be considered. At the west there is the narthex which contains the only preserved doorway leading into the southern aisle. Further west a narrow atrium seems to have bordered with the *cardo*.

As mentioned before, the Nea Church was actually a complex of buildings which must have spread over a fairly large area beyond the church itself. The next step in ascertaining the limits of this complex was not far away. During 1976-1977 we excavated in an open area adjacent to the southern city wall, where there were plans to build an underground parking lot ("the terminal") for the Jewish Quarter. Some 40 meters north of the city wall, we encountered an east-west wall (3, p. 233) 66 *278* meters long and 7.6 meters high, which contained a series of vaulted openings with relieving arches above; abutting it was a building of the Crusader period. It soon became clear that the long wall was actually the southern supporting wall of the Nea Church complex; such a wall was necessary to support the earth fill which had been used to expand the level area of the construction site for the church on its southern flank. Assuming that the general plan was symmetrical, the supporting wall enabled us to estimate that the overall width of the complex extending to the north was about 105 meters.

The most dramatic development in our discovery of the Nea Church was still to come. The Jerusalem Foundation had planned to build a small, open garden-theater in the inner angle of Burj Kibrit, the tower at the corner of the city wall (Area T-7, p. 32). The intention was to exploit the convenient topography of the site, which would facilitate sloped seating on the concave, semicircular hillside. The resulting garden-theater would face south, toward the city wall and overlooking the southern part of the Kidron Valley—a most picturesque and natural backdrop. But the necessity for archaeological investigations prior to any construction, and for preserving any ancient remains revealed, have forced the planners to change the theater plan radically, to accommodate a unique architectural monument and preserve it for posterity.

The task of excavating here was difficult and drawn out, primarily because of the danger that the tower debris which formed a steep scarp here might collapse. Suddenly, one day, an event occurred which had almost become commonplace in our excavations. The mechanical excavator clearing the upper debris hit the ceiling of a subterranean structure, breaking a hole through into the interior. In the past we had often discovered cisterns in this manner, for they are a very regular feature of ancient Jerusalem. Throwing stones and burning paper into the gaping hole, we found that this cistern was very deep indeed, much more so than usual. A rope

282 ladder was brought, and when we descended some 10 meters into the interior, we beheld a most impressive sight—enormous vaulted halls, entirely plastered over, with arches resting upon massive pillars and deep niches built into the walls. Two such halls were intact, but the continuation to the west seemed to be destroyed. To the north, a sort of long corridor led down into this structure. What could this have been? While the plastered walls suggested some sort of huge water reservoir, none of us had ever encountered a cistern of this sort.

Only later did we find that earlier explorers of Jerusalem had visited this spot a century ago, when the entire series of six vaults was still intact. Thomas Lewin, in describing his dramatic visit, relates how he and his companion, Dr. Barclay, were lowered by rope into the "subterranean depths" and landed upon a large wooden board afloat in the water. They explored the vaulted chambers and, in one of the niches, found the skeleton of a man who had apparently fallen into the cistern and was unable to get out. In keeping with the spirit of his time, Lewin describes the impressive structure in dramatic terms, ascribing it to the House of Ananias, High Priest in the days of the Second Temple!

Charles Warren, the famed pioneer excavator, visited this cistern and even published a schematic plan of it which, for some unknown reason, he called a "columbarium" (dovecote), but he gave no description. Conrad Schick, too, knew of the cistern, and reported the collapse of several of its vaults. He was astonished by the construction of such a cistern and agreed with Warren's identification of it as a "columbarium." This is a very strange assumption on the part of an architect of Schick's experience in archaeology, but it is certainly indicative of the uniqueness of the unusual construction. It occupied our attention for some time, not because of its monumental size as such, but because of its close ties with the Nea Church.

The interior of this structure (2, p. 233) spreads over an area of some 9.5-17 x 33 meters, and comprises a series of six adjacent vaulted halls. The archways connecting them are borne on massive pillars, 3.5 to 5 meters square. The entire structure is built of compacted rubble covered over with a strong, pinkish plaster. In the

279 northern wall there are two tiers of deep niches, behind which is a long, stepped
281 gallery leading down into the cistern. The upper doorway of the gallery was blocked by the collapse of the ceiling, but we have cleared the debris and opened it up.

All the evidence, in particular the specially plastered walls, and two pottery pipes, show that these vaults had been used for the storage of water. But this was not their main function; such a massive and complex construction would have been built primarily as a substructure for some building originally rising above it. Indeed, above the vaulting we did find remains of walls and pavements. These walls were built in alternating strips of courses of stone and brick, a technique also used in the *289* northern part of the vaults below and one very typical of the Byzantine buildings in Constantinople. This technique was apparently derived from there by builders familiar with it.

This led us to associate the vaulted cistern with the Byzantine Nea Church, close by to the north (1). Moreover, in 1981 the brick-and-stone constructions were *278* found to continue to the north, thus connecting the vault complex with the building of the church. In this context, we assume that the cistern was originally intended to support one of the wings of the Nea Church complex, built over the slope. The construction of this church was an imperial enterprise of monumental proportions, and its execution was entrusted to Theodoros, an architect from Constantinople. As Procopius relates (*Buildings* V, 6):

> The Emperor Justinian gave orders that it be built on the highest of the hills, PROCOPIUS'S DESCRIPTI
> specifying what the length and breadth of the building should be, as well as the
> other details. However, the hill did not satisfy the requirements of the project,
> according to the Emperor's specifications, but a fourth part of the church,
> facing the south and the east, was left unsupported, that part in which the
> priests are wont to perform the rites. Consequently those in charge of this work
> hit upon the following plan. They threw the foundations out as far as the limit
> of the even ground, and then erected a structure which rose as high as the rock.
> And when they had raised this up level with the rock they set vaults upon the
> supporting walls, and joined this substructure to the other foundation of the
> church. Thus the church is partly based upon living rock, and partly carried in
> the air by a great extension artificially added to the hill by the Emperor's
> power.

This is precisely the situation found by us—the local topography, the remains of the Nea Church founded upon bedrock, the vaulting built on the southern slope with the traces of constructions above it, and the supporting wall of the terrace on the south. There is little doubt that our subterranean vaulting is identical with the vaulted substructures mentioned by Procopius. The method of creating an artificially flat expanse by means of subterranean vaulting is a known principle in ancient architecture, and it was one used particularly in Jerusalem. An immediately comparable example is that of the famous "Solomon's Stables" beneath the southeastern corner of the Temple Mount. The vaulted substructure of the Nea Church was apparently considered by its builders to be a particularly worthy achievement; this can be seen in the fact that, besides receiving full credit in Procopius' description, they saw fit to commemorate the achievement in a monumental inscription fixed on one of the walls of the cistern. The discovery of this inscription was, in its own way, the climax of our investigations in the Nea Church. But before telling the story of this discovery I should like to describe a disturbing accident in the field which hampered our work for a while.

A SETBACK IN WORK   While clearing the debris from within the vaults which had collapsed, our "Shoveldozer" removed large quantities of debris from a narrow space some ten meters deep. Abner, its operator, had to execute various breathtaking acrobatics in order to carry out his task, but as he was approaching the floor of the cistern at one spot, the tractor suddenly slid under one of the vaults and sank into the mire up to the top of its tracks. All of Abner's efforts to extract it by its own power came to nought, and it seemed as if the tractor would remain there as an archaeological-technological monument to the 20th century A.D. Quite precariously, a second tractor was sent down into the cistern to rescue its sister out of the mud-hole and onto dry ground. But then the "dry ground" suddenly sank again under Abner's tractor and it was stuck a second time in the mud. With even less room to maneuver now, the rescue tractor was forced to withdraw lest it, too, should sink. Since there was no way for heavy cranes to be brought into effective play, the first tractor remained forlorn, abandoned to its fate.

But not so Abner. In desperation, he resorted to means which reminded me of the man who, having sunk into a quagmire, tried to get himself out by pulling on his own hair. But sure enough, it worked! When the engine was ignited, Abner found that he could move the tracks within the mud, much like car wheels spinning in sand. The tractor moved slightly, but then immediately settled back; and this happened over and over. Then someone suggested putting stones in the space which opened up each time the tractor was put into gear. This, too, was done repeatedly and "dry" ground was slowly built up beneath the tracks. The tractor gradually rose until it could move out and onto true *terra firma*. All in all, it had been rather difficult on the nerves, and a week had been lost in getting the tractor out of the mud, out of the cistern and to freedom. Now we could all breathe freely once again, and everyone was anxious to get back to normal work.

280. Removing debris from the vaulted cistern by tractor

On 8 May 1977, while the tractor was still engaged in removing the earth from the collapsed vaults, the debris within the cistern was still quite high, almost reaching the ceiling. The clearing had been undertaken by an earthmoving contractor, under the supervision of Shlomo Margalit of our staff. At 4:30 pm, my home phone rang and Shlomo excitedly told me that a Greek inscription had been found on the wall. "It's getting late and I'm here all alone. What should I do?"

Had I heard him correctly? A wall inscription? In our excavations? In almost a decade of work in the Jewish Quarter, we had not come across anything like a monumental inscription. I shot over to the excavations like an arrow, and could not believe my eyes. At the top of the southern wall of one of the vaults was a large

tabula ansata (a tablet with "ears") containing a Greek inscription of impressive size, in large, clear letters. Below it was a big cross. All of this was executed in plaster relief, and I had never seen anything like it anywhere in Israel.

After I had brushed away the remaining grains of dirt and began reading, the first thing I saw were the Greek words ERGON ("work") and BASILEOS IOUSTINI-ANOS ("Emperor Justinian"). I knew immediately that what we had found was a building or dedicatory inscription of Justinian himself—as good as his calling card! Precisely what one would have expected in such a spot, but we never believed it would be found.

285. Initial treatment of the Greek inscription discovered on the southern wall of vault 4

I jotted down the inscription excitedly and left together with Shlomo, just as it was getting dark. By midnight, however, I had already returned twice, to make certain that everything was in order, for darkness alone was guarding the precious inscription. The next morning we placed a 24-hour guard over it.

That same night I spent several hours deciphering the text of the inscription. Even though I am not an expert in Greek epigraphy, the contents and significance of the inscription were abundantly clear to me. I telephoned Dr. Yoram Tsafrir and invited him to come to the excavations the next morning. He had recently finished his doctoral thesis on Byzantine Jerusalem, and I knew that the inscription would prove a thrilling experience for him; and later he was to contribute much toward its interpretation. Père Benoit, who was following our excavations closely, was so excited when he saw the inscription that he could only keep mumbling "Unbelievable! Unbelievable!"

For the next few days the local archaeological community descended into our vaults to see the inscription on the wall before we removed it for preservation. In the light of possible danger from current and future construction work, it was thought best to transfer it temporarily to a safer spot, and eventually to return it to its original location. The difficult and delicate task of removing such a large plaster inscription from the hard surface of the wall was successfully undertaken by the staff of the laboratory at the Israel Museum, under the direction of Dodo Shenhav and Rafi Brown.

Removing the inscription from the wall

288. The inscription of Justinian

289. Wall built of alternating strips of stone and brick, above the vaults

Following Roman custom, the inscription is framed by a *tabula ansata* measuring 1.58 meters long; the inscription itself is 1.2 meters long, and the letters are about 8 to 10 centimeters high. Arranged in five lines, the letters were formed in the wet plaster in high relief, and painted red when dry. Despite the fact that several letters were slightly damaged, the almost perfect condition enabled a full reading of the Greek text. In translation, it reads:

> And this is the work which our most pious
> Emperor Flavius Justinianus carried out
> with munificence, under the care and devotion
> of the most holy Constantinus,
> Priest and Hegumen, in the thirteenth (year of the) indiction.

The inscription thus commemorates the building of a structure undertaken on behalf of Justinian, its patron and donor (from other sources, it is known that he contributed toward the building and maintenance of the Nea Church), under the direction of Constantine, abbot of the monastery. The mode of dating—according to the "indiction"—was based on a 15-year cycle between assessments of property for purposes of taxation throughout the Byzantine empire. Justinian's reign covered three such cycles, which fell in A.D. 534/35, 549/50 and 564/65. The second date, A.D. 549/50, was six years after the dedication of the Nea Church and this is most likely the date of construction of this associated structure.

The location of the inscription, in almost total darkness some 8 meters above the floor within a subterranean cistern, indicates that it was not intended to be a display inscription. It was probably made solely for the dedication ceremony, like many foundation inscriptions. The inscription seems to refer not only to the vaults themselves but also to the building above, which has not survived. It was surely one of the buildings of the Nea Church complex, and may even have been the very monastery over which Constantine was abbot.

We are fortunate in that this "hegumen" Constantine can be identified, and his association with the Nea Church confirmed. He was one of the abbots of the monastery of the Nea Church, and is mentioned in Patristic literature: in the late 6th century or the early 7th century A.D. the monk John Moschus wrote of "Abba Constantinus the Hegumen of the (Church of the) Holy Mary, Mother of God, of the Nea." Not only did this clinch the connection between Constantine and the Nea Church, but it infers that the vaulted cistern was indeed part of the church complex.

This brings our episode of the Nea Church to an end for the time being. It represents a rare interlacing of literary source, pictorial descriptions, and architectural remains, as well as epigraphic evidence. This combined material has enabled us to uncover and identify the remains of one of the greatest and most renowned buildings of Byzantine Jerusalem, a structure which influenced the architectural image of the city for several centuries. It has also vividly brought to life an important chapter in the history of the Byzantine city. The cast of this drama includes Justinian, the emperor who lavished much wealth upon the city, the Abbot Constantine, who supervised some of that lavishment, the historian Procopius who perpetuated it in his books, and the anonymous but skilled mosaic artist who tried to capture it graphically for eternity. All these were brought into focus by our excavations, which fully confirmed their accuracy and reliability.

When we place the Nea Church in its proper setting along the southern portion of the *cardo maximus* — for we can now regard them as contemporaneous, and possibly even the enterprise of a single emperor — we can fully realize the great and imposing momentum behind the planning and construction which characterized Byzantine Jerusalem.

290. A gold coin of Anastasius I (A.D. 491-518), minted at Constantinople

CHAPTER SIX

IN THE MIDDLE AGES

Muslim and Crusader Remains

After the conquest of Byzantine Jerusalem by the Muslims, in A.D. 638, the Umayyad rulers instituted widespread building activities around the Temple Enclosure. For the first time since the destruction of the Second Temple in A.D. 70, the Temple Mount again assumed a sacred character, and the Arabs began calling the city *al-Quds*, "The Holy." Caliph Abd al-Malik (A.D. 685-705) erected the Dome of the Rock — the jewel of Early Islamic architecture — and Caliph al-Walid (A.D. 705-715) built the al-Aqsa Mosque (which later underwent major modifications at the hands of the Crusaders). Large buildings were also constructed south and west of the Temple Mount (remains of which have been uncovered in the recent excavations of the Mazar expedition). In the 9th and 10th centuries, Abbasid and Fatimid rule deprived Jerusalem of much of its importance and the city dwindled. But though Jerusalem preserved its sacred status, the seat of rule passed to the newly founded town of Ramle.

We found no Umayyad or other Early Arab building remains in the Jewish Quarter excavations. Since a similar situation prevailed in the excavations of the Kenyon expedition in the Armenian Garden, this entire area was apparently uninhabited in this period.

CRUSADER REMAINS   Jerusalem underwent a decided change, however, after the Crusader conquest in A.D. 1099. As capital of the Crusader kingdom, it again rose to become an administrative and religious center. After the initial slaughter of the Muslim and Jewish inhabitants, Jerusalem remained a purely Christian city, and it was richly embellished with churches, monasteries, and large markets — a focal point for pilgrims from all over Christendom.

Several of the numerous Crusader churches in Jerusalem are still functioning today. Two of them are truly outstanding: the Church of St. Anne near St. Stephen's Gate — the most attractive of all the Crusader churches; and the Crusader-renovated Church of the Holy Sepulcher, a mere shadow of its Byzantine predecessor. Both these structures are typical of Crusader architecture in Jerusalem and of the Romanesque style of the 12th century in general. Complete buildings of the Crusader period have been preserved in the markets as well as in the Citadel. Crusader remains were also discovered in the recent excavations on Mount Zion and in the Armenian Garden; and in Misgav Ladakh Street in the Jewish Quarter,

the ruins of the Church of St. Mary, which had belonged to the Teutonic Order, have been cleared and restored by the Jerusalem Foundation.

Crusader remains came to light in our excavations too. We found vaulted structures reutilized in the present-day shops along Jewish Quarter Street (these were not actually excavated, but rather cleaned of the earth which had filled them in over the years). They had formed part of the medieval bazaars built over the *cardo maximus*, all the way from the Damascus Gate down to the end of Jewish Quarter Street. Many of these Crusader shops had been the property of the Church of St. Anne, as is revealed by inscriptions bearing the legend "SANCTA ANNA," found in some of the shops. Such an inscription was found in secondary use in one of the shops which we cleared in Jewish Quarter Street. A façade of three Crusader shops, with shallow-arched entrances, came to light at the northern end of the Byzantine *cardo*, where a part of the First Wall was discovered (Area X-2). Most of the stones of this facade bore stonemasons' marks of the 12th century.

292. Façade of a Crusader building in Area X-2 (p. 222)

A different sort of remains from the Crusader period came to light in our excavations in the large, open area near the southern city-wall. This area, spreading *293* over a length of some 160 meters, had long served as a dump, the refuse reaching a height of more than six meters. In one typical instance, near a new Armenian residential building on the southern continuation of Ḥabad Street, we found two upright columns forming a north-south line. This roused our curiosity, for the columns lay on the assumed line of the *cardo maximus* (this was still before we had found any remains of the *cardo* itself). We dug a trial pit near one of the columns, in order to see whether it stood in its original place and to find what type of pottery might be at its base. When we reached the bottom, we found that the column was standing on a makeshift base. Amusingly, we also found a medicine bottle from a local "Mother and Child" Clinic from the days of the British Mandate over Palestine, among the various rubbish at the very bottom of the pit, at a depth of some five meters below the present street level!

The proximity of this locale to the city wall lends it a special importance for the topographical problems here, which can be solved only through archaeological excavation. But the spot was covered by enormous quantities of earth and rubble, which would have to be cleared away before we could even begin to excavate methodically. The roadway, too, would have to be moved aside before any archaeological work could commence. Had it not been for the ambitious plan of the Jewish Quarter Reconstruction and Development Company to construct an underground parking lot ("terminal") here, to serve the needs of the entire Jewish Quarter, we would have avoided this far from promising site.

The daring plan for such a parking lot raised quite a row, the public being divided on whether to go ahead with the project or not, whether or not it was to the benefit of the local inhabitants, and whether it might not detract from the special character of the Old City. Although a final decision has yet to be made, whatever the outcome it is clear that the proposal was very beneficial to archaeology. For in the meantime certain groundwork proceeded, including the clearance of the refuse, and archaeological excavations. Without this plan, the site would never have been excavated, and precious archaeological data on the history of Jerusalem would have been left buried forever. Thus, whatever the fate of the "terminal" project, we must be thankful for its very inception.

Among the other structures in this area, we uncovered a Crusader building some 62 meters long (6 in fig. 278) abutting the southern supporting wall of the Byzantine Nea Church complex. As is usual in buildings adjoining such high terrace walls, considerable portions of the Crusader structure have survived, in particular a large *295* hall measuring 11.4 x 16.3 meters, with four stout columns arranged in a square. These massive columns, with attractive Attic bases but no capitals above, had supported a ceiling of nine cross-vaults, only traces of which have survived on the northern wall. The height of the vaults from floor to top was 7.4 meters. Along the walls they were supported by stylized Corinthian capitals resting upon elbow-*297* shaped consoles embedded in the wall. These capitals, as well as the peculiar consoles, are typical of the Crusader architecture of the 12th century. Smaller capitals of this type, found in the debris within the hall, may indicate the former

249

293. Removal of massive debris, prior to excavations in Areas T-2 and T-4 (p. 32)

existence of an upper story, also hinted at by the thickness of the walls. However, we are unable to determine the precise function of this impressive public hall. After the Crusades, apparently in the Mamluk period, various installations were established within the hall, serving some craft which required large quantities of water.

Such an impressive building should have found mention in contemporaneous literary sources, and it might still be possible to identify it more positively. At present we tend to assume that it was the basement of a Crusader church, the ground floor of which has entirely disappeared. Crusader sources mention a "Church of St. Peter ad Vincula" in this general vicinity. The Crusaders would often use the remains of Byzantine structures for building their own churches and, in the present instance their church (?) was placed adjoining the supporting wall of the Nea Church complex.

In the eastern part of the Crusader building we uncovered a hypocaust, the fire-chamber beneath the hot-room of a bathhouse. It was built of pillars of stone, which had been damaged severely by the fire and the high temperatures. In order to strengthen the ceiling of this chamber, large fragments of round basalt millstones had been inserted as supports. The walls of the bathing chamber itself were not lined with pottery flues for heating it, as in the Byzantine bathhouse discovered in our Area C (p. 32). The few pottery flues within the walls here had served merely to ventilate the hypocaust.

294. Start of excavations between the Crusader building and the city wall (Area T-3, p. 32)

278

Some 30 meters south of the Crusader building near the present-day city wall, another wall 2.5 meters thick and 45 meters long, was uncovered (7, p. 233). It was built on the foundations of the Byzantine wall bordering the stepped street (5) mentioned previously, and its continuation to the east runs beneath the Turkish city wall. This wall contains a gate with two towers jutting inward, which we tend to regard as part of the southern Crusader city wall. One would expect the Crusaders to have built a more impressive fortification here, and this might actually have been part of the earlier Abbasid fortification which the Crusaders reutilized. Many scholars have assumed that the southern Turkish city wall was founded upon the Crusader line of fortification here, but the facts are clearer now. Moreover, there is a stretch of some 45 meters of the Crusader wall here which is not covered by the Turkish wall.

AN AYYUBID TOWER

298

The Crusader wall was cut on the west by a mighty tower which also cut through the stepped Byzantine street. This tower spreads over an area of 23 x 23 meters and contains a chamber measuring 12 x 13 meters with a pillar at its center. It is built of large ashlars with dressed margins. Though some twelve courses of the solid base of the tower are preserved, only fragments of the upper courses have survived above the floor level of the chamber.

The present-day Turkish wall passes over the southern wall of the tower in such a manner that only a thin strip of it juts outside the Old City. This part of the tower

295. The columned building from the Crusader period, looking north (Area T-2, p. 32)

296. Within the Crusader building

had been uncovered by M. Broshi prior to our discovery of the tower within the walls. Among the fallen ashlars there, there were stones which Broshi ascribed to the gate of the tower; the precise position of this gate is not known. One of these ashlars bears a monumental Arabic inscription ascribing the building of the tower to the Ayyubid Caliph al-Malik al-Mu'azzam 'Isa of Damascus, in 1212. In 1219, only seven years after the tower was built, a Muslim historian relates that al-Mu'azzam 'Isa ordered the walls of Jerusalem to be dismantled in order to prevent them from falling into the hands of the invading Crusaders. What forced al-Mu'azzam 'Isa into this desperate act was the realization that he had little chance of preventing the capture of the city. Though painful even to the Muslims themselves, this act was in keeping with the "scorched earth" policy so often practiced in that day. Most of the inhabitants fled the city after the walls had been razed. It would seem, however, that al-Mu'azzam 'Isa was somewhat hasty, for the Crusaders hesitated in coming and it was not until 1229, ten years later, that the open city fell

297. The Crusader capital

298. The Ayyubid tower

into their hands without a fight. According to other historical sources, the walls of Jerusalem remained in ruins for an extended period. In 1488 Rabbi Obadiah of Bertenoro, who visited the Holy City, wrote home to his father: "The greater part of Jerusalem is destroyed and desolate, not to mention that it has no walls." The city wall was not rebuilt until 1538, under the Turkish Sultan Suleiman the Magnificent.

These events find expression in our archaeological excavations. The stones of the dismantled Ayyubid tower were scattered about by the hundreds, on and around the ruins of the tower. At one spot they spilled over an adjacent building, showing that even nearby dwellings were intentionally destroyed. The heaps of stones lay in place for hundreds of years without being disturbed, until the mid-16th century when Suleiman the Magnificent laid down the not so magnificent foundations of the Turkish wall — directly over the toppled rubble, as can be seen in our *299* photograph.

The suggested gate of the Ayyubid tower is located opposite the *cardo maximus*, THE NAME OF THE GATE the long north-south axis of Roman-Byzantine Jerusalem. The existence of an internal gate here in Byzantine times is documented in the Madaba map, as noted in the previous chapter. The name of the gate in this late period is not known for sure. In Crusader maps of the city, the gate located here is called "Zion Gate." The building of the Ayyubid tower brought about the total destruction of any possible earlier gates on the site.

It has been suggested that the Arabic name for this gate was "*Bab al-Tih,*" mentioned in the list of gates of Jerusalem by the famed Arab geographer Muqaddasi (around 985) and appearing also in a work by Yaqut (around 1225), another Arab geographer, though with a minor change in the Arabic spelling, reading *Bab al-Nih.* The French scholar Clermont-Ganneau suggested a century ago that this second spelling reflects the correct name of the gate (the interchange of *t* for *n* in Arabic is a common misreading, for the two letters are almost identical); he interpreted the name as the "Nea Gate"! Clermont-Ganneau did not, of course, know of the exact site of either the gate or the church. But now — after the discovery

Turkish city wall, built directly over the rubble of the ower

300. Oil lamps of the Mamluk period, found in a potter's kiln. Their form is similar to that of lamps of the Iron Age (7th century B.C.)

of the Ayyubid tower and the remains of the Nea Church only some 50 meters to the northeast — this identification (recently suggested by Y. Tsafrir and M. Sharon) seems quite reasonable. After the deliberate destruction of the Ayyubid tower in the 13th century, no gate was rebuilt on this site. With the construction of the Turkish walls in the 16th century, the Zion Gate was shifted some 120 meters farther to the west.

MAMLUK REMAINS   Going back somewhat, to the Mamluk period, Muslim religious and secular building increased in Jerusalem under the rule of the Egyptian Mamluks (1250-1517). Religious academies, hospitals, pilgrim hostels, and bazaars were established, and pilgrim traffic to the city grew — for Jerusalem is the third Holy City of Islam. These buildings, most of which still stand, have given the city its Islamic architectural character, as can best be seen in the Muslim Quarter of the Old City.

There are no significant buildings of this type among the houses of the Jewish
300   Quarter. We discovered the scattered remains of structures, potters' kilns, pottery, glass, and the like in our excavations, all witnessing to the occupation of this area in the Mamluk period. But no outstanding finds were made, certainly nothing particu-
302   larly worthy of mention in our brief review here, except possibly a choice group of Mamluk pottery.

THE TURKISH WALL   The Ottoman Turks captured Jerusalem in 1517, ushering in their 400-year rule over the city, which came to an end only when the British Army entered its gates in 1917. The Ottoman period is actually outside the framework of our archaeological survey, and, in any event, our excavations have contributed nothing to the history of this period. Most of the ruined buildings cleared away to make room for the reconstruction were of this period, though there were some medieval structures as well. We have already mentioned one major Ottoman project, the construction of the city walls under Suleiman the Magnificent, and this wall still frames the Old City of Jerusalem, protecting the historical and cultural heritage concealed within.

255

301. The photographers at work

...azed pottery and an ornamented glass bowl (center), of the Mamluk period

Visitors watching the discovery of a
...ic floor in Area O-2 (p. 32)

304. In the courtyard of the rebuilt Batei-
Maḥse, a meeting-point of remains of the
past and the generation of the future

EPILOGUE

In reviewing the results of our excavations in the Jewish Quarter as presented in the previous chapters, we may say that they have brought the Upper City of Jerusalem out of the realm of oblivion and into the light of day, adding new dimensions to the history of the city and its material culture. We, the excavators, have been following the tracks of Jerusalem's history for a full decade. We have trodden unknown paths, and have viewed scenes not observed by man for many centuries.

During the course of our work it became evident that, despite the repeated destruction which befell Jerusalem, there were sufficient archaeological remains to facilitate the reconstruction of the Upper City and its history. We were able to see this city unfold from a totally unknown entity—a bare concept—into a tangible reality, before our very eyes. Equally fascinating was the correlation of our archaeological findings with the ancient literary source, which enabled us to view our discoveries in a proper historical framework. Even if the picture now before us is still far from complete, our excavations have put the investigation of ancient Jerusalem on a new track and advanced it by leaps and bounds. This work has not come to an end with the conclusion of our excavations, and it is deeply hoped that future excavations will continue to reveal the hidden treasures of the Holy City.

Despite great disturbances to the various archaeological strata, there were still some areas remaining where we could determine the precise stratigraphy of the locale, from the earliest settlement till modern times. And these enabled us to ascertain, beyond the shadow of a doubt, that the area was initially settled in the 8th century B.C.

The Western Hill of Jerusalem had not yet been settled in the days of David, Solomon, and the early kings of Judah, except perhaps by a few isolated farmers. It was not until the confines of the City of David were too pressing that the first urban settlers came to the hill from the walled town near the Gihon spring. This process apparently began early in the 8th century B.C., possibly in the days of Amaziah or Uzziah. The process quickened after the northern Kingdom of Israel was conquered by the Assyrians in 722 B.C., when a large number of refugees poured into the city. The population was further swelled by an influx of rural Judeans who sought refuge in the capital after Sennacherib's campaign of 701 B.C. The new residential quarters seem to be mentioned in the Bible under the names *Mishneh* and *Makhtesh*. At first these suburbs were entirely undefended, but eventually they came to be encompassed by a mighty city wall. The thick wall and the massive gate-tower which were part of this fortification were revealed in our excavations. These two discoveries are located on the northern line of defence of the city, confirming Josephus' description of the existence of a city wall on this flank from the period of the First Temple. We have assumed that our thick wall was built under Hezekiah, and that it encompassed the entire Western Hill, joining up with the walls of the City of David on the south to form a single, unified city. The position of the tower indicates that changes were eventually made in the northern course of this wall. The traces of a conflagration which we found near the tower, along with arrowheads, point to fierce fighting here — undoubtedly the final siege by Nebuchadnezzar in 586 B.C.

Our excavations reveal that there was a break in occupation on the Western Hill after the destruction of Jerusalem by the Babylonians. This stratigraphic-chronological gap lasted several centuries, for no archaeological remains of the Persian period were found here. In the days of the Return from Exile, the population was apparently too small and poor to populate more than the limited confines of the City of David; the Western Hill therefore remained barren and uninhabited for a considerable time.

It was not until the 2nd century B.C. that the city once again spread to the Western Hill. This was certainly a gradual process, which began early in the century. But only after 152 B.C., under the Hasmoneans, was the hill again fortified with a city wall, today known as the First Wall. We have uncovered the remains of this wall and a tower on its northern line. Interestingly, the Hasmonean structures were integrated with remains of Israelite fortifications.

During the period of the Herodian dynasty, Jerusalem attained a grandeur never before seen in the city. This growth is expressed mainly in public building projects such as the Temple Mount, the fortifications, and the public water supply. However, the Jewish Quarter excavations uncovered another Jerusalem — a secular, everyday Jerusalem with a residential quarter whose splendor outshone everything previously known in the city. This was a very wealthy quarter, with large mansions embellished with frescoes and colorful mosaics, complex bathing installations, luxury goods, and artistic objects — all "status symbols" of the times. These were well-cultivated homes lavishing under the influence of a style common throughout the Hellenistic-Roman world. This newly revealed character of the Upper City emphasizes the uniqueness and significance of our excavations.

This flourishing quarter met a violent end when Jerusalem was destroyed by the Roman army in A.D. 70: a month after the Temple was burnt, the Roman legions captured the Upper City and put it, too, to the torch. The remains of that fierce conflagration could still be seen in the buildings uncovered along the eastern edge of the quarter, opposite the Temple Mount.

Over the ruins of Jewish Jerusalem arose a Roman city which Hadrian named Aelia Capitolina. This new town spread over the northern part of the Old City, but no Roman building remains have been identified in the south, in the area of our excavations. The southern part of the city remained desolate throughout this Roman phase, except for the camp of the tenth legion, and this area was rebuilt only in the Byzantine period, when Jerusalem became a Christian metropolis. We uncovered the remains of two monumental architectural enterprises of this new period of splendor: the main street of the city, actually a Byzantine southern extension of the Roman *cardo maximus*; and the famed Nea Church built by Justinian in the 6th century A.D. Our discovery of this church was crowned by the finding of a dedicatory inscription in Greek, naming Justinian.

After the Arab Conquest, Jerusalem declined to the status of a provincial town. Its only importance stemmed from its religious significance to Islam, focusing upon the mosque and shrine built in the Temple Enclosure. Only sparse remains of this period were found in the Jewish Quarter excavations, the most outstanding of which is a defensive tower of the Ayyubid period. In contrast, we uncovered extensive Crusader building remains, many of them now integrated into structures of Mamluk and Ottoman date which are, in turn, part of the present-day tangle of buildings.

Having now completed our historical tour of the archaeological remains in the Jewish Quarter, I should like to point out that during our decade of work there, as excavators, we were witness to another historical process. This new process, which is still evolving before our very eyes, reflects the pattern of the past—war-destruction-restoration—patterns which have repeated themselves throughout the long course of Jerusalem's history. Much of the Jewish Quarter was destroyed in the Arab-Israel War of 1948, when the Jewish inhabitants of the quarter were forced from their homes. But Jews returned to the Old City after the Six-Day War of 1967, and began clearing the ruins and rebuilding their homes and synagogues. Now, after a decade of this restoration in the quarter along with our archaeological excavations—the Jewish Quarter is once again coming to life, and the voices of children are resounding in its streets. With this in mind, we recall the words of the prophet Isaiah (52:9): "Break forth into singing, you waste places of Jerusalem, for the Lord has comforted His people, He has redeemed Jerusalem!"

CHRONOLOGICAL TABLE
5000 YEARS OF JERUSALEM'S HISTORY

Date	Period	Rulers / Persons	Events	Notes
B.C. 3000	Early Bronze Age			— Earliest settlement on Eastern Hill
2500				— Salim (Jerusalem?) mentioned in Ebla Texts
2000	Middle Bronze Age	Patriarchal Period		— Jerusalem mentioned in Egyptian "Execration Texts"
1500				
1400	Late Bronze Age	El-Amarna Period		— "Abdi-Ḥeba, king of Jerusalem" appears in Amarna Letters
1300				
1200		Period of the Judges	— Israelite Conquest of Canaan	
1100				
1000		Saul / David / Solomon		— "Jebus"
				— David captures city, renames it "City of David"
900	Israelite Period (Iron Age)		— Division of Israelite Kingdom	— Solomon builds Temple and palace
800				— Western Hill first settled
700		Uzziah / Hezekiah / Manasseh / Zedekiah	— 722, Fall of Samaria and Northern Kingdom	— Hezekiah builds Siloam Tunnel and city wall on Western Hill
600			— 701, Sennacherib's Invasion	
500			— 586, Fall of Jerusalem and Kingdom of Judah	— Destruction of Jerusalem
400	Persian Period	Nehemiah		— Restoration of city wall; resettlement of City of David; Western Hill abandoned
300			— 332, Alexander the Great conquers Palestine	
200	Hellenistic Period	Antiochus IV / Judas Maccabeus / Jonathan/Simon / Alexander Janneus	— 167, Outbreak of the Maccabean Revolt	— Western Hill resettled
100	Hasmonean Period			— City Wall on Western Hill rebuilt
0	Herodian Period	Herod the Great / Herod Agrippa I	— Ministry of Jesus	— Temple rebuilt by Herod
A.D. 100			— 66, Outbreak of First Jewish Revolt	— 70, Destruction of entire city. Roman army camp on Western Hill
		Hadrian	— 135, Outbreak of Bar Kokhba Revolt	— 131, "Aelia Capitolina" founded by Hadrian; Western Hill largely abandoned
200	Roman Period			
300		Constantine the Great		— Church of Holy Sepulchre built
400		Eudocia		— City wall on Western Hill rebuilt
500	Byzantine Period	Justinian		— Southern cardo maximus and "Nea" Church built
600			— 614, Persian Invasion	
700			— 640, Muslim Conquest of Palestine	— 691, Dome of the Rock built
800		Umayyads		
900	Early Arab Period	Abbasids		
1000				
1100			— Crusader Kingdom	— 1099, Crusaders conquer Jerusalem
1200	Crusader Period	Mu'azzam 'Isa		— 1212, City walls rebuilt, dismantled 7 years later
1300				
1400	Late Arab Period	The Mamlūks		
1500		Suleiman the Magnificent	— 1514, Ottoman Turks conquer Palestine	— 1537, Suleiman rebuilds city walls (still standing)
1600				
1700	Ottoman Period			
1800				
1900			— 1917-18, British conquer Palestine	— 1867, First archaeological excavations in Jerusalem
			— 1948, State of Israel established	— 1948, Arab Legion occupies Old City; Jewish Quarter partly destroyed
				— 1967, Jerusalem reunified under Israel
				— 1968, Jewish Quarter rebuilt
				— 1969, Archaeological excavations in the Jewish Quarter

Ed. R. Grafman

Selected Bibliography*

General, Summaries:
F.J. Bliss and A.C. Dickie: *Excavations at Jerusalem, 1894-1897*, London, 1898.
L.-H. Vincent: *Jérusalem antique*, Paris, 1912.
L.-H. Vincent and F.-M. Abel: *Jérusalem nouvelle* I-III, Paris, 1914-1926.
L.-H. Vincent and M.-A. Steve: *Jérusalem de l'ancien Testament* I-III, Paris, 1954-1956.
J. Simons: *Jerusalem in the Old Testament*, Leiden, 1952 (and the Bibliography there, on pp. 505-508). A comprehensive summary including also later periods.
M. Avi-Yonah, ed.: *Sefer Yerushalayim* I, Jerusalem-Tel Aviv, 1956*.
Kathleen M. Kenyon: *Jerusalem. Excavating 3000 Years of History*, London, 1967.
Kathleen M. Kenyon: *Digging Up Jerusalem*, London, 1974.
B. Mazar: *Cities and Districts in Eretz-Israel*, Jerusalem, 1975, pp. 11-44*.
Y. Yadin, ed.: *Jerusalem Revealed. Archaeology in the Holy City, 1968-1974*, Jerusalem-New Haven, 1976.
Encyclopedia of Archaeological Excavations in the Holy Land II, ed. M. Avi-Yonah, Jerusalem, 1976, s.v. Jerusalem, pp. 579-647.

Excavations in the Old City, especially on the Western Hill:
C.N. Johns: "The Citadel, Jerusalem. A Summary of Work since 1934," *Quarterly of the Department of Antiquities in Palestine* 14 (1950), pp. 121-190.
A.D. Tushingham: "The Armenian Garden," *Palestine Exploration Quarterly* 100 (1968), pp. 109-111.
Ruth Amiran and A. Eitan: "Excavations in the Courtyard of the Citadel, Jerusalem, 1968-1969. Preliminary Report," *Israel Exploration Journal* 20 (1970), pp. 9-17.
B. Mazar: *The Excavations in the Old City of Jerusalem near the Temple Mount. Preliminary Report of the First Season, 1968*, Jerusalem, 1969; *Preliminarty Report of the Second and Third Seasons, 1969-1970*, Jerusalem, 1971.
B. Mazar: "Herodian Jerusalem in the Light of the Excavations South and South-West of the Temple Mount", *Israel Exploration Journal* 28 (1978), pp. 230-237.
N. Avigad: "Excavations in the Jewish Quarter of the Old City of Jerusalem (Preliminary Reports)," *Israel Exploration Journal* 20 (1970), pp. 1-8, 129-140; 22 (1972), pp. 193-200; 25 (1975), pp. 260-261; 27 (1977), pp. 55-57, 145-151; 28 (1978), pp. 200-201.
N. Avigad: *Archaeological Discoveries in the Jewish Quarter of Jerusalem*, Second Temple Period; Israel Museum Catalogue No. 144, Jerusalem, 1976.
D. Bahat and M. Broshi: "Excavations in the Armenian Garden," in Y. Yadin, ed.: *Jerusalem Revealed*, Jerusalem-New Haven, 1976.
M. Broshi: "Excavations in the House of Caiaphas, Mount Zion," in Y. Yadin, ed.: *Jerusalem Revealed*, Jerusalem, New Haven, 1976.
M. Broshi: "Along Jerusalem's Walls," *Biblical Archaeologist* 40 (1077), pp. 11-17.
Ute Lux: "Vorläufiger Bericht über die Ausgrabung unter der Erlöserkirche in Muristan in der Altstadt von Jerusalem in den Jahren 1970 und 1971," *Zeitschrift des Deutschen Palästina-Vereins* 88 (1972), pp. 185-201.
Y. Shiloh: "City of David Excavation 1978", *Biblical Archaeologist*, 42 (1979), pp. 165-171; *ibid.* "The City of David Archaeological Project: The Third Season — 1980", *BA*, 44 (1981), pp. 161-170.

The Expansion of ancient Jerusalem to the Western Hill:
M. Avi-Yonah: "The Walls of Nehemiah — A Minimalist View," *Israel Exploration Journal* 4 (1954), p. 239.

---

* Publications in Hebrew are marked with an asterisk

Ruth Amiran: "The Necropolis of Jerusalem in the Time of the Monarchy," *Judah and Jerusalem. The Twelfth Archaeological Convention*, Jerusalem, 1957, pp. 65-72*.

E.-M. Laperrousaz: "L'extension préexilique de Jérusalem sur la colline occidentalle," *Revue des études juives* 134 (1975), pp. 3-30; *ibid*. Le problème du "Premier Mur" et du "Deuxième Mur" de Jérusalem après la réfutation décisive de la "Minimalist View", *Homage à Georges Vajda*, ed. G. Nahon et Ch. Touati, Lovain, 1980, pp. 13-35.

M. Broshi: "The Expansion of Jerusalem in the Reigns of Hezekiah and Manasseh," *Israel Exploration Journal* 24 (1974), pp. 21-26.

A. Mazar: "Iron Age Burial Caves North of the Damascus Gate, Jerusalem," *Israel Exploration Journal* 26 (1976), pp. 1-8.

G. Barkay and A. Kloner: "Burial Caves North of Damascus Gate, Jerusalem," *Israel Exploration Journal* 26 (1976), pp. 55-57.

D. Davis and A. Kloner: "A Burial Cave of the Late Israelite Period on the Slopes of Mt. Zion," *Qadmoniot* 11 (1978), pp. 16-19*.

H. Geva: "The Western Boundary of Jerusalem at the End of the Monarchy," *Israel Exploration Journal* 29 (1979), pp. 84-91.

A.D. Tushingham: "The Western Hill under the Monarchy," *Zeitschrift der Deutschen Palästina-Vereins* 95 (1979), pp. 39-55.

Ancient sources on the topography of Jerusalem in Second Temple times:
Flavius Josephus' *Antiquities of the Jews* and his *The Jewish War* (both available in "Penguin" editions).
1 and 2 *Maccabees* in the Apocrypha.

Varia:
A. Strobel: "Die Südmauer Jerusalems zur Zeit Jesu," in O. Benz, et al., eds.: *Josephus-Studien*, Göttingen, 1974, pp. 344-361.

J. Wilkinson: "The Streets of Jerusalem," *Levant* 7 (1975), pp. 118-136.

Y. Tsafrir: "The Location of the Seleucid Akra in Jerusalem, *Revue Biblique*, 82 (1975), pp. 501-521.

For specific comparative material see:
Y. Yadin: *Masada*, New York, 1966.

S.S. Weinberg: "Tel Anafa: The Hellenistic Town," *Israel Exploration Journal* 21 (1976), pp. 86-109.

V.J. Bruno: "Antecedents of the Pompeian First Style," *American Journal of Archaeology* 73 (1969), pp. 305-317, pls. 67-70.

R. Ling: "Stucco Decoration in Pre-Augustan Italy," *Papers of the British School of Rome* 40 (1972), pp. 11-57, pls. I-XV.

On the matter of early blown glass, see:
Yael Israeli: "Sidonian Mold-Blown Glass Vessels in the Museum Haaretz," *Journal of Glass Studies* 6 (1964), pp. 34-41.

Gladys D. Weinberg: "Glass Manufacture in Hellenistic Rhodes," *Archaiologikon Deltion* 24 (1969), pp. 143-151 (Athens, 1971).

Gladys D. Weinberg: "Hellenistic Glass from Tel Anafa in Upper Galilee," *Journal of Glass Studies* 12 (1970), pp. 17-27.

D.F. Grose: "Early Blown Glass," *Journal of Glass Studies* 19 (1977), pp. 9-29.

Gusta Lehrer: *Ennion—A First Century Glass-maker* (Exhibition Catalogue, Museum Haaretz), Tel Aviv, 1979.

On the *menorah* symbol, see:
B. Narkiss: "The Scheme of the Sanctuary from the Time of Herod the Great," *Journal of Jewish Art* 1 (1974), pp. 6-14.

N. Avigad: *Beth-Shearim* III, Jerusalem-New Brunswick, N.J., 1976, pp. 268-274.

On ritual baths, see:
J. Schönberg: *Miqwaot* ("Ritual Baths"), Jerusalem, 1973*.
R. Reich: "Mishnah, Sheqalim 8:2 and the Archaeological Evidence," *Jerusalem in the Second Temple Period* (A. Schalit Memorial volume), ed. A. Oppenheimer et al., Jerusalem, 1980, pp. 225-256*

On stone carving in Jerusalem, see:
N. Avigad: *Ancient Monuments in the Kidron Valley*, Jerusalem, 1954, esp. pp. 84-85, figs. 46-47*.
N. Avigad: "The Burial-Vault of a Nazirite Family on Mount Scopus," *Israel Exploration Journal* 21 (1971), pp. 185-200.

Material relating to the Jerusalem stone tables:
Gisela M. Richter: *The Furniture of the Greeks, Etruscans and Romans*, London, 1966.
L.Y. Rahmani: "Table-top of the Late Second Temple Period," *Sefunim* 5 (1976), pp. 67-71.
Uza Zevulun and Yael Olnik: *Function and Design in the Talmudic Period* (Catalogue, Museum Haaretz), Tel Aviv, 1978, pp. 3-6.

On bone gaming-pieces, see:
M. Rostovtzeff: "Interpretation des tessères en os," *Revue archéologique* (IVe serie) (1905), pp. 110-124.
M.M. Bieber: *The History of the Greek and Roman Theater*, Princeton, 1961, pp. 186, 246-247.
Elizabeth Alföldi-Rosenbaum: "The Finger Calculus in Antiquity and in the Middle Ages, Studies on Roman Game Counters I," *Frühmittelalterliche Studien* 5 (1971), pp. 1-9.
Elizabeth Alföldi-Rosenbaum: "Alexandriaca, Studies on Roman Game Counters III," *Chiron* 6 (1976), pp. 205-239.

On Byzantine Jerusalem, see:
M. Avi-Yonah: *The Madaba Mosaic Map*, Jerusalem, 1954.
Y. Tsafrir: *Zion—The South-Western Hill of Jerusalem and its Place in the Urban Development of the City in the Byzantine Period* (unpublished Doctoral Thesis, Hebrew University, Jerusalem, 1975)* (with English Summary).
J.T. Milik: "La Topographia de Jérusalem vers la fin de l'époque byzantine," *Mélanges de l'Université Saint Joseph* (Beyrouth) 37 (1960-1961), pp. 127-189 (esp. pp. 145-151, on the "Nea" Church).

For Byzantine colonnaded streets, see:
C.A.R. Radford: "Justinia Prima (Tsaritsin Grad): A 6th Century City in Southern Serbia," *Antiquity* 109 (1954), pp. 15-18.
D. Claude: *Die byzantinische Stadt im 6. Jahrhundert*, Munich, 1969, esp. "Kolonnaden-strassen," pp. 60-63.

On the "Nea" Church, see:
Procopius: *Buildings* V, 6 (Loeb edition, ed. by H.B. Dewing and G. Downey, London, 1954, pp. 342-343).
N. Avigad: "A Building Inscription of the Emperor Justinian and the Nea in Jerusalem," *Israel Exploration Journal* 27 (1977), pp. 145-151.
Y. Tsafrir: "Muqaddasi's Gates of Jerusalem—A New Identification Based on Byzantine Sources," *Israel Exploration Journal* 27 (1977), pp. 152-161.
M. Ben-Dov: "More on the Nea Church", *Biblical Archaeology Review* 4 (1978), pp. 48-49.

For Umayyad building in Jerusalem, see:
M. Ben-Dov: "The Omayyad Structures near the Temple Mount," in B. Mazar: *Excavations in the Old City of Jerusalem near the Temple Mount. Preliminary Report of the Second and Third Seasons, 1969-1970*, Jerusalem, 1971.

Illustration Credits

Most of the black-and-white photographs were taken by Avinoam Glick, and some by Zeev Radovan, David Harris and Photo Emka.
The color photographs of the excavations were taken by the author, except Nos. 132-140, by Zeev Radovan.
The color photographs of the objects were taken by Zeev Radovan, David Harris and the author.
The other photographs are by: Dan Bahat (1); Pantomap (3-4), J. Schweig (17); Jerusalem District Police Photo-Lab (18); The Israel Museum (127, 197); and Palphot Ltd. (264).
The drawings are by: Peter Bugod (63, 67, 92, 121, 130); Florica Vainer, Israel Museum (96); Alina Friedlander (115, 196, 214); J. Schmeisser (220); and Leen Ritmeyer (86, 90, 91, 180, 270).
The plans and topographical maps were prepared by the expedition staff.

Abbasids, 247
Abraham, 41
Adonizedek, 24
Aelia Capitolina, 205-207, 212, 225, 226, 227
Aelia Capitolina gates, 206
Agrippa I (*See* Herod Agrippa I)
Agrippa II, 94
Ahimaaz, 44
Ahrensburg, B., 137
Ain Feshkha, 127, 174
Akra, 63, 64-65
al-Aqsa Mosque, 247
Alexander Balas, 64, 73
Alexander Janneus, 73, 75, 85, 147, 191
Alexander the Great, 63
Alexandria, 193, 194
Alföldi, E., 194
Amiran, Ruth, 20, 45, 67
Ananias, 82
Antiochia, 63, 64, 162
Antiochus III, 63
Antiochus IV Epiphanes, 63, 64, 162
Ararat, 211
Araunah the Jebusite, 24
Arch of Titus, 148
Ark of the Covenant, Holy, 24
arm, **135**, 137
Armenian Garden, 29, 30, 45, 247
Armenian Quarter, 20, 63, 71, 205, 206
arrowheads, **52**, 53, **53**, **70**
Ashdod, 23
Assyrians, 24
Avi-Yonah, Michael, 64, 162
Ayyubid gate, 254
Ayyubid tower, 251, 253-254, **254**

B

Bab el-Amud (*See* Gate of the Column)
Babylonians, 29
Bahat, Dan, 20
Barag, Dan, 189
Bar-Kokhba, 146
Bar-Kokhba Revolt [Second Jewish Revolt], 205
Batei Mahse, 230, **257**
bath, ritual immersion [miqveh], 111, 139-143, 140, 141, 143
bath room, 104, **104**, **154**, **160**, 210
Benaiah, 44
Ben-Dov, Meir, 232
Benoit, Pierre, 231, 242
Bethel Synagogue, 161
Bethlehem, 175
Bieber, M.M., 193
Birket el-Hamra (*See* Lower Pool)
Bliss-Dickie expedition, 14, 60, 67

bone objects, **193**, **199**, **200**
bowls, **74**, **75**, 117, **117**, 118, 179, **187-188**, **198**
Brand, J., 174
Broad Wall, 62
bronze spoons, **199**
Broshi, Magen, 20, 45, 67, 150, 253
Brown, Rafi, 242
Bugod, Peter, 216
Burj Kibrit, 232, 234
Burnt House, 106, 120-139, **121**, **124**, **126**, **133-136**, 195
Byzantine captials, **225**

C

Caesarea, 82, 149
Caliph Abd al-Malik, 247
Caliph al-Malik al-Mu'azzam 'Isa, 253
Caliph al-Walid, 247
Canaan, 23
cardo maximus, 49, 205, 211, 213-229, **213**, **214**, **215**, **217**, **222-224**, 246, 248, 254
Central Valley [Tyropoeon Valley], 26, 29, 54, 55, 57, 229
Chen, Doron, 225
Christian Quarter, 20, 29
Christian Quarter Road, 206
Church of St. Anne, 247, 248
Church of St. Mary, 248
Church of St. Sion, 208, 212
Church of the Holy Sepulchre, 205, 208, 213, 226, 227, 247
cisterns, **105**, 235-239, **237**, **238-239**, **240**, **241**
Citadel, 20, 45, 62, 71, 206, 247
City of David, 24, 26, 27, 28, 29, 54, 55, 77
Claudius Caesar, 94, 195
Clermont-Ganneau, 254
coin mold, **129**
coins, 75, **75**, **76**, 77, **77**, 170, 194-196, **194**, **195**, **200**, 246
column base, 151-152, **152**, 161, 177, **221**
Constantine the Great, 208, 226
Constantinople, 236
cooking pots, 119
Corinthian capital, 151, **151**, **178**
Crusader remains, 218-220, 247-251, **248**, **250**, **251**, **252**, **253**
Crusader wall, 251
Cyrus of Persia, 61

D

Damascus Gate, 59, 205, 211, 228, 229, 248
Dan, tribe of, 42
David, 24, 26, 27, 28, 29
David Street, 53, 206, 212

David's Tomb, 26
decumanus, 205, 206
Delos, 174
Demetrius I, 72
Demetrius II, 64
Der Deutscher Platz, 230
de Saulcy, F., 13
Didyma, 161
Dome of the Rock, 82, 247
Double Gate, 20
Dura-Europos, 146

E

Early Wall (*See* First Wall)
Eastern Hill [Ophel Hill], 24, 26, 27, 29, 30, 62, 77
Ebla [Tell Mardikh], 23
Egypt, 23
Eitan, Avraham, 20, 45, 67
el-Amarna, 23
el-Wad (Valley) Street, 212
Essene sect, 143
Eudocia, 208, 229
Execration Texts, 23
Ezra the Scribe, 61

F

Fahn, A., 98
Fatimids, 257
figurines, **36**, **40**
First Wall [Early Wall], 37-39, 47, 48, 50, 50, 56, 65-74, 248
Fish Gate, 54
fresco, 103, **112-114**, **157-159**

G

Gate of the Column [*Bab el-Amud*], 212
Gennath Gate, 69
Geva, Hillel, 46, 60, 216
Gihon Spring, 23, 24, 26, 27, 56
glass blowing, 189-191, **190**
glassware, 107, **108**, 117, 186, **187-188**, 189, 192
Golden Gate, 212

H

Habad Street 212, 216, 249
Hadrian, 205, 228
Hamalakh Street, 216
Haram al-Sharif (*See* Temple Mount)
Hasmonean tower, **68**, **69**, 70, 71
Hasmonean palace, 65
Hasmoneans, 29, 30, 65, 71, 72, 77
Hazor, 23
Hebron, 43
Heraclius, 208
Herod Agrippa I [Agrippa I], 29, 60, 194, 195
Herod Archelaus, 194
Herod the Great, 81-82, 84, 144, 147, 162, 194

Herodian Residence, 84-95, **84**, **85**, **86**, **90**, **91**
Herodians, 77
Herodium, 82, 149
Herod's palace, Masada, 142
Hezekiah, 24, 43, 56, 60
Hezekiah's Tunnel, 24, 27
Hinnom Valley, 26
Hippicus Tower, 82
Hofri, Sara, 129
House of Ananias, 235
Huldah the Prophetess, 54
Hurvah Synagogue, 88

I

inkwell, **127**
inscriptions, 129-131, 196, **201**, **202**, **202**, **203**, 240-245, **242**, **243-244**, 248
Ionic capitals, 161-162, **161**, **162**, **163-164**, 165
Isaiah, 55
Israeli, Yael, 117
Israelite tower, 49-54, **51**, **52**
Israelite wall, 46-49, **47**, **48**

J

Jaffa, 23
Jaffa Gate, 26, 205, 212
jars, storage, **73**, **80**, **128**, **132**, **184**, **185**
Jason, 63
Jehoiachin, 24
Jehoiakim, 24
Jericho 146, 149, 150
Jewish Quarter, 16-19, 20, **22**, 31, **32-33**, 43, 45, 46, 49, 62, 64, 65, 81, 88, 95, **138**, **139**, 142, 144, 146, 148, 149, 186, 194, 207, 209, 211, 225, 226, 230, 247
Jewish Quarter Street, 53, 212, 216, 229, 248
Jewish Revolt, First, 97, 123, 146, 151, 195, 196
Jewish Revolt, Second (*See* Bar Kokhba Revolt)
John Hyrcannus I, 73
John Moschus, 245
Johns, S.N., 45, 67
Jonathan, 64, 72
Josephus, Flavius, 26, 29, 50, 57, 59, 64, 65, 67, 82, 94, 123
Joshua, 24
Josiah, 24
Judah bar Hassenuah, 54
Judean Desert Caves, 146
Judas Maccabeus, 64
jug fragments, **78**
Julian "the Apostate", 208
Justinian, 208, 226, 228, 245

K

Karatepe, Turkey, 41
Kenyon, Dame Kathleen, 14, 27, 29, 30, 45, 48, 60
Kerch, Crimea, 194

Kidron Brook, 95
Kidron Valley, 234
Kuntilet Ajrud, 44

L

Lachish, 23, 54
Lachish Letters, 44
lamelekh stamps, 43, 44
lamps, **88, 204, 255**
Lewin, Thomas, 235
Lion Gate [St. Stephen's Gate], 212, 247
Livy, 172
Lower Pool [Birket el-Hamra], 60

M

Maccabean Revolt, 63, 196
Maccabeans, 72
Madaba map, 59, 205, 211-212, **212**, 225, 227, 230, 254
Magen, Menahem, 228
Makhtesh, 24, 28, 54
Mamluk remains, 255
Mansion, 95-120, **96, 97, 98, 99, 100**, 110-116, 139, 144, 149, 150, **153**
Manasseh, 24
Maoz, Zvi, 196
Margalit, Shlomo, 206, 240, 242
Margovsky, Yizhaq, 20
Mariammne Tower, 82
Masada, 82, 102, 142, 144, 146, 149, 150, 165, 196
Mattathias Antigonus, 63, 75, 81, 147
Mazar, Ami, 46, 122, 147
Mazar, Benjamin, 20, 55
Megiddo, 23
Melchizedek, 41
Menorah graffito, 147-149, **147, 148**
Middle Gate [*sha'ar ha-tawekh*], 59
millo, 24
miqveh (*See* bath, ritual immersion)
Misgav Ladakh Street, 95, 122, 247
Mishnah, 86, 119, 142, 174, 176, 183
Mishneh, 24, 28, 54, 55
mortars and pestles, **127**
Mount Moriah, 24, 26
mosaic pavements, 115, 144, 145, 146, 154-156, 209, 257
Mount of Olives, 23, 95
Mount Zion, 20, 24, 45, 62, 71, 208, 209, 212, 247
Muqaddasi, 254
Muristan, 29
Muslim Quarter, 20, 255
Muslims, 247

N

Nabateans, 186
Nahal David, 190
Narkiss, Bezalel, 149

Nea Church [New Church of St. Mary], 208, 211, 213, 227, 229-246, **231, 232, 233,** 255
Nea Gate, 212, 226, 254
Nebuchadnezzar, 24, 54
Nehemiah, 61
Nehemiah's Wall, 61-62
Nero, 195
New Church of St. Mary (*See* Nea Church)
Nineveh, 54
Niv-Krendel, Esther, 216

O

Old City, 13, 14, 20, 23, 29, 55, 205, 206, 212, 226, 228, 255
Ophel Hill (*See* Eastern Hill)
Ophel Wall, 62
Ottoman Turks, 255

P

paved street, Herodian, 94
Pelugat Hakotel Street, 49, 50
Phasaelis, 82
plaster fragments, 149-150, **149**
Pompeii, 99, 102, 103, 150, 172, 204
Pompey, 81
Poseq, A., 149
pottery, **40, 80, 86, 87**, 116, 117, **128**, 183-186, **226, 257**
Procopius, 229, 230, 234, 236, 245
Ptolemies, 63, 72
Ptolemy I, 63

Q

Qumran, 127, 142

R

Rabbi Obadiah of Bertenoro, 254
Rahmani, L.Y., 172
Ramat Rahel, 44, 77
Rambam Synagogue, 161
Ramle, 247
Rashi, 142
Reich, Ronny, 46, 106, 122
Rhodian jar handles, 77
Ritmeyer, Leen, 59
Robinson's Arch, 20, 94
Rogel Spring, 26
Romans, 81
Rome, 193
roof tiles, **206**
Rostovtzeff, M., 194
Rothschild House, 230
Royal Portico, 20, 167

S

Sadducees, 83
Salim, 23
Samaria, 149
Samaria Ostraca, 44

Sardis, 161
Sassanians, 208
Scharef, Zeev, 46
Schick, Conrad, 230, 235
seal impressions, 43-44, **43**, **45**, **63**, **78**, **79**
Seleucids, 63, 72
Sennacherib, 24, 54
Sha'ar ha-tawekh (*See* Middle Gate)
Shallum, 54
Sharon, M., 255
Shebanio, 44
Shenhav, Dodo, 242
Sheshbazzar, 61
Shonei Halakhah Street, 50
Siloam Pool, 60, 208
Simeon, 64, 65, 72
Six-Day War, 14, 55
Socoh, 43
Solomon 24, 26, 27, 28, 29
Solomon's Stables, 236
Souq Khan ez-Zeit, 206, 212, 228
St. Mark's Street, 67, 216
St. Stephen's Gate (*See* Lion Gate)
stone tables, 106-107, **107**, 126, 167-172, **169**, **170**, **173**, 197
stone vessels, 127, **132**, 174-176, **175**, **176**, **181-182**, **183**
stone weight, **94**, **129**, **130**
stonework, 165-167, **166**, **167**, **171**
Street of the Chain, 49, 206
stucco fragments, **101**, **102**, **103**
Suleiman the Magnificent, 254, 255
sundial, Mansion, 119-120, **119**
Syria, 23

T
Tel Anafa, **102**, 190-191
Tell Mardikh (*See* Ebla)
Temple, Second, 20, 27, 29, 30, 31, 46, 64
Temple, Second (Herod's), 81, 82, 147, 148, 161, 162, 174, 196
Temple, Solomon's (First), 13, 27, 28, 29, 30, 31, 33, 46, 54
Temple Enclosure, 20, 29, 49, 63, 64, **95**, 122, 131, 165, 208, 247
Temple Mount [*Haram al-Sharif*], 13, 14, 20, 26, 27, 28, 29, 65, 82, **94**, **109**, 165, 230, 247
Temple of Augustus, 162
Temple of Jupiter, 205

Tenth Legion, 205, 206, 207
Terminal area, 249
terra sigillata ware, **88**, **91**
Teutonic Order, 248
Theodosius II, 208
Theodorus, 236
Tiferet-Israel Synagogue, **89**, **144**
Titus, 205
Tomb of Queen Helene (*See* Tomb of the Kings)
Tomb of the Kings [Tomb of Queen Helene], 13, 151
Transversal Valley, 26, 49
Tsafrir, Yoram, 242, 255
Turkish wall, 255, **255**
Turmus-Aya, 172
Tushingham, A.D., 29, 45
Tyropoeon Valley (*See* Central Valley)

U
Umayyads, 247
Uzziah, 24, 44

V
Varro, 172
Venus of Jerusalem, 36
Via Dolorosa, 206

W
Warren, Charles, 13, 14, 20, 235
Weinberg, Gladys, 189
Weinberg, Saul, 190
Western Hill, 27, 28, 29, 30, 41, 45, 46, 49, 54, 55, 60, 62, 64, 71, 77, 82
Wilson's Arch, 65

Y
Yadin, Yigael, 143, 146, 149
Yaqut, 254
Yehud, 61, 77
Yeshivat Hakotel, **95**, **144**

Z
Zechariah's Tomb, 161
Zedekiah, 26
Zephaniah, 44, 54
Zerubabel, 61
Zion Gate, 254, 255
Ziph, 43

Discovering
Jerusalem